D0119769

FALSE BELIEF AND THE MENO PARADOX

False Belief and the Meno Paradox

ELLY PIROCACOS

Ashgate

Aldershot • Brookfield USA • Singapore • Sydney

Published by
Ashgate Publishing Ltd
Gower House
Croft Road
Aldershot
Hants GU11 3HR
England

Ashgate Publishing Company
Old Post Road
Brookfield
Vermont 05036
USA

British Library Cataloguing in Publication Data
Pirocacos, Elly
    False belief and the Meno paradox. - (Avebury series in
    philosophy)
    1. Truthfulness and falsehood
    I. Title
    177.3

Library of Congress Catalog Card Number: 98-73400

ISBN 1 84014 852 7

Printed and Bound by Biddles Short Run Books, King's Lynn

Contents

Acknowledgements

The preparation of this book began at King's College London under the supervision of Dr. Mary Margaret Mackenzie and was completed under the supervision of Prof. Richard Norman at the University of Kent, at Canterbury. I am indebted to Prof. Norman both for his wisdom and encouragement in the writing up of this book, and to Dr. Mackenzie for introducing me to Plato and getting me started on the topic of false belief. I would also like to thank the *Onasis Foundation* for their financial support in the way of a scholarship.

I would also like to thank my colleagues at Deree College for their support and for their insightful comments. I would also like to thank the computer lab curators and assistants at Deree College for their invaluable assistance in preparing this book for publication.

Erratum

Page 1, lines 4 to 14 should read as follows:

The argument presented in the *Theaetetus* to illustrate the impossibility of false belief includes the premise which states, all thinking requires knowledge. However, though the actual treatment of falsehood will not turn on this discussion, it seems that the all-or-nothing assumption found in the *Theaetetus* hinges on the view that the mind thinks pictorially so that it seemed to make sense to talk of the objects of thought only in terms of these representing the real objects which these merely reflect in thought. This premise will be referred to as the all-or-nothing condition since it suggests that either something is completely known and for that reason can be thought; or else, something is absolutely unknown, and cannot therefore be thought.

Introduction

A Vested Interest in Falsehood: Philosophical Implications Following from Its Impossibility

The ambition of this book is to present a discussion of the problem of false belief that ties in its relevance to wider Platonic themes which are philosophically interesting. The topic of falsehood is tackled in Part II of the *Theaetetus* and resolved in the *Sophist*. The argument presented in the *Theaetetus* to illustrate the impossibility of false belief includes the However, though the actual treatment of falsehood will not turn on this discussion, it seems that the all-or-nothing assumption found in the *Theaetetus* hinges on the view that the mind thinks pictorially so that it seemed to make sense to talk of the objects of thought only in terms of these representing the real objects which these merely reflect in thought. premise which states, all thinking requires knowledge. This premise will be referred to as the all-or-nothing condition since it suggests that either something is completely known and for that reason can be thought; or else, something is absolutely unknown, and can not therefore be thought. Mostly this assumption is viewed as problematic in terms of intolerable implications which follow from it; for instance the impossibility of falsehood. True it makes sense to think of objects in this way but surely what will follow from the discussion of falsehood first in the *Theaetetus* and then in the *Sophist*, is that not all words which are employed for thought are meaningful because they correspond to something in the world. This will introduce a distinction between getting something or some object in mind (pictorially) and reflecting about something, some object or matter.

The implication of the all-or-nothing premise introduces wider Platonic themes which centre around the status of the elenctic method. In the *Meno* there is a famous passage where Meno presents what is known as the Meno Paradox. This paradox also springs from this all-or-nothing premise. It states, if something is either known completely or not at all, then either inquiry is pointless because I already possess knowledge, or else inquiry can not get started because there is no way to entertain beliefs for which there is no knowledge. The impasse to inquiry, together with the impossibility of false belief puts the Socratic elenctic method in contradiction with itself. For the elenchus, the Platonic Socrates would argue, is interested in engaging in joint inquiry in the pursuit of knowledge. If knowledge can not be had by inquiry then there is no reason to engage in the elenchus. Historically this is significant because Socrates had been hard pressed to distinguish himself from the sophists who used eristic methods of argument in their attempts at persuasion. The two methods of Socrates and the sophists are, of course, similar in that both embrace the all-or-nothing condition. However, for Socrates it is something that he can not afford because it renders the elenchus self-defeating, whereas, for the sophists, the eristic method remains unchallenged. In the case of the sophists the all-or-nothing premise will follow straightforwardly from their epistemological relativism, whereas in the case of Socrates the all-or-nothing premise follows from his belief that the ability to identify something to think requires knowing it completely. A challenge would seem to present itself since the very assumption which Socrates painsakingly acknowledges time and time again and which finally culminates in the Meno Paradox also places the sophist in a comfortable epistemological niche which impedes the elenchus but substantiates sophistry.

Turning to the *Sophist* this discussion unfolds as a challenge first fully understood by Parmenides. The *Sophist* opens with Socrates suspended of his inquisitive role. Looking to Socrates' warning in the *Protagoras* regarding the status of the men to whom neophyte philosophers entrust their souls, we should be weary of his replacement. Curiously we find an alleged companion of Parmenides, though still a stranger to us, assumes the executor role of leading the philosophical inquiry. The topic of the day is falsehood which given the sketched dynamics would put any attentive reader on his guard. For falsehood is the trade attributed to the sophists by Plato, and the executor role of inquiry is reserved for the philosopher who exclusively seeks the truth. Still the stranger could easily be mistaken for a philosopher in the same way that Socrates had be mistaken for a sophist. The warning can not be accidental given that we are told at the end of the *Theaetetus* that the dialogue must end prematurely as Socrates must meet with the King Archon regarding the charges brought up against him for having presumably corrupted the youth with sophistic trickery. The next day the discourse continues in the *Sophist* where the course of discussion is guided by the Eleatic Stranger who speaks of the words of his philosophical father, Parmenides. With five failed definitions of the sophist, the sixth is immediately followed by the daunting words of Parmenides, 'never shall this be forcibly maintained that the things that are not are'. The sixth definition accounts for the sophist as an 'image maker who reproduces not with accuracy but with deceptive expertise such that, his listener would be deluded into embracing contradiction and falsehood'. The Eleatic Stranger anticipates the ensuing paradox (236c-237a) and spelling it out for the neophyte makes explicit that thinking falsely is 'thinking what is not', precisely the words which Parmenides had said could not possibly be maintained (236e). Still the Eleatic Stranger does not accept the status of the Parmenidean argument on his philosophical father's word alone, and says that it must first be 'put to a mild torture, [so that] studying it on its own merit, [we could] (to) thereby discover the truth' (237b1-4). A challenge unfolds which I will refer to hereafter as *the Parmenidean Challenge*.

An Exposition of the Parmenidean Challenge[1]

That Plato understands Parmenides as presenting a challenge to the way that language had until his time be understood to work, and that such a view could be defended needs some consideration. Parmenides is traditionally understood as defending monism but the interpretation I will argue for establishes that Parmenides did not set out to defend anything. Instead, Parmenides set out to present a challenge by drawing this intolerable monistic conclusion from a chain of seemingly valid deductive arguments. It will be shown that the driving problematic assumption throughout is what is referred to as semantic atomism; namely that for each word there is a corresponding thing in the world that it represents.

Parmenides' poem is divided into two related, and yet antithetical parts. The first, *Alitheia* is presented as the Way of Truth, and it is occupied in frs.2-7 with providing a preliminary conclusion, which is expanded in a series of deductive arguments throughout fr.8, where it reaches its full potential in its striking conclusion, radical monism.[2] Taking its start by rejecting the world of appearance, it is led to a world in which plurality cannot be countenanced. The second, *Doxa* depicts the Road of Opinion traversed by mortal men; notably Parmenides and his reader. And positing a plurality presents a need for an argument for cosmogony. Why does a pluralistic account of what exists (in the cosmogony) follow the apparent refutation of such a world in the deductively conclusive monist argument in *Alitheia*? The reason has often been sought in providing a consistent interpretation of the cryptic remarks of the goddess regarding mortal opinion.[3] So that, though *Doxa* is as extensive in material as *Alitheia*, because it has generally been accepted that the bulk of the philosophical debate is restricted to the latter, I will consider the arguments presented in *Alitheia*, and restrict reference to the antithetical character of *Doxa*[4] only in support of conclusions immediately drawn from the Way of Truth.[5]

Apart from the obvious allegoric material alluding to a philosophic journey of enlightenment in the proem[6] the journey from night to light,[7] etc.—what is of deep philosophical significance is the dialectical[8] context in which the goddess escorts Parmenides' on his pedagogic journey. Appearances suggest that the Way of Truth is recounted in the form of a monologic dictum from the lips of the goddess (i.e. only the voice of the goddess is, in fact, heard); and this in turn negates the possibility of dialogue. What then of the dialectical context? It is not a requirement of the dialectical context that there be an actual exchange of ideas between at least two persons, thereby calling for the overt participation of each party. Rather, the requirement is more subtle, and, as it will be shown, contributes to the delicate structure of the poem in its entirety. Parmenides does not permit himself and his readers—mortal men—direct access to the goddess because she is the embodiment of the inaccessible world discovered at the end of the Way of Truth.[9] The very world which denies the possibility of human existence—in fact, of any existence—could not be asked to recognise a discursive counterpart; but that the goddess cannot hear Parmenides (because for her he cannot exist) does not preclude the possibility of an attentive listener. Moreover, the conditions required to support the dialectical context are confirmed by the underlying discursive nature of the poem. Namely, that the goddess sets out to teach Parmenides the Way of Truth—the only true way—presupposes that Parmenides is there,[10] and that he is attentively following, and thus reflecting upon the arguments presented to him by the goddess. The significance of this is not immediately obvious until the connection between the Way of Truth and Persuasion at fr.2.4 is drawn. Not only does this presuppose the dialectical context—in its most economical form, that there is a speaker and a listener—but suggests a symmetrical relationship; (a) truth is by its very nature persuasive; and (b) that a belief is persuasive because it attends upon truth. The former (a), implies that (i) someone be persuaded of that truth, and (ii) that the truth persuade someone of something. The latter (b) imposes a restrictive use of persuasion. A general understanding of persuasion requires that someone be induced to adopt a particular belief, where emphasis is given to some psychological state of mind; whereas this strict use argues that someone is induced to adopt a particular belief, and that the belief is true, where emphasis is placed on the content of the belief. Hence, though not explicitly argued, it must be the case that Parmenides believed that the merit of truth is that it generates knowledge (fr.2 emphasises the association between truth and knowledge); and that knowledge is ineffective if it is not applied. It is thus crucial to the Way of Truth that the dialectical context be maintained. The two-facedness of the structure of the poem already suggests that the Way of Truth is impotent to sustain itself; and yet that it is not easily dismissed given the puissant Authority of our teacher, the goddess.

That enquiry begins when Parmenides leaves the experiential world of sense-perception behind, and ascends to the heavens of godly insight, suggests that, Cartesian-like,[11] enquiry assumes no knowledge, but from logical principles establishes truth. What then has established the truth of the dialectical context, i.e. two rational thinking agents? In order to explain what I think Parmenides is doing here, I want to compare and contrast his enterprise with that of Descartes' 'cogito' argument. Descartes is engaged in an entirely first-person exercise. He addresses his argument only to himself, and convinces himself of the truth 'I exist insofar as I am thinking'.[12] This establishes only his own existence, it says nothing about the existence of others, and so it leaves him with the problem of solipsism. Descartes could have used an analogous argument to tackle the problem of the existence of others. Acknowledging that his use of language presupposes the possibility of dialogue, he could have argued similarly 'You exist insofar as you are thinking'. This Descartes fails to do, but Parmenides does it. Parmenides is explicit about the dialectical context[13] of his argument. It is an argument in the second person, addressed to him by the goddess. And this is why, despite the apparently monistic conclusion of the argument, I maintain that Parmenides cannot be committed to that conclusion, because he remains committed to the existence of a plurality of thinkers. The exposition of Parmenides' arguments below also defend this view.

Here the proem ends, and the anticipated arguments begin. Providing the prologue to the subsequent arguments the proem is restricted in scope, being not exclusively introductory in content, however. The purpose is introductory in that it sets out to specify what is to follow. Yet, it is also unusually persuasive and personal; and it is this aspect which furnished the structural context presenting both the prospective challenge and the prescribed reference of interpretation of all subsequent arguments. The reference is backward looking therefore, and we should expect everything which follows to conform to it.

The major argument is presented in the form of a logical law: either *esti* or *ouk esti* (fr.2). It has uncontroversially be taken as stating an exhaustive list of logically exclusive possible routes that enquiry can take; either *esti* (Way of Truth); or *ouk esti* (No Way); or the conjunct *esti and ouk esti*[14] (Road of Opinion).[15] The second way is an 'altogether indiscernible track' because 'you could not know nor indicate what is not' (fr.2.5-6), so that following its explicit exposition in fr.6, it becomes evident that we are now discussing the ontological status of the objects of enquiry. Since the refutation of the two wrong roads and the acceptance of the right road hinges on the acceptance of this premise, to which Parmenides attaches explicit significance in his cautionary clause at fr.6.2-3, some time ought to be spent on clarifying what it says, and what the logical implications of its acceptance suggest.

At fr.6.1 Parmenides argues for the co-extensiveness of being and thought. His reasoning seems obvious; to the assertion, 'I am thinking', the obvious response is 'of what?'. If 'I am thinking', it must be that I am thinking of something, for otherwise there is no object of thought. With nothing present to the mind, the object of thought is empty, which is just nonsense. Thought presupposes content. The choice between *esti* or *ouk esti* thus suggests itself as a choice between thinking of something—understood that it exists—and thinking nothing. Hence we must choose *esti*. Criticism directed at mortal men is in not choosing; two-headed (*dikranoi*) 'they believe that to be and not to be are the same and not the same' (fr.6.8-9). Given the existential reading of *esti*, it must be that fault is found with mortal men because they speak of non-existent things as if they, in fact, existed. The assertion, 'Homer does not exist', entails—on the basis of the argument brought against *ouk esti*—the possibility to identify or pick out the object of thought, and that requires that 'Homer exists'; and yet the assertion is that 'Homer does not exist', and the result is self-contradiction ('...and the path taken by them is backward-turning' fr.6.9-10).

So far the suggestion is that *esti* has an existential reading. Of course, that the word *esti* can take a number of different, though compatible readings, is a matter which will establish what can and can not be said of the poem. The (a) existential use—something exists—is distinguished from (b) the veridical use—it is true of *x* that such and such (c) the predicative use—something is *F* (some property is attributable to *x*)—and (d) that of identification—*x* is (the same as) *y*. The contextual dimension set out in the proem at least suggests that the veridical usage may be a likely candidate. For, the journey from the world of *Doxa* to the world of *Alitheia* presented not a cosmological problem but a problem regarding the search for knowledge. Subsequently fr.6 cast this search in terms of what there is for knowledge to be of. Parmenides, as the path of Persuasion already introduced, is concerned with the object of knowledge, where, of course, any statement involving that object would also have to be true of it. Statements are complex sentences which assert some truth about the object in question; and Parmenides will expect (fr.8) that any statement can be broken down into atomic structures themselves also accessible to thought because they too are some-one-thing. It is the relationship between Parmenides' understanding of something and truth which reveals that a correspondence theory of truth must be in play here. This would, in turn, expose the existential usage of *esti*. To begin, this perfectly conforms to the conclusion and the challenge that has been argued for. If there are no statements which can be entertained by thought, then a correspondence theory of truth is self-defeating precisely because there is nothing for truth to correspond to. In other words, a correspondence theory of truth must *suppose* that there is an *existent* world to which beliefs, when true, strictly correspond. Falsifying its existence on its own terms naturally looks like a reduction ad absurdum which, when taking the proem seriously, can not mean that Parmenides set out to refute such a view, but rather to reveal the challenge which it manifests. In fr.2 the Way of Persuasion is identified with truth because it is then that thought involves 'what is and is impossible to not be' which is in standing contradiction with the indiscernible track which could be postulated as 'what is not and what is needful to not be because it cannot be indicated'. Of course, given that the third way of mortal men is presented as commonplace, the choice between thinking in the first and second instance does not suggest that thought cannot entertain 'what is not', so that the infallibility of thought would follow as a consequent. What he is saying is that whenever the mind is occupied by thoughts of 'what is not' that it is impossible that it also be true. The first and most obvious point being made in fr.2 is that thought must be full, and that because 'thinking what is not' is given as impossible, it follows that an ontological claim is being made about the objects of thought. 'What is not' has no corresponding reference and strictly speaking does not exist to be thought of. This ontological claim suggests that there is a causal relationship between the objects of thought and the thinking mind attending upon them, and this would presuppose that there is an existent external world which furnishes the mind. When the mind, in fact, strictly attends upon these corresponding objects, thoughts or verbatim statements about them will be true because thought is just of that thing.

To reiterate: Fr.6 explicates fr.2, the object of thought and speech must be of what exists because only what exists is there to be picked out by thought; whereas nothing is not. It is not possible to identify a non-existent because it is simply not there to identify. The validity of this reading is further strengthened by the co-extensiveness of thought and existence as it appears in fr.3. ('what can be thought is identical to what exists'). So that finally, the restraint of choosing *esti* can not tolerate the formulation of any belief which takes the form of *ouk esti*, since that necessarily implies *esti* and their contradictory conjunct.

It is not until fr.7 however that the sweeping force of this restraint is made explicit, 'never shall this be forcibly maintained, that things that are not are...'; the implications of which are elaborated in fr.8.5-49. Having argued that every object of enquiry must exist, fr.8 sets out to deduce which names, if any, can properly be used to describe the object of enquiry, where clearly those attributes must also be something that exist. Fr.8.5-49 demonstrates that for this reason *esti* cannot tolerate any qualification whatsoever, and the result is radical monism.[16] Predicative monism follows as a straightforward consequent since all the arguments throughout fr.8 demonstrate that 'what is for thought' can tolerate absolutely no qualification. However, given that all subsequent arguments were derived from the condition that whatever occupies thought must be something which exists, numerical monism also follows by implication. That which remains unsaid, though implied, is that from the parallel between thought and the existent world, not only is thinking going to be impossible (i.e. thought is always complex) but the world, for which we assume plurality, is comprised of a single homogenous stuff, and this may suggest material monism also. And here looms the Parmenidean challenge.

I have presented a rather unorthodox interpretation of Parmenides' poem and have argued that this interpretation is encouraged by what happens in the *Sophist* and is therefore what Plato too must have understood by it. What has been called semantic atomism is responsible for the monistic conclusion which Parmenides' poem concludes with, but I have argued that the context of the poem shows that Parmenides could not have believed that conclusion to be true. Moreover, it is evident that Plato picks up the Parmenidean challenge in the *Sophist* because he replaces Socrates with one of Parmenides' followers in a dialogue which seeks to set things right on the problem of falsehood, or thinking 'what is not is'. We are not told that this is, in fact, impossible. In fact, in the *Sophist* the Eleatic Stranger embarks on the search for an explanation of falsehood saying 'never shall this be *proved*—that the things that are not are', followed by the challenging remarks, 'we have this great man's testimony, and the best way to obtain a confession of the *truth* may be to put the statement to a mild torture...and study it on its own merits' (237b). The reader is asked, therefore, to scrutinise the statement on the terms that it was laid out on. The impossibility of this statement is found in the Way of Truth, and the terms of its impossibility were given for thought and speech.[17] The challenge which is being referred to as the Parmenidean Challenge is, therefore a language problem about getting straight on the semantic atomism which has been responsible for the chain of deductive arguments which got stuck in monism.

An Exposition of the Sophistic Challenge

In the case of the sophists, Protagoras' Man-Measure argument is the source of their acclaimed epistemological relativism which is the target of Plato's antagonism and the strength upon which their tenet that 'anyone can rightfully argue for any claim' rests. The question which this popularised notion immediately raises is, given an acknowledged awareness of the diversity of opinion, often contradictory, on what grounds are all opinions equally valid? Based on strong empiricism the sophists advocate an anti-realistic view, arguing, and thus rejecting the naturalistic contrast between reality and appearance, that knowledge is limited to 'the way things appear to each person; and that as they appear, so they are'. The truth of a belief is determined by the relative circumstances from which the belief is derived and from the particular perspective of the person who acquires the belief. Consequently, all belief is infallible because it is restricted to the private world of the individual. Therefore, no matter how deviant a person's experiences, the judgements he is led to will be true for him, providing him with the knowledge of how things are for him. It is for this reason that the sophist is entitled to pursue suasion and to employ whatever means necessary to manipulate the manner in which persons view the world. Since there is nothing beyond appearance the subjective criterion of truth guarantees that all judgements will be true and no one truer than another.

The thesis attributed to Protagoras which advocates that 'contradiction is impossible, and that this amounts to saying that it is impossible to speak falsely',[18] must thus infer that because knowledge attends upon the privileged access to experience for which each person is the sole authoritative judge, our beliefs are about different things, namely, the knowledge of how things appear to each person. And its corollary, because knowledge is perception, appearances are necessarily true (for each person whose appearances they are) precisely because this thesis holds that all things are to each person exactly as they appear to him, and thus no one can be mistaken about the reality that confronts him. In which case the sophist should not be condemned for committing the Pittacusian offence—passing-off a false statement for true—but at most for not recognising the weakness and cost of their epistemological subjectivism.

Having thus obliterated the distinction between truth and falsehood, the only recourse open to discussion is the presentation of individual opinions where its form can either be purely descriptive or disputive. Given the nature of rhetoric the sophist must have claimed that the beliefs of others can be affected by argument. The way that things appear to each person can be affected by the way that argument can make them appear to each person. Therefore, if someone can be persuaded that things are such and such (true), things will appear in such and such a way to that person; and clearly it must be this avenue that the sophist claims to travel. The packaging and presentation of opinions in the most believable and appealing form for consumption is the commercialism which the sophist is most ardently reproached for in the *Sophist*.

Granted that not all men are of the same opinion, and given that all opinions are equally valid, the sophists are reprimanded not primarily for their conclusions, but for the arguments they rely on.[19] In light of the difficulty to decide which of all the equally valid beliefs should be endorsed, opposing views seem to cancel each other out, thus undermining any possible consensus. Rather than submit to the scepticism of this resulting indecision, the sophists turned it to their advantage; and for a price would sponsor any of the existing beliefs by eristic methods of argument.

The Sophistic challenge seems thus to entail the eristic method and the epistemology it depends on. By sophistic account everything we think or speak of is necessarily true; but the cost of this epistemological perfection must have proved too high for Plato to be expected to sanction, the significance of which the famous Socratic disavowal of Knowledge, *en gnorizo ouden gnorizo*, attests to. Not only does this challenge the Platonic search for truth but it also empowers the sophists with the opportunity to pass off any of their chanced opinions as received wisdom in Greek society irrespective of their consequences.[20] Therefore, if Plato could establish that false belief is possible then the epistemological foundation of sophistic professionalism would be undermined, and their persuasive power diminished.

Unlike the sophist who hides from us, the philosopher is impenetrable because we—mortal men—are ignorant of the truth of his Way.[21] Consequently, the relativism of eristic teaching awaits as the only other alternative laid open to us. The choice between Parmenides' only two logically possible routes to inquiry (the indiscernible track is no way at all) expose man as too lazy or too ignorant to appreciate that a choice needs to be made. They are 'two-headed for helplessness guides the wandering thought in their breasts, and they are carried along, deaf and blind at once, dazed, undiscriminating hordes, who believe that to be and not to be are the same and not the same' (fr.6.5-8). It would be anachronistic to suggest that the sophists or the method of sophistry are anywhere in Parmenides' thoughts. However, there is more than just a hint that mortal men overcome by eristic reasoning could well be described in this fashion. We should not forget that the objective of any sophistic debate is the contest; that the best professionals pride themselves on being capable to argue either side of the same debate with equal precision; and that the persuasive form of any argument is eristic, hence only apparently sound. We should not forget then, that the sophist hides the face of his argument from the scrutiny of curious eyes, and desires to vanquish any on-looker. So too is the Way of *Doxa* for Parmenides the path traversed by the multitudes whose thoughts are guided not by the dictates of their reason but by their own personalised experiences, and subsequently, they indiscriminately accumulate beliefs that are contradictory in kind. The Way of *Alitheia* and the Way of *Doxa* correspond to two contrary methods of inquiry; the first deductive a priori, the second, inductive a posteriori. The Way of *Doxa* is comfortable and easily accessible; the alternative is arduous; in fact, it is at least momentarily inaccessible, and consequently bewildering. For the first, there is no knowledge to be gained; for the latter nothing to gain it from. All this followed as a result of semantic atomism and the particular mess this created for *what is not*.

Summary of Chapters

In the final section of this Introduction I shall set out the main claims which I shall be making in subsequent chapters. The overall aim of the thesis is to show that the problem of falsehood is worth consideration because it is entangled in a complex philosophical web that centres on the puzzle of 'thinking and speaking of what is not'. This is what makes the sophists and Parmenides pertinent. The sophists claimed that the impossibility of thinking or speaking of 'what is not' makes it impossible to think or speak falsely. I argue that this is directly relevant to the status of the elenctic method because (1) it supports the sophists' eristic method which rests on the assumption that all beliefs are equally valid, and (2) it consequently renders the elenctic search for objective truth meaningless. It would then follow that, in virtue of their common application of antilogic, the Socratic elenctic method would become indiscernible from the eristic method. This would provide some justification for the charges which were made against Socrates at his trial, and which Plato regarded as such a travesty of justice.

In Chapter One I shall outline the form of the eristic method, and show why the elenchus would be confused with the eristic method if the search for truth were indeed impossible. I shall set out the well-known paradox of enquiry in the *Meno* which is known as the Meno Paradox, and I shall argue (3) that the paradox follows from the following premise: that the ability to identify something to think of presupposes knowledge of that thing, and that something can either be thought of and is therefore known, or else is not known and can therefore not be thought of. This premise I shall refer to as 'the all-or-nothing condition'.

In Chapter Two I shall argue (4) that the same problematic premise is responsible for the impasse concerning falsehood. In the *Theaetetus* the original problem is re-formulated as an epistemological problem. In Chapter Two I shall show (5) that Plato's problem about knowledge again follows from a misunderstanding of what thinking involves, confusing the object of thought with the process of thinking itself. A pictorial view of thinking is adopted, which again rests on the problematic assumption that to identify an object of thought is to know that object. The discussion in the *Theaetetus* turns to the problem of falsehood, and Plato tries three models for reinstating its possibility. First the Allodoxia Model is presented as a choice between 'thinking of something without actually identifying it' and 'identifying something without actually knowing it; the Wax Tablet Model suggests how this could happen when perception is involved, and finally the Aviary Model, restricting the inquiry to thought, argues for the possibility of two levels of knowledge. Each attempt to reinstate the possibility of falsehood fails.

In Chapter Three I look at how, in the *Theaetetus*, the original inquiry about knowledge is resumed and promises to get us straight on the question of what is really involved when something is known. Knowledge is defined as true belief plus an account, or the ability to justify a given claim as true. Three models of 'an account' follow, and I argue (6) that each fails because once again a misplaced understanding of the relationship between the objects of thought and the thinking process itself leads to a preoccupation with the actual objects. Consequently, it becomes obvious that there must be something more to justifying a belief as true than just referring to parts of the given object. I argue that this again rests on a view of the word-object relation which I call 'the proprietary assumption'.

Finally, in the *Sophist*, the problem of falsehood, which had originally been set up as the problem of 'thinking what is not', is recognised as following from misconceptions about how language works. The reader of the *Sophist* is led to discover that he is as much in the dark about 'being' as about 'not being'. In Chapter Four I argue (7) that this prevailing confusion between the objects of thought and thinking itself is shown in the *Sophist* to have plagued all theories, so that materialism might perhaps go as far as to say that the thoughts of objects are the objects themselves, and idealism might say that what really is, and therefore truth, can only be found amongst the immutable forms, which places them beyond human accessibility.

In the *Sophist*, Parmenides is then brought on the scene, and it is shown (8) that the view that to think of something (truthfully) means thinking of that thing in terms of what it is and nothing else (what is being called 'the proprietary assumption') would exclude the possibility of meaningfully talking about any given thing. It would involve employing words (naming things) that in no way correspond to the thing in question (its parts), but in a way which nevertheless makes meaningful thought possible.

In Chapter Five I show (9) that Plato in the *Sophist* then picks up on the word-object assumption and makes sense of why it is meaningful to talk about something without this involving any of the usual paradoxes, because thinking is different from stating or claiming that something is true. Language works in such a way that sentences become meaningful when something gets asserted, but what is asserted need not correspond to what is actually the case in the world. The epistemological puzzle, which originally concerned the possibility of having in mind a false thought, is modified so that the question is now about how it is possible to meaningfully state what is false. I argue (10) that the account offered by Plato of how false judging or stating is possible can provide a partial solution to the Meno Paradox. The understanding of meaningful thinking makes it possible to explain how a claim can be both meaningful and false. Consequently, it would be possible for Socrates' interlocutors to make claims which turn out to be false, because belief no longer presupposes knowledge. The *Sophist* does not provide an answer to the question of how knowledge is actually acquired. Nevertheless enough has been done to show how the elenchus can get under way, and this would restrict the kinds of argument that could be meaningfully employed. The arguments could thus be evaluated for consistency, and so the sophist would be forced to retract his use of fallacious argumentation as a means of persuasion.

Notes

[1] See E. Pirocacos (1998) *Philosophical Inquiry*, 'Parmenides: Rationalism Falls Short of Truth'. In this paper I present a slightly variant view of Parmenides' philosophy. Instead of arguing that Parmenides sets up a challenge for an

exposition of our understanding of truth, I claim that he defends that the truths of logic are not empirical truths of fact and are therefore inapplicable to the world. This need not present a problem for the reading herewith since the objective was to present a reading of Parmenides which is both plausible and consistent with *Plato's* understanding of him.

[2] It is controversial whether Parmenides actually argued for numerical—this is the view which is traditionally provided in introductory texts—predicative, or material monism, or indeed a combination of any of these. Though it is not necessary to the argument of this chapter to enter this debate, I will show that a strong monist position is required to support the Parmenidean challenge as it is outlined here. For a discussion outlining these three kinds of monistic possibilities in Parmenides see P.K. Curd (1991) 'Parmenidean Monism', *Phronesis*. See also T. Gomperz (1964) *Greek thinkers: A History of Ancient Philosophy*, where he argues that the implied material monism of preceding cosmologists is extended by Parmenides by logical argument to include predicative monism as well.

[3] See G.E.L. Owen (1971) 'Eleatic Questions', p. 52: 'The assumption of which the debate (regarding the status of the cosmogony) depends is to examine the general character which the goddess attributes to her statements regarding human opinions.'

[4] It has been argued from antiquity (see Plutarch, and Simplicius in his *Physics 38.24*-8) until the present day that the Way of Opinion or *Doxa* corresponds to the second of the two promised things that the goddess will teach, namely the 'deceitful opinions of mortal men'. As a result, the second part of Parmenides' poem, *The Way of Opinion*, is often thought to represent the *Way of Falsity* or still for those who understand the fruitlessness of taking such a journey, argue instead that it is the *Way of Plausibility*. This is not the view that will be supported here. In fact, it will be argued that the mistake germinates in the misplaced understanding of the poem in its entirety. That once the overall argument is made clear, the *Way of Truth* and the *Way of Opinion* are contrary but not contradictory, and hence not altogether incompatible.

[5] For an explicit exposition of the view that Parmenides' poem is concerned with the problem of knowledge, and specifically the problem of the search for knowledge, rather than cosmogony; and that this is made lucidly clear from the start, namely in the proem, see Charles H. Kahn (1969) 'The Thesis of Parmenides', *The Review of Metaphysics* 22, p. 704-6.

[6] Barnes recognises only this obvious aspect of the proem and argues that the only further aspect of philosophical importance in the proem occupies lines 30-32 where the goddess promises to teach Parmenides both the well-rounded way of truth, *and* the unreliable opinions of mortals. For Barnes' viewpoint see J. Barnes (1982) *PreSocratic Philosophers*, chapter IX 'Parmenides and the Objects of Inquiry', pp. 155-175. However, for readings which favour the view that the proem is rich in philosophical content, see J. Burnet (1962) *Greek Philosophy: From Thales to*

Plato; M.M. Mackenzie (1982) 'Parmenides' Dilemma', *Phronesis*; Charles H. Kahn (1969) 'The Thesis of Parmenides', *The Review of Metaphysics* 22, and others.

[7] For a completely opposed reading of the direction of the journey from light to night, and thus the apocalyptic nature of the proem Furley offers an intriguing analysis in, D. Furley (1973) 'Notes on Parmenides', *Phronesis*.

[8] Derived from ancient Greek the meaning of the term dialectic, notably in the Socratic method of enquiry, is 'to converse' or 'discourse'; and is often distinguished from eristic discourse.

[9] In the proem Parmenides leaves the world of sense-perception behind in order to meet the goddess; and though she says that she will teach Parmenides both truth *and* the unreliable opinions of mortals, it is clear that she is the embodiment of the well-rounded truth for two reasons. First, we cannot associate the goddess with the way of opinion both because mortal opinion is faulty and she wants to show why it is, and it belongs to the world of sense perception which has already been rejected. Second, at fr.2.5 the Way of Truth is designated as the only true way, and the only way by which persuasion is possible. Indeed, the only way by which She too can persuade Parmenides of Her truth. Therefore, not only does the goddess want to convince Parmenides that the Way of Truth is the only possible route of enquiry, but She must also adhere to the rules set out in the Way of Truth in its exposition.

[10] This is confirmed by his journey to meet the goddess in fr.1.

[11] The comparison between Descartes' first principle and Parmenides is often made; see M.M. Mackenzie (1982) op cit.

[12] R. Descartes, *Meditations on First Philosophy*, trans., J. Cottingham, p.17

[13] M.M. Mackenzie (1982), op cit., p. 1.

[14] See. D. Furley's essay, 'Truth as What Survives the *Elenchus*' in *Cosmic Problems*; where he gives an interesting analysis of the logical function of the word *elechein*. He argues that the acceptance of *esti* is based on providing a refutation for the other two possibilities which make up the exhaustive list of possible responses to the question, *esti* or *ouk esti*. In other words, Furley supports that the overall logical form of Parmenides' argument is disjunctive.

[15] The way in which this choice between these three exhaustive alternatives are set up seems to imply that the logical form of the argument that Parmenides aims to support is disjunctive. Though the strength of the arguments presented here are not directly affected by this debate, I should say that I disagree with this view. To begin with it is my view that Parmenides is not, in fact, strictly *arguing* for the truth of a conclusion. Moreover, the strength of the 'argument' which overthrows the route of *ouk esti* is founded on a more important assumption which is hidden and which is responsible for the troubles throughout the Parmenidean journey. That assumption concerns semantic atomism. Also, the route of *esti and ouk esti* is not rejected outright; all that is said of this route is that it renders unintended (I say unintended because the speakers believe that their words are conveyed

successfully, and curiously, others receive such words successfully) contradictions. I will say no more on the subject due to a lack of space.

[16] Since at fr.8.1-5 Parmenides provides an outline of the program for the remainder of fr.8, and indicates the intention of arriving at a case for monism, it is unimportant to the present discussion to consider either each deductive argument in turn, or whether he does so successfully.

[17] This is reinforced again later in the dialogue when the discussion of images is underway at 240a-b. There the Eleatic Stranger reminds the sophist who is looking to evade the possibility of falsehood, that the discourse must not transgress the specified task of accounting for thinking and speaking of *what is not*.

[18] Note that in the *Euthydemus* (286b-c) Socrates indeed attributes this thesis to Protagoras; but, the argument is in reverse order and he first argues for the impossibility of false judgement and from there builds the view that contradiction is also impossible.

[19] See T.H. Irwin (1992) 'Plato: The Intellectual Background', in Kraut's *A Companion to Plato*.

[20] This is a recurring theme in Platonic dialogue; see for instance the *Protagoras* where the fear of the power delivered in the hands of the sophists and their possible misuse of such power is raised.

[21] It has also been argued that sophistic and Socratic argument are similar in that they employ similar methods; the first, what is called antilogic (though perhaps the sophists are essentially eristic-minded and employ antilogic as one of the many techniques of rhetoric); and the second, dialectic. 'Antilogic...[is] the procedure of arguing by means of contradictory propositions. In antilogic we start from a basic idea and work mutually contradictory from it, arriving, as may be expected, at a dead-end.' This is similar to the aporetic dialogues; the difference between the two cases is in their intention. The first aims at victory in argument, and the second the search for truth. See. H.D. Rankin (1983) *Sophists, Socrates, Cynics*, pp. 21-23.

1 The *Meno*

Introduction

The *Meno* is commonly believed to be a transitional dialogue which means that the ideas presented in the *Meno* move beyond what can reasonably be supposed to represent Socratic, as opposed to Platonic philosophy. Whether there is any legitimate historical content in Plato's dialogues, and whether he can at any time be counted on to present any ideas other than his own is still a controversial issue which may find no resolution.[1] What can be said about the transitional nature of this dialogue however is that it sets up, and attempts to resolve a fundamental question which each of the dialogues which preceded it inadvertently raised. Specifically, the unique nature of the *Meno* is that it (i) locates a serious logico-methodological problem for the so-called Socratic elenctic method; (ii) that this problem finds expression in the so-called Meno Paradox, (iii) that (ii) raises serious epistemological questions where the topic of false belief will be central; that (iv) a sample elenchus (the slave boy) is presented to illustrate the proposed solution; and that (v) the proposed solution is the Theory of Recollection.

The most immediately compelling aspect of the early Socratic dialogue is the non-constructivist and provocative force of its aporetic end. All encounters with Socrates end when one of his interlocutor's beliefs are shown to be inconsistent with the conjunct of a number of his other beliefs. A minimum conception of the elenchus thus reveals that at least one of these beliefs must be rejected in order to maintain consistency. But the perplexity lodged in the belief-set of the interlocutor does not make the location of the faulty belief an accessible task, since the only epistemic requirement of the elenchus is that the participants sincerely express their beliefs, namely that they believe that they are true. If the participants believe all their beliefs true, a revealed inconsistency demonstrates that at least one of their beliefs must be false, without indicating which one. It is this end that has generated feelings of animosity amongst elenctic participants,[2] as well as misgivings regarding the pedagogico-epistemological merit of the method it is most remembered for. Not until the *Meno* however does Plato discuss the logical form of the elenchus explicitly and ask whether it can achieve the purpose for which it has been exercised given its form, namely a search for truth. Since this is the catalytic question which prompted Plato to embark on this philosophic expedition, the formulation of it will provide a key to all subsequent sections in this chapter.

This introduces an engaging problem which does not find Socrates and Plato in complete agreement. For Socrates the moralist, elenctic inquiry begins with existing beliefs and at the end makes the status of these available to his interlocutors for scrutiny. This already implies the opinion that belief is short of knowledge, and that belief can be converted into knowledge. I will argue that Meno's version of the paradox corresponds to the elenctic method as practised by Socrates, and is therefore consistent with the implications mentioned above. I will also argue that Socrates' reformulation of the paradox which is marked by the insertion of the all-or-nothing assumption reflects deeper concerns that may be attributed to Plato. Specifically, I will argue that two things are going on. Firstly, the 3-stage paradox as developed by Meno starts off with the ability to get inquiry started and therefore also with the distinction between belief and knowledge. Secondly, the all-or-nothing assumption gets inserted by Plato through Socrates, and this is an assumption about thinking or the required ability to identify an object to then go on to think about. Meno's formulation of the paradox is incongruous with what the all-or-nothing assumption would have us accept since it would stump inquiry from the beginning. That this does not occur, I have already said, is consistent with the elenchus. The problem commonly raised for the elenchus even by Plato in his dialogues is that it is similar to the sophistic method. On the grounds that indeed it can get started, and the antilogic that both methods use, we could easily confuse the elenchus with sophism. Hence, the description of the elenchus as contentious; a word normally used to describe sophistry. This suggests that fault is usually found with the elenctic method not because it can not get underway, but because it can not convert belief into knowledge.

So two things are going on here. There is what Plato is confused about genuinely, namely how the mind ever grabs hold of something to think without knowing that thing completely, hence the all-or-nothing assumption. This is a genuine concern for Plato, but presumably the reason for inquiry is that he believes that it must be somehow mistaken. The other thing is the similarity of the elenchus and the sophistic method which is a related but separate problem about knowledge. Specifically it is about the problem of converting belief into knowledge. The remainder of the *Meno* following the Meno Paradox is reserved for answering the problem of knowledge acquisition, and the assumption which Socrates inserts is saved for a discussion first in the *Theaetetus* and later in the *Sophist* which will introduce the puzzles on the impossibility of falsehood.[3] Plato does therefore recognise the self-defeatingness of the elenchus and accepts the commonplace notion that belief short of knowledge is possible as well as that inquiry is possible. However, Plato remains perplexed by the all-or-nothing assumption and he will work out epistemological and semantic puzzles from the underlying thrust of this assumption. By the end of the *Sophist*, which is the dialogue in which Plato presumably makes concrete headway, we should expect Plato to be able to show us, not that inquiry is possible but rather how inquiry thoughtfully proceeds and how truth and knowledge may be gained thereby. The proposed solution takes Plato into deep semantic waters since the challenge that Plato here sets himself requires that he can explain what 'thought and speech' involve and how beliefs may be meaningful and still short of truth or knowledge. I argue that the all-or-nothing assumption is a problem for thought and that it is because Plato is concerned with the objects of thought and how it is that the mind can grab hold of these that the puzzles for both inquiry and falsehood follow. In turn, I also argue that once Plato takes on board the view that belief is short of knowledge and that thinking is meaningful irrespective, that he will be required to rethink his assumption about how and what the mind thinks. This would require that thought is not understood to merely involve strings of identified objects somehow, but some manner in which reflection can take place. Finally, I would like to point out that if it were the case that Plato was really convinced that 'something is either known completely or not at all' surely Meno's paradox and Socrates' so-called reformulation of it would be different in no way whatsoever; in which case, Plato would also have to accept that inquiry is indeed impossible. We would expect him therefore to either embrace sophism or abandon the pursuit for truth. As it is, Plato was an ardent defender of the elenchus and though perplexed by this assumption which has strong roots in what has been coined the Parmenidean Challenge, he was not committed to its truth. In fact, his mission is to overthrow this epistemological and semantic challenge. It must be possible to have belief short of knowledge and beliefs must be meaningful even when false.

In light of what has already been argued in the Introduction regarding the sophistic method, the *Meno* and the Meno Paradox are important to the philosophical framework of the topic of false thinking. That is, the elenctic method in opposition to the eristic method stands to gain a great deal from the debate since the possibility of false thinking will by implication undermine the relativism of sophistry. More than this, the problem divulged by the Meno Paradox for the elenchus will be shown to overlap with the epistemological puzzle leading up to the paradox of false thinking. The job here is to show that the epistemological puzzle raised by the Meno Paradox does not deviate from the central problem of false thinking explicitly discussed in the *Theaetetus* and *Sophist*. The Meno Paradox hinges on a misplaced understanding of what thinking involves, so that the ability to think of something or the ability to identify something for thought—for want of making a mockery of thought and speech altogether—presumes complete or exhaustive knowledge of that thing. Again, the infallibility of thought follows as a consequent, but here it flies in the face of the elenchus since unlike the sophistic eristic method, it is inconsistent with its epistemological basis, and consequently the end of Socratic inquiry, namely knowledge. This chapter has, therefore, a twofold task: (i) to set out the elenctic method in full; and (ii) to exhibit the paradoxical epistemological starting point of the elenchus, and how this obstructs its own pursued end, which will be shown to overlap in philosophical interest with the topic of false thinking.

Elenctic Form

Agreement regarding the structural form of the elenchus[4] is unanimous; however, the intention and rules of its exercise are not wholly unified in interpretation. Does Socrates intend to establish the falsehood of his interlocutor's thesis, or is he content to deflate their unjustified conceit of knowledge by revealing the inconsistency of their belief set? Must the counter-argument itself be a sound argument, or will it suffice that its exposition is based on those beliefs sincerely held by the interlocutor? Is it imperative that the interlocutor himself also comprehend the logical necessity of his self-contradictory conclusion, or is it intended as an exercise for the reader of the dialogue? Is the Socratic disavowal of knowledge sincere, or is it an eristic trick?

Elenchus has consequently been variously defined; sometimes as examination, cross-examination, censure, but more often as refutation. But the word elenchein, Vlastos argues, is used by Plato to describe, rather than baptise, what he does,[5] so that, though all elenctic arguments are shown to refute, at least in a limited sense, the refutand, this is a consequence of the method, not necessarily its intention; and this may say more about the status of our beliefs, rather than the method itself.

The Formal Structure

(1) The interlocutor asserts a thesis, say p, in response to a typical Socratic 'What is x?' question.[6]

(2) To a series of secondary questions Socrates manages to get the interlocutor to agree to a number of further premises, say q and r.

(3) Socrates argues and the interlocutor agrees that q and r entail not-p.

(4) Socrates argues and the interlocutor agrees that p and not-p can not both be true at the same time; and therefore, at least one of his beliefs must be false.

Further elaboration of this method requires that we first specify the objective of the elenchus (O); and the rules (R) by which the method is meant to proceed in order to secure (O). As defined by (O) and (R) these constraining conditions will be shown to suggest that the elenctic method is logically limited to exposing the inconsistency of the belief-set of the interlocutor, rather than prove the falsehood of the refutand; and that the problems raised for the elenchus by the Meno Paradox logically follow from this interpretation.

With respect to (O) the distinctive nature of Socratic, as opposed to sophistic argument, is telling. Though the use of antilogic is common to both, it was argued in the Introduction, that unlike the sophist who sought to persuade his audience to adopt a particular belief by whatever means, Socrates was committed to two distinguishing principles.

Two pertinent conditions apply for (O):

(O1) that assent to belief be restricted to those beliefs that can be proved true.

(O2) that the elenchus should reveal to the interlocutor that his conceit of knowledge is unjustified.

In turn, three further conditions can be inferred for the Rules by which inquiry can proceed:

(O1) introduces (R1) which is an epistemic constraint, which provides that the concluding belief is accepted only if the argument in support of it is both valid and sound.

(O2) introduces (R2) or the availability constraint which provides that the interlocutor must be in a position to follow the argumentative method which reveals the inconsistency of his beliefs.

and finally (R3) or the doxastic constraint[7] provides that all the beliefs sincerely belong to the interlocutor (i.e. that he believes them).[8]

In summary then, the success of the method is achieved when the interlocutor (R2) deduces the falsehood of his original belief, from a number of other beliefs that he also believes are true (R3), and when his reasoning has been both valid and sound (R1).[9] In other words, the conclusion of the counter-argument must be both valid and sound, and the interlocutor must comprehend the logical necessity of its conclusion.

The incompatibility of the epistemic condition at (R1) on the one hand, and the psychological condition at (R3) on the other hand, generates a paradox which logically restricts the elenctic method to its traditionally accepted non-constructivist aporetic interpretation. It is because the beliefs being used to test the truth of the original thesis are also beliefs that are simply accepted as true by the interlocutor, and are not already known to be true, that at the end of the elenchus it is unclear which of all those beliefs is false. The interlocutor expresses the belief that p is true; and to a number of further questions he expresses that q, and r, are also true. The interlocutor is equally committed to the truth of each one of these beliefs; and in case we are worried that he is just repeating popular opinion, he is asked specifically by Socrates to boldly express only those beliefs that he accepts as true. By way of deductive argument, Socrates then demonstrates to the interlocutor for his understanding, that the conjunct of these beliefs {p,q,r} is self-contradictory, in which case at least one of these beliefs must be false. But which one? Unless each of these beliefs in turn is submitted to the elenchus the truth-value of each will remain unknown. And yet, given (R3), this would again introduce a number of other beliefs that the interlocutor has that may or may not be consistent with his other beliefs. The interlocutor is at a loss, and since he is unable to think himself out of this logical entanglement, the dialogue unsurprisingly ends. In other words, unable to render judgement regarding the soundness of the counter-argument the dialogue ends with the only logically inferable conclusion, inconsistency.

Vlastos On the Socratic Elenchus[10]

Convinced that Socrates is not over-stating when he says in the Gorgias, 'has it not been proved that what was asserted [by myself] is true?' (479e), Vlastos attempted to provide a novel reading of the elenchus that would justify this bold claim, i.e. that the refutand is proved false. This demonstration hinges on the acceptance that (1) (R3) is incomplete because the interlocutor's beliefs must not only be his own but Socrates must also accept or believe them to be true; and (2) that Socrates has elenctic knowledge[11] which verifies to him that his belief-set is consistent, and therefore, true. This view is obviously inconsistent with the above and it will be shown to be unacceptable; yet, Vlastos raises a significant point at (2) that deserves elaboration.

That textual support is restricted to a single quote from the Gorgias is already reason enough to doubt that Socrates at all aims at proving anything more than inconsistency. However, whether textual evidence can, in fact, support this view is a secondary issue; what is more interesting is if, given its structure and rules of exposition, it can logically prove that the refutand is false.

Already Vlastos' concession (1) is troubling. If Socrates is going to accept and use in the elenctic process only those doxastic beliefs (R3) that he accepts are true (presumably he asks leading questions which he is already convinced will render the 'right' belief), then in retrospect both Socrates' pedagogic and knowledge disclaimer is an eristic trick used to manipulate his respondents into answering his questions with the intention to shame them. In turn his use of antilogic would become indistinguishable from the sophistic use that Plato seems so determined to keep clearly apart.

Regarding (2) Vlastos introduces an adventurous assumption A which he says Socrates could justifiably have inferred as a meta-elenctic statement, and from which two further assumptions are derived B and C.

A Anyone who ever has a false moral belief will always have at the same time true beliefs entailing the negation of that false belief.

B The set of moral beliefs held by Socrates at any given time is consistent.

C The set of moral beliefs held by Socrates at any given time is true.

The truth of A is inductively inferred from the outcome of numerous elenctic arguments which show that 'every time he [Socrates] tangles with people who defend a thesis he considers false and he looks for true premises among their own beliefs from which he can deduce its negation the needed premises are in place; they are always where they should be if A is true. So he has this purely inductive evidence for A'.[12] It follows that a consistent belief-set must be sound, for given A, any belief-set that contains at least one false belief must also contain true beliefs entailing its negation, in which case it would be an inconsistent belief-set. And from the same kind of inductive reasoning, Socrates is satisfied that his own belief-set is consistent, in which case, given A, his beliefs must also be true. What in effect Vlastos is arguing is that Socrates drew from a history of elenchi, and incorporated—at some point unknown to us—this knowledge in the method itself in order to surmount the so-called early destructive aim of the elenchus, and make some positive propositional claims that he now knows must be true on the basis of the evidence provided by past elenctic conclusions.

On the basis of amended (R3), the elenchus can thus secure the truth of not-p; since the beliefs used in the deductive elenctic counter-argument have been selected on the basis of Socrates' belief-set, and therefore must be true. As the conjunct of these true beliefs entails the negation of the refutand, it must be false. But Vlastos himself admits that Socrates could only claim probability for A; that on the strength of an inductive inference this is most probably a true assumption. Given that it is only probable, can A yield certain truth? Clearly, it cannot.

Vlastos is counting on A to show that at (3) Socrates will accept only those beliefs which he already elenctically knows to be true, in which case, if those beliefs could be false, there is still no reason to be convinced that the elenchus can show any more than inconsistency. Given that A is inductively true, there is room for mistake; therefore, those beliefs could be false. Further, even if we were to credit certainty for A, that A has been established by the elenchus, begs the question. This assumes that the elenchus has been refuting his various opponents all along; i.e. his confidence that q and r are true, and therefore that the refutand is false, is dependent on the elenchus showing just that.[13] But can the elenchus demonstrate truth? This is the question with which we began; the argument is viciously circular, and must therefore be rejected.

These powerful arguments leave little promise for the endorsement of Vlastos' innovative attempt to rewrite the story of the Socratic method; but it is not without shedding new light on our understanding of the method. Although Vlastos' A and B do not meet the challenge, they do make a point of the obvious; namely, that the consistency, or lack of consistency, of any argument can only speak about the relationship that holds between the variously affirmed propositions; and can say nothing of the truth-values of each proposition as such. The extravagance of A-C was introduced exactly for this reason; that without it nothing could be said for the truth-value of the propositional claims being made, and therefore, whether the refutand or any or all of the premises used in the counter-argument were true remained unknown.

Deductive Reasoning and Vlastos

A deductive argument claims that if its premises are true, then the truth of its conclusion necessarily follows. What is important is not whether the premises and conclusion are true, but that it is not possible for the premises to be true and the conclusion false when the argument is valid. Validity refers to the special relationship that holds between the premises and conclusion of a deductive argument. Validity is not interested in the actual truth of the beliefs expressed in an argument, but whether the belief of the conclusion may be logically inferred from the expressed beliefs of the premise set. That means that a valid argument is one which affirms logical consistency for its belief set; indeed, it may be the case that one or more of its beliefs may be false (it is, of course, also possible that an invalid argument be comprised of all true premises and a true conclusion).[14]

> All fishes are mammals
> All whales are fishes
> _____
> Therefore all whales are mammals

Here, we have a valid argument with all false premises, and a true conclusion. Yet, is it the consistency of the argument that tells us that the premises are false? In fact, it is not. However, it does tell us that IF the premises were true, that the conclusion would have to be true. And this is important—and also suggests why Socrates chooses the deductive method for 'refutation'—because it tells us that when our beliefs are inconsistent, and our argument is therefore invalid, our understanding of the beliefs affirmed in our premise set is somehow mistaken. Specifically, inconsistency doesn't evaluate whether the propositional claims do correctly correspond to what is affirmed about the external world (that is, if they are, in fact, true); but reveals that the meaning of the terms employed in the premise-set have not been wholly understood. For instance, in the Republic I (338c-341c) Thrasymachus asserts about justice that,

> justice is what is in the interest of the stronger/ruling party

and from a related belief, he also asserts,

> It is just to obey the laws prescribed by those in power written in their own self-interest[15]

but because, as Socrates suggests and Thrasymachus agrees, those in power are fallible, and may sometimes prescribe laws that are not truly in their own self-interest, they must conclude that,

> it is just to do what is not in the self-interest of the stronger party.

Clearly this conclusion and the second premise can not both be true at the same time (Law of Contradiction);[16] and the inconsistency with which

Thrasymachus employs the term reveals that he, in fact, does not really know what justice is. Rather than leave Thrasymachus with the task of venturing a 'guess' at the faulty belief however, Socrates proceeds with the inquiry only to reveal that not even Thrasymachus could possibly agree with his original thesis because his understanding of 'ruler' renders it self-contradictory;[17] i.e. because he has conceded that no ruler ever enjoins his own advantage (342c), the original thesis now reads, 'justice is what is in the interest of the ruling party who never prescribes what is in his own self interest'.

In this way Socrates blocks the easy route of dropping one of the two contradictory beliefs, and intimates that it is because Thrasymachus does not know what justice is, that he is bound to employ predicates which won't always consistently apply, and it is for this reason that a deductive argument could always be used to refute him. In other words, as Vlastos himself argues though for very different reasons, 'Socrates is convinced that when he shows his interlocutors the inconsistency of their thesis with the conjunction of premises to which they have agreed, they will never succeed in saving their thesis by retracting conceded premises...'.[18]

Though Socrates could not have drawn this inference from inductive elenctic experience (as has already been shown), he could have deductively inferred it. To understand this it is important to be aware of two factors: (i) that at (1) Socrates is searching for an exhaustive definition of x that will satisfy all possible affirmations about x consistently.[19] That is, no matter what predicates are used to describe x, all such predicates must consistently correspond to the given meaning of x. This in turn suggests, and Socrates makes no secret of this, that (ii) for each term employed or used to describe x, the appropriate definition must also be available (*Meno* 75d);[20] and so forth for the terms of that definition, ad infinitum; and hence an infinite regress. It is therefore for this reason that even if the interlocutor were to choose the apparently easy route and withdraw one of his previously conceded beliefs, unless he could meet this infinite regress the deductive method would eventually reveal some inconsistency within his belief-set. Socrates on this view is fittingly characterised a sceptic; indeed knowledge is beyond human capacity, and his disavowal of knowledge is quite consistent.

Though no argument has presented itself to counter this problem apart from Vlastos' heroic attempt, it does seem that Socrates supposes that this deductive feat consists of almost extracting from these words meanings or definitions which entail the meanings of these constituent terms such that a pyramidal skeleton of these definitions of terms would become apparent. One would imagine Socrates working from the top descending to its smallest composite parts by determining, as he often acclaims, what all things that could be called by such a name would have to have in common. An answer to this question would have us identify one or more further qualities whereupon Socrates would propose to determine the rightful meaning of these via the same process until finally we arrived at a number of terms which required no further qualification. What reason could there be for this? Would the process of unpacking the meanings of words end where words meant only what they named? Would it end where the last strand in the string of deductive inferences implied the first? For this no evidence can tell. Still, as gallant a fight as this final plea may be, it can not establish knowledge. Once more we are left with the question, 'how when starting from the top—presuming that we know the top—of the pyramid can one be sure that the meaning supposedly extracted from it is actually correct, or wholly correct?' Here we may borrow Vlastos' A and by putting it to a slightly variant purpose say that a life time of elenctic pursuits had indeed found Socrates always prepared to supplant the appropriately related belief in order to overthrow his interlocutor, and if nothing else this showed that the moral terms he commonly disputed must be comprised of the particular constituent terms he proposed. Still, for the reasons already discussed A is insufficient to make such a bold claim.

Can the deductive method alone, however, be counted on to render knowledge? Given the hypothetical scenario where the challenge of the infinite regress has been met, does an albeit exhaustively consistent belief set demonstrate knowledge? Though the deductive method is perfectly suited to the destructive objective of the elenchus; it is doubtful that an achieved consistency is all that is required for knowledge. For it has already been argued that even a valid or consistent belief set can say nothing about the truth-value of each individual belief, or indeed whether, in fact, its author knew it to be true. For this reason the deductive elenctic method can not be used for the reverse purpose; namely to build knowledge. The logical inference here deductively drawn regarding invalid arguments and its implication (i.e. that the terms employed have been somehow mistakenly understood) can not be drawn for valid arguments. Inconsistency does demonstrate lack of knowledge; but consistency or validity (alone) does not by implication render knowledge.

For Socrates the deductive method was never used to build knowledge, but only to reveal that his interlocutors do not have knowledge, and to this focused task the deductive method is ideal. Understanding that, is understanding both the Socratic elenctic method, and the peril of Plato's mission to reveal the problem of then moving on to a positive constructivist method to attain knowledge.

Setting Up the Paradox

Meno opens the topic of debate with the kind of question which we would expect the Platonic Socrates anxious to find a satisfying response to. He asks, 'can virtue be acquired by teaching or practice, or if neither by teaching nor practice, then does it come to man from nature, or what other way?' (70a)

Given that the Socratic method is exclusively concerned with moral questions and that the elenchus must, at least in a limited sense, aim at somehow affecting the beliefs of its participants (i.e. the doxastic and availability constraint), so that they part having 'learned' that what they previously believed to know with certainty they now know to be not true—i.e. the conjunction of their contradictory beliefs must be false,[21] it is imperative that the elenchus therefore be able to justify the effectiveness of appealing to the method for moral questioning and thereby establish that virtue, which is after all the encapsulation of all moral ideals (i.e. the 'Unity of Virtues', see the Protagoras), is somehow teachable. In other words, if the elenchus is unfit to teach anything about morality then why submit moral practice to the scrutiny of the elenchus?

Having in this limited sense set the stage for a rebuttal or defence of the elenctic method Socrates replies in a manner typical of the method; he says,—first alluding to the sophistic prejudice of Meno's training (i.e. following Gorgias' visit to Thessaly Meno has been accustomed to a bold manner of speaking which becomes those who know)—that he is not only unable to render an answer regarding the source of virtue, but he could not even say what virtue is. To make his point Socrates asserts, and Meno agrees, that if he did not know Meno, he could not say anything about him or in any way describe him. Meno misses the implication—that knowledge of what the object concerned is, is logically prior to knowing anything else about it—and in disbelief asks if that is what he is to report back to

Thessaly about Socrates. Socrates concedes, and adds, as if to entice Meno to carry on and provide an answer to the newly established question of Socrates' choosing, that he in fact has never known of anyone else who did in his judgement know what virtue is. Because Gorgias—Meno's teacher— supposedly has advanced a view on virtue which both he and Socrates have heard, but which Socrates has forgotten, Meno is asked to recapitulate since his views are consistent with Gorgias'.

Meno has not yet understood why the knowledge of what virtue is, is logically prior to knowing anything about virtue; in fact, Meno can not even appreciate the difference between the two kinds of questions which is, in fact, responsible for his failure to provide a satisfactory reply; and in Socrates' effort to enlighten Meno they are inevitably led down the dark path to the Meno Paradox. The is/about distinction marks a significant epistemological point and for this reason will take italic throughout. To say that x is y implies identification, whereas to say x is F implies predication. Looking back to Parmenides, predication becomes impossible when we adopt the view that for each word there is a corresponding object in the world in virtue of which names become meaningful and true when the name is used accurately for its object.

Despite Meno's ineptness, he nevertheless proceeds by first attending to this question. Meno answers boldly, but in his arrogance stumbles, and Socrates in his usual manner remarks that though he had asked for one virtue, he is presented with many; i.e. Meno describes a virtuous man, woman and child (72a). Socrates shows Meno by way of analogy that the case of bees is no different from that of virtue; for all things that can rightly be called a bee share a quality by which they are not different; hence he must direct his attention to identifying that quality commonly shared by each instance of virtue, and according to which they are rightly referred to as virtuous. Meno says that he is beginning to understand, and the subsequent example about strength verifies this; yet, he is unable to draw the general inference in order to apply this understanding to the case of virtue. Meno is committed to the view that a man and woman are not virtuous for the same reason; a virtuous man knows how to administer the state, whereas a virtuous woman keeps house and obeys her husband. Must Meno admit that a virtuous man too must by the same token also keep house in order to satisfy Socrates with an answer to his question and by doing so provide a single quality against which all things may rightly be described as virtuous? In Socrates' effort to show Meno that this is what makes a virtuous man different and not the same as a virtuous woman—in the same way that there are bees of varying shape and colour— he argues that each in turn can only rightly be referred to as virtuous when they perform their distinctive tasks with justice and temperance (72e-73d). Satisfied that he has subsequently understood the object of the Socratic question, Meno makes a second attempt to say what virtue is, namely 'the power of governing mankind' (73e). To this Socrates adds, and Meno agrees, that 'the government must be just', for after all 'justice is a virtue'. In reply Socrates asks, is justice a virtue, or virtue itself?

Meno is once again at a loss; and, Socrates once again in his customary manner refers Meno to an example to clarify. Roundness, he says, is a shape, but not shape itself since there are various other examples of shapes, and likewise justice is a virtue, not virtue itself since there are many other kinds of virtues. Anxious to display his understanding Meno thereby furnishes examples of the various kinds of virtues as courage, temperance, wisdom and magnanimity. Much to his dismay however, he has yet again found many virtues when Socrates' search was directed at one; the same mistake, in fact, that he made at the beginning of their inquiry, though, as Socrates is careful to point out, it is a mistake of a different order (74b).

In this latter case Meno has mistakenly arrived at a number of universal terms; whereas, in the former case he had concluded with a number of particular instances of virtuous acts. The very significant difference between the two kinds of mistakes is that for any universal term there must be a corresponding definition of its meaning against which any particular thing may rightly or not be described as such. In other words, because the universal is the property predicated or used to describe a particular thing, defining or knowing the meaning of xness is logically prior to naming or identifying a thing as x. Hence, before expressing any beliefs about things we must first be certain that the meaning we assign to a given universal term is correct; i.e. we must know what xness is. This is, in fact, precisely the reason given to support Socrates' intent on first working out whether his interlocutor has such an understanding/knowledge of the terms employed in his beliefs. The previous analysis of the elenctic method demonstrates that the interlocutor could not possess such an understanding/knowledge, for if he had, no logical inconsistencies could possibly emerge regarding his relevant beliefs. For as previously argued, a derived inconsistency does reveal a lack of understanding/knowledge since it is the knowledge of xness which guarantees that something could not falsely be described as x because I know all the necessary and sufficient characteristics that something must possess in order to be described as x. Still focused on the task of exhibiting his knowledge to Socrates however, Meno hasn't yet reached this realisation.

Still in this epideictic mode of inquiry (typical of sophistic discourse) Meno is blinded to the devastating problem raised by the above enumeration, and so the Platonic Socrates tries, once again, to help Meno understand the objective of their task. Socrates is unwavering in his direction, and explains to Meno by way of example[22] that justice, temperance, and so on, must all share some quality in virtue of which they can consistently be called virtues. Exploiting the example of figure Socrates provides a sample definition as, 'figure is the only thing which always follows colour' (75c). Meno thereby raises an astute objection in the form of a question, and asks what Socrates would reply to a person who were to say that he does not know what colour is, any more than what figure is?' (75b). Socrates' reply is significant. He says that 'he would make use of the premises which the person interrogated would be willing to admit' (75d)—therefore, he would appeal to the already existing beliefs of his interlocutor (i.e. the doxastic constraint) in order to arrive at a definition of the particular term in question. Once again however, the application of these arbitrary beliefs could in no way guarantee that the definition derived would be anything more than internally consistent; that is, it could not thereby be established as true. In fact, Socrates seems to be alluding to the arbitrary status of the proposed definition of colour immediately following since he says that Meno is impressed with this response only because it is what he is in the habit of hearing.

Meno offers a poet's saying as the third definition of virtue; 'he who desires the honourable and is able to provide it for himself' (77b). The elenchus is unceasing and in its usual destructivist manner shows that what Meno believes about the honourable and desirable (the terms employed in his definition) renders his definition too broad; and what he believes about the means of its acquisition uninformative. That the acquisition of any goods is virtuous only when the means are just and pious; yet this only says that what is done with part of virtue is virtue. That again is begging the question; Socrates wants to know what virtue is, so that he can thereby recognise something as virtuous. Meno is unable to follow the pattern of definition earlier framed by example since he is employing terms which couldn't very well be known since knowing them is dependent upon already having a satisfying answer to their original question, 'what is virtue?'. To define the meaning of these given terms—as in the case of colour—by reference to their generic class (in this case virtue) first requires defining virtue itself.

Frustrated, and for the first time demonstrating insightful confusion, Meno takes a turn at asking the questions, and in what follows sets the agenda for the remainder of the dialogue. Specifically, Meno asks three penetrating questions known as the Meno Paradox: (1) 'how, if you do not know what virtue is, will you look for it?, (2) what sort of thing among the things that you do not know will you set before yourself as the object of your search?, and (3) if you did chance upon it, how would you know that it was the thing that you did not know to begin with?' (80c). Socrates replies by reformulating (1)-(3) in order to show how these questions lead to an impasse of inquiry since (4) in the case that x is already known there is no point in searching for it; and (5) in the case that x is unknown the search remains undirected since you do not know what you are searching for. Numbers (4)-(5) do not strictly correspond to what Meno had said, and suggest that this is a Socratic Dilemma. The impasse proposes a logico-epistemological dilemma: either (i) knowing x is incompatible with searching for x, or (ii) not knowing x is incompatible with searching for x.

A Preliminary Analysis

A prior analysis of the structure of the exposition of the Meno Paradox (MP) must first spell out what weakness the paradox could have been logically expected to expose for the elenchus before proceeding to 'the problem' and a recipe for its solution. The MP has often been described as a problem for inquiry. Inquiry is either (5) impossible because you do not know what to look for; or (4) pointless because you already know what it is you are looking for; and hence, inquiry stops before it begins. There is nothing however, in the dialogue that supports such a reading except for Socrates' treatment and re-appraisal of the paradox in terms of points (4) and (5). However, Socrates' reappraisal presents a problem in itself since, as will be shown, the Meno Paradox identifies the elenctic deadlock not at the start of inquiry, but at the end of inquiry. Therefore, inquiry does not stop before it begins; and the MP can not legitimately be renamed a 'problem for inquiry'. Inquiry, indeed is possible; in fact, it is commonplace; Socrates engages in inquiry all the time. We must search elsewhere to locate the essence of the logical puzzle Meno presents, therefore.

The MP asks three distinctive questions, which are often subsumed by Socrates' treatment of them in terms of (4) and (5), which will be referred to as the Socratic Dilemma (SD). Two main arguments have been advanced to justify this treatment of the MP. The first argues that Socrates reformulates the paradox in order to expose the contentious[23] nature of the argument that Meno—consistent with his training—is leading up to. By implication we need not bother with the slight discrepancy regarding the way in which Socrates reformulates the paradox originally expressed by Meno. The second argues that because (1)-(3) rest on establishing that inquiry (1) is incompatible with either (i) knowing or (ii) not knowing, that questions (2)-(3) are conditional upon its solution, and therefore uninteresting as a separate problem.

The first argument however is unable to account for the deliberate and elaborate development of the arguments leading up to the MP and its solution, which suggests that the adjective eristic or contentious is used not to describe the status of the paradox itself but the dubious status of the elenctic method specifically. Whereas, the second argument can not say why Meno didn't, in fact, ask only one question, namely 'how, if you do not know what virtue is, will you search for it?'.

Contrarily there are strong reasons in favour of treating the MP and the SD as separate, yet certainly related, puzzles. Questions (1)-(3) introduce three successive stages of inquiry; each movement assuming the preceding stage: (1) concerns the impetus of inquiry or the conditions required for inquiry to begin; (2) concerns the hypothetical knowledge-claim or subject of inquiry; and finally (3) refers to rendering proof or securing the proposed end of inquiry; i.e. finding the answer. Meno could have no other reason for proposing all three successive stages unless he also believed that the elenchus could obstruct the paradox both at (1) and (2), but that the conditions of the elenchus would be found incompatible with (3). Obviously *Meno* would have had no need to go beyond (1) if it could counter the possibility of inquiry from the beginning.

That the SD suggests that the paradox is damaging only if inquiry is found to be incompatible with both (i) knowing, and (ii) not knowing (because for each respective case inquiry is rendered either meaningless or literally unthinkable) is curiously incongruous with the above since Meno doesn't raise this point until (3). Specifically, (4) does not figure in (1)-(3) at all (no where does Socrates fret about the meaninglessness of searching for professed knowledge), but is introduced on the strength of the assumption which (5), taken from (3) makes. At (5) Socrates argues that in the absence of the knowledge of what x is, inquiry must be rendered impossible for, as (3) advocates, judgement regarding the authenticity of something must be suspended prior to knowing the necessary and sufficient conditions which constitute what it is. This, in turn, implies that knowledge of this kind would be complete or exhaustive and therefore inquiry would be pointless.

What justifies this incongruity, and what gives cause to Socrates' derogatory referral to the dilemma as contentious—which he was given cause to raise on the basis of (3)? Textual evidence and the logical form of the elenchus provide an answer. The paradox is the offspring of Meno's eventual inability to prove what he 'professed to know' at the beginning of the dialogue on the terms or conditions of the method. Immediately preceding the paradox Meno likens Socrates to a sting-ray—an animal which catches and incapacitates its prey—objecting that 'prior to submitting himself to the Socratic method of inquiry, he had delivered many high calibre speeches to many people, but can now not even say what virtue is' (80b3-4), because, following the MP, the elenchus has disqualified all attempts of defining virtue by reference to terms that are themselves conditioned on already knowing what virtue is. Therefore, if the Socratic method has incapacitated Meno in his pursuit to 'prove his knowledge' in the same way that the sting-ray does its prey, then if this, in turn, raises a problem for inquiry, the elenchus has inadvertently been stung by its own tail; i.e. the objective of the elenchus is incompatible with its method of pursuit. Therefore, the elenchus is internally inconsistent, in which case either its objective or method of pursuit must be rejected as unsound. The SD implied that the paradox is damaging only if inquiry is incompatible with both (i) knowing and (ii) not knowing; but the elenchus may suffer further damage, and may also be rendered contentious, if it is also unable to consistently maintain its high standards for the pursuit of truth.

The analysis of the MP depends upon both the structure and conditions of the elenctic method as well as the historical evidence which portrays Socrates as the spokesperson for the elenchus. That would mean that for Socrates inquiry is indeed possible, and since there is nothing in the *Meno* preceding the MP which contradicts this view, quite the contrary in fact, the interpretation of the paradox should be expected to reflect this. The point is that we do engage in inquiry, indeed Meno is led to his paradox whilst engaged in inquiry; but, if the SD is to be taken seriously, we would have to admit that inquiry is stumped altogether from the outset, (4) and (5). Most would agree that inquiry presupposes the absence of knowledge (at least at some level). Socrates, even Plato, must have believed this, since, after all the pursuit for knowledge is always preceded by the destructive exercise of deflating the unwarranted conceit of an interlocutor, and to then start afresh. The acknowledgement of this distinction, implies that the argument which is going to show how 'knowledge acquisition' is possible may be different from the argument which will show how it is possible 'to think something in order to then inquiry about it'. There is an important incongruity between what the elenchus, now as always, is entitled to do and what the stringent condition for thought given at (4) and (5) entitles it to. The elenchus must be able to get started since the paradox as presented by Socrates is also the result of inquiry; but the all-or-nothing condition for thought clearly renders the conclusion that this is logically impossible.

The Meno Paradox

The MP is threefold. Taking its start from the problem raised by the 'priority of definition' which the SD lucidly spells out, three successive questions are raised for inquiry (1-3).The three questions of inquiry are as follows:

(1) What is the appropriate method of inquiry [or (R)]?
(2) What is the object of the inquiry?
(3) What is the end of the inquiry?

It is being argued that (1) and (2) are not regularly taken to be problematic and the elenchus is never shown to be defective in these ways; but that (3) has often been acknowledged as a problem for the elenchus both historically in terms of the sophists, and epistemological in terms of the traditional aporetic end of the early Socratic dialogues.

On the basis of the all-or-nothing condition provided by Socrates, it is always going to be impossible to entertain thoughts unless the object of that thought is somehow (e.g. TR) already known. It would follow straightforwardly that all the beliefs normally acquired from the interlocutor for inquiry to both begin and carry on already constitute knowledge. All the beliefs on the grounds of the all-or-nothing premise would already comprise knowledge; for again anything less would be impossible. All the beliefs used in the elenctic search constitute knowledge and inquiry stops before it begins. That takes care of (1). In turn, it is also impossible to name something as the object of inquiry (2), or supplant one of the interlocutor's existing beliefs as the subject of the search, because once again this requires knowing that thing, and hence it is pointless to search for it. Finally, (3) is concerned with the ability to distinguish truth from falsehood. Specifically it asks which of all the beliefs the interlocutors submit for discussion in the elenctic pursuit for knowledge are true, and which false. All of this is just a little queer because each question, (1)-(3), presupposes that an answer has been given to its preceding question. But we have already seen that on the basis of Socrates' all-or-nothing premise a possible answer to each of the three questions is faced with the same paradox. Moreover, all of this must be pertinent to the elenchus. It is strange how all the so-called true beliefs which constitute knowledge at (1) can get the interlocutors stuck in contradiction. And (3) doesn't even begin to make sense unless you have already admitted that you can have some true and some false beliefs; and that both are held with equal conviction. It is for the reasons outlined that it is important to notice that (1) and (2) do not strictly apply to the elenchus.

Despite the fact that the paradox as such lies with (3), the final frame of the paradox could not have revealed why the elenchus is necessarily committed to an underlying argument which renders the efforts of inquiry contentious without (1) and (2). The first two frames show that despite the priority of definition—as the Early Platonic dialogues attest to—Socratic inquiry does nonetheless proceed; and apart from the otherwise well-known intention of the elenchus to discover truths, its only requirement is that his interlocutors honestly employ their own beliefs, without the further stipulation that these beliefs are also true. Inquiry is thereby able to proceed but at great cost. For at the end of the elenchus, following (R2), the belief-set of the interlocutor is affected—though negatively—because he understands that the 'refutand' and its contradictory cannot both be true at the same time (Law of Contradiction); and that either the one or the other must be true (Law of the Excluded Middle). Hence given that both the 'refutand' and its contradictory are derived from the interlocutor's already existing beliefs, then from the outset Socrates must be assuming—in fact counting on the fact—that his interlocutor has some or partial knowledge regarding his proposed knowledge-claim, which constitutes the straight contradiction that they 'both know and do not know at the same time'. Notice that Socrates' reformulation of the paradox subsumes the three staged development by Meno under the paradox of the hit-or-miss contention regarding knowledge and hence the identification of belief with knowledge.

This underlying contradiction is important not just because it reveals that the elenchus is internally inconsistent, but because it suggests that if Socrates is unable to show the possibility of (R1), that given (R3), he will be hard pressed to show that the truth is not relative to what each individual just happens to believe is true. As Protagoras—the protagonist of sophistic teaching—has said, 'man is the measure of all things that are, that they are; and of all things that are not, that they are not' (*Tht.* 152 a2-5), because knowledge is necessarily restricted to what 'appears to be the case for each person'. Despite the radical empiricism (i.e. knowledge is perception), sophistic relativism does not differ from the kind of relativism which Socrates is forced to admit in the absence of proof for (R1). In either case the problem is that the only thing we can know with 'certainty' is what we believe. So when restricted to the conditions of (R2) and (R3) Socrates can only travel the road of sophistic inquiry which also appeals to the existing beliefs of his interlocutor [i.e. (R3)], but chooses to affect [i.e. (R2)] those beliefs via the so-called contentious means of eristic argument employed for the purpose of persuasion alone. Finally, the paradox of elenctic inquiry is shown to rest on an underlying argument which exposes its contentious character because without (R1) the elenchus is subsumed by sophism.

An analysis of the structure of the elenchus has shown that Socratic inquiry is a response to a hypothetical knowledge-claim proposed by an interlocutor, and that, drawing from the belief-set of the same man, Socrates sought to establish if the claim were sound. However, a breakdown of the elenctic conditions of inquiry showed them to be necessarily restricted to the destructive task of invalidation. Hence, the elenchus was shown to embark on inquiry intent on searching amongst the given beliefs of his interlocutor for the justification of the proposed knowledge-claim made at the outset. That inquiry can proceed in this way—based upon the arbitrary status of the belief-set of the interlocutor—suggests that for both (1) and (2) the elenchus is not obstructed by the problem posed by the priority of definition. It also suggests that the inauguration of knowledge-claims are helplessly limited to the dubious status of our beliefs. For successfully obstructed by (3) or the inability of the elenchus to prove the soundness of a proposed knowledge-claim, all inquiry, though obviously possible, will be based on the agglomeration of persuasively and perhaps validly arranged beliefs. The MP thus leads to the argument which reveals that elenctic inquiry, like sophistic inquiry, is possible; but, it is nonetheless unable to render truth. In fact, for the same reasons that Socrates has referred to sophistic inquiry as contentious, in the absence of objective truth, Socrates must also admit that all beliefs are relative to what appears to be the case. Note that appearances show that the beliefs which follow validly must also be true, but it does not also necessarily make them true.

Subsequent sections will show that the Platonic Socrates dissolves this contradiction by introducing (a) the distinction between knowledge and belief, and (b) the Theory of Recollection (TR) which, like Vlastos' A, provides the means of distinguishing true from false beliefs about what something is like (poion ti) on the basis of latent knowledge concerning what a thing is (ti esti). It will also be argued that Plato does not bother to show where these beliefs (as opposed to knowledge) come from; but is involved with the specific, yet restricted, task of providing a theory on the basis of which knowledge acquisition is possible. Moreover, despite criticism to the contrary, it will be argued that the Method of Hypothesis (MH) is part and parcel of the proposed solution of the TR.

The Theory of Recollection

The Theory of Recollection (TR) is being used to counter the impasse to inquiry introduced on the merit of the MP. However, as the preceding section has shown the MP is a threat only to the possibility of knowledge acquisition (3). By implication the form of the elenctic method should remain unaffected by the TR; and should be seen as providing the means to move beyond the aporetic destructivism of early(ier) Socratic dialectic.[24] This addition to the method must consist of the logical grounds or method by which the executor[25] be able to judge which of his contradictory beliefs is true; which for Socrates would necessarily comprise knowledge (i.e. the Priority of Definition or PD). For it is the lack of knowledge (PD) which is responsible for this impasse, since this is tantamount to no knowledge whatsoever (i.e. knowledge is an all-or-nothing affair). As a result all beliefs were left to the same desolate fate of indiscriminable status, which was shown to be the consequence of sophistic epistemology, and the motto (i.e. all beliefs are equally true) of sophistic inquiry, which we want to keep clearly apart from Socrates' mission.

The TR should not be viewed as challenging the PD; but as providing an argument that makes it possible to 'possess' knowledge prior to inquiry but, at the same time, in a (psychological) state of ignorance. Such a state would permit Socrates to argue that inquiry is not incompatible with not-knowing. For the TR to be successful it must show (a) why this still doesn't commit Socrates to the straight contradiction that he knows and does not know the same thing at the same time; (b) how prior or innate knowledge acquisition does not collapse into the same problem Socrates is trying to solve; (c) how this so-called prior knowledge differs from current or a posteriori knowledge; and (d) why the elenchus is the necessary route for the attainment of current or a posteriori knowledge.

The Slave Boy Example as Testimony

That the sample elenchus—renowned as the Slave Boy Example—has been set up to illustrate to Meno how the TR resolves the problem of the MP in general is uncontroversially accepted on Socrates' word (82a-b6; esp. 82b5-6); so that, if it can be shown that in this example the elenchus is unchanged, and that the TR merely introduces the means of attaining knowledge, it may be inferred with confidence that Plato means to exceed the destructivism of Socrates. Therefore, evidence that the TR is pertinent to elenctic inquiry only after the interlocutor or executor has arrived at that contradictory proposition which reveals his false conceit of knowledge, will be sufficient to prove that the MP raised the specific problem of knowledge acquisition; and that the elenchus prior to this was exclusively destructive in scope.

Though the sample elenchus is not obviously identical to the elenctic structure outlined in the section Elenctic Form, the running commentary to which Socrates refers us does suggest the relevant distinctive marks of each stage.[26] The distinctive feature of the first stage is characterised by the interlocutor's over confident reply to Socrates' original question. At 82e4-7 Socrates comments 'you see, Meno, that I am not teaching him anything, only asking. Now he thinks he knows the length of the side of the eight-foot square'. Here we have the proposed knowledge-claim with which elenctic inquiry begins; and seeks to evaluate as a legitimate claim to knowledge.

Stages 2-4 transpire over a relatively short span where Socrates asks the interlocutor to answer a number of relevant questions which the slave boy honestly and boldly (82d-e) responds to (hence consistent with the doxastic constraint), but gets himself into ever deeper confusion, until finally the inconsistency of his variously expressed beliefs lead him to conclude 'It's no use Socrates, I just don't know [the correct answer]' (84a2).

Based on his own belief-set,[27] the Slave boy advocates as a proposed knowledge-claim that 'doubling the side of a given square would produce a double sized figure' (83a); or belief {p}. However, the interlocutor, when questioned, is revealed to be equally committed to the belief that, q, 'a double sized figure/square must be equal on all its sides, such that, r, each side is double, so that, s, when dissected into equal parts, it contains four squares, each equal to the size of the original four-foot square' (83b1-10); or beliefs {q,r,s}. Yet, beliefs {q,r,s} entail the belief that a square twice the size of a four-foot square must be four times bigger than the original corresponding to its four dissected parts (83b12); or not-p, which contradicts his originally proposed reply p. These two movements coincide with stages two and three of the elenchus where a conclusion is rendered on the basis of the interlocutor's belief-set which is logically inconsistent with what his originally proposed knowledge-claim advocated.

Inquiry does not however end there. Socrates sets up another mathematical exercise implying that the knowledge required to work out the answer to the original question would be sufficient for working out any other related problem. That is, if the slave boy is right about this latter belief,[28] and believes that he knows the right answer, he should be able to draw the right knowledge-claim for any similar mathematical problem. Yet, still confusing the comparative size and occupied space of the related squares, the slave boy has not yet drawn the general inference regarding the criteria or mathematical formula which determines the right answer. It is the lack of knowledge which constitutes his general failure to respond to the question, and this nicely parallels his final knowledge disclaimer (84a2) and corresponding fourth and last stage of early Socratic elenctic inquiry. Hence, knowledge is not just sufficient for rendering the right answer about related problems, but it is also necessary. Whereas he originally felt confident he could work out the right answer to the given question, he now does not even know how to go about answering it; or as Socrates puts it '[previously] he thought he knew it and answered boldly, as was appropriate—he felt no perplexity. Now however he does feel perplexed. Not only does he not know the answer; he does not even think he knows' (84b1). That is, because the truth of his latter belief, {not-p}, was not available to the slave boy, but was derived from the logical inferences drawn from those beliefs Socrates revealed he did possess, in the absence of knowledge he could follow how this was related to the original question; it was just one amongst many equally affirmed beliefs. Aware of the inconsistency of his beliefs, the slave boy is in the psychologically uneasy state of aporia.

Apart from the discerned similarities of the slave boy conversation with the elenchus generally, Socrates, immediately following the interlocutor's expressed aporia, and immediately prior to embarking on the TR proper, explicitly tells us that 3 (secure truth and knowledge) can only begin once the conceit of knowledge has been dispelled.[29] From 84b-c9 Socrates takes a breather to comment on the results rendered by the method so far, and equates it with the given results of his conversation with Meno before the paradox. At 84b5 Socrates describes the resulting perplexity that the elenchus has stirred up in the slave boy as

...numbing him like a sting ray...

These are the same chosen words used by Meno to describe the annoying aporetic end of the elenchus at 80a5 just before introducing the MP. He says,

...you are exactly like a sting ray that one meets in the sea. Whenever anyone comes into contact with it, it numbs him, and that is the sort of thing that you seem to be doing to me now. My mind and my lips are literally numb, and I have nothing to reply to you.

And extending the parallel between these two instances he says, speaking for the slave boy

> up till now, he thought he could speak well and
> fluently, on many occasions and before large
> audiences, on the subject of a square double the size
> of a given square, maintaining that it must have a side
> of double the length (84b11)

which are precisely the words used by Meno to express his frustration, and perhaps to make the point that the elenchus is destructive in nature;

> yet I have spoken about virtue hundreds of times, held
> forth often on the subject in front of large audiences,
> and very well too... (80b)

Even if this parallel were accidental, Socrates could have no other reason to argue that he had done the slave boy a service in inducing in him this perplexity and aporia (84b9-10; 84c4-8)—the same perplexity that Meno had experienced—because it is

> ...starting from this state of perplexity, [that] he will
> discover by seeking the truth in company with me,
> though I simply ask questions without teaching him.
> (84c11-d)

except to make the point that it is only after the default-conclusion rendered by the elenchus (i.e. early Socratic elenctic method) that the TR can take over to yield conclusive results. In fact, Meno's and Socrates' inquiry preliminarily ended with the following remark from Socrates, 'I am ready to carry out with you, a joint investigation and inquiry into what it is' (80d7-8). So that again making the same point, having driven you to the state of perplexity that Socrates enjoys, they may now nonetheless set out together to define virtue; or the knowledge of what virtue is.

It was this joint perplexity and, therefore ignorance, of course, which led Meno to the logically substantive view that knowledge-acquisition is impossible for the elenchus. Now, having therefore led the slave boy to aporia, Socrates has satisfied the first frame of the MP; only in a legitimate psychological state of ignorance—when you do not think you know—is inquiry possible or sensible. For irrespective of whether you do, in fact, have the right answer or true belief, so long as that truth is for you unrecognisable you do have a genuine subject for inquiry. Hence, Socrates is pushing for the 'compatibility of not-knowing with inquiry'; and is therefore, left with the task to show that 'a state of ignorance' can render knowledge. In fact, had Socrates not opted for the compatibility of not-knowing with inquiry, the destructivism of the Socratic method would have remained unaccounted for. He has now shown that this is what the elenchus achieves, and has expressed its positive reinforcement as a developmental stage leading up to knowledge-acquisition, but he has not yet proved its necessity—i.e. could the TR work independently without this preliminary stage? Whether indeed the TR is logically separable from this so-called preliminary and destructive stage of inquiry may however miss the mark. For given that the elenchus seeks to affect the belief-set of his participants (availability constraint) in the absence of conscious doubt, in fact, given the existence of arrogant conceit, the elenchus would lack the persuasive vigour required to uproot them from their dogmatic slumber.[30] As Socrates himself argues, 'in fact we have helped him [the slave boy] to some extent toward finding out the right answer, for now not only is he ignorant of it but he will be quite glad to look for it' (84b9-11).

The TR and Knowledge-Acquisition

Following this destructive stage which accurately parallels the end of early Socratic dialectic, Socrates begins the 'interrogation of the slave boy's own opinions' (84d2-3) for the same subject all over again. So that, as Socrates clearly confirms in his summing up of this stage of elenctic development (85c-d7), this is where recollection proper takes off; namely from ignorance.

In his usual manner, Socrates does not instruct or explain anything to the boy; he merely asks a number of questions to which he is granted assent. These questions are conspicuously more appropriately leading...to the right answer, which the slave boy does eventually derive, however.[31] For instance, 'by suggesting that the required length must be between two and four, Socrates almost prompted the slave to give the wrong answer, 'three'; but when he pointed out that this was wrong, and led him on to the correct solution, the slave was able to 'see' that what was said was true'.[32] Then, Socrates, even more suspiciously, provides the boy with the technical name for the mathematical operation from which the right answer was derived. Socrates manages to squeeze this addition in without causing too much fuss. However, this is indeed an eyebrow raiser, for though Socrates offers it in the name of expediency, he does explain (as the name itself suggests) that 'the square on the diagonal of the original square is double its area' (85b8). Despite the fact that he introduces it as 'an opinion that the boy already possessed' (i.e. 'it is your personal opinion that...'.), the boy did not and could not have drawn this as a general inference by himself, for that would have required his acknowledged assent to a belief he recognised as being true. And it is this 'recognition of a true belief requirement' which presupposes knowledge that got the MP on its way. Overlooking this concern, the running commentary argues that the slave boy has indeed advanced beyond the previous stage of doubt, to a stage of true belief. The previous stage ended in the boy's recognised defeat—'I do not know'; whereas he is now once again responding in the same zealous fashion he had prior to his aporia. Nonetheless, there are no distinguishable marks of wisdom that persuade us that this state is any different in quality from his original one. Is it not possible that he could have just as easily committed himself to a bunch of contradictory beliefs had Socrates posed them in a fashion that the slave boy would have found appealing?

In fact, Socrates almost admits as much in the final stage where he explains that the boy's 'present opinions, being newly aroused, have a dreamlike quality. But if the same questions are put to him on many occasions and in different ways, you can see that in the end he will have a knowledge on the subject as accurate as anybody's' (85c11-d). So that 'knowledge will not come from teaching but from questioning' (85d2-3); in fact, from the appropriate questioning.

A lot seems to depend on the kinds of questions put forth for answering. In other words, without further questioning of the same sort the boy would remain in this state of affirmed belief; but would not understand why his affirmed belief is, in fact, true. But this begs the question the paradox is raising. It is the absence of knowing why or what makes a particular belief true that necessarily discredits any attempt at fixing belief; for in the absence of knowledge there is no way of distinguishing a true from a false belief.

Therefore, in the absence of some sign that the boy managed to at least draw some general rule on the basis of the logical relation of his affirmed beliefs, there is nothing to distinguish the first stages from the latter stages except the content of the questions; and Socrates' claim that the slave boy has arrived at a true belief—notably because he (and Meno) knows the right answer. Unless, therefore, the theoretical account of the TR can somehow show how the mental state of the slave boy at stages 1-2 differed in quality from stages 3-4, and explain how the boy could have alone recognised his belief at stage 3 as being true, especially given that knowledge acquisition requires being able to 'tie down its truth by working out its cause' (aitias logismos) at stage four, the paradox remains unanswered. For once again until this can be demonstrated it remains impossible to determine whether, in your ignorance, you have mistakenly got hold of a false, rather than a true, belief; and thereby wrongly satisfied yourself that you possess knowledge. It is important to remember that the interlocutor 'believes' that he is in a state of knowledge; and that the purported arguments that turn out to be invalid on the elenctic account, provide its reasons. But these supporting beliefs are problematic because even though the elenchus can establish that after all the interlocutor's originally proposed knowledge-claim is self-refuting, he is unable to tell which of all his beliefs are false, and which are true. It is capable only of showing that his belief-set is self-contradictory; and that according to the Law of Excluded Middle, either the belief or its contradictory must be true. And therefore, knowledge must be both necessary and sufficient to the task of distinguishing a true from false belief, and there lies the MP; if knowledge acquisition is possible it must have always been in the interlocutor's possession, for were it not, it would be impossible to figure out which of all existing beliefs are true.

At the 4th stage the point is that true belief can be converted into knowledge, and that this involves 'tying down its cause' or aitias logismos. Presumably, what we are talking about here is justification. That is, a true belief is converted into knowledge when we can work out the reasons for its truth. Though it is not obvious what Socrates means by justification here, the suggestion would seem to imply that knowledge can be inferred from other truths. The structure of the elenctic method would seem to support such a view. The arguments in the elenchus proceed by deductive reasoning, and the premises employed belong to the belief-set of Socrates' interlocutor. Not knowing whether the existing beliefs of the interlocutor are true or false, the elenchus is able to draw conclusions which shed light on the truth-value of these beliefs. This is accomplished by asking questions pertinent to the meaning (and application) of the moral terms under question. Where the inferences yield contradiction, the implication is that one of the beliefs must have been invalidly drawn from a number of other implicit beliefs regarding indirectly related moral terms, for instance. Looking back to the section Deductive Reasoning and Vlastos in this chapter, a likely suggestion would be that the elenctic method can yield knowledge by assisting the interlocutor to realise the implications of the beliefs he already possesses. Of course, that which remains puzzling is the status of the interlocutor's existing beliefs, as well as the process by which these beliefs are acquired. The first question is important because the invalidity of an argument can not also expose which belief making up the premise set is false. This was precisely the problem which Vlastos could not answer. Again in the section Deductive Reasoning and Vlastos of this chapter, it was argued that the elenchus indeed gives the appearance of proposing the possibility of knowledge a priori, and that this knowledge can be acquired through validly inferring beliefs from the meaning or definition of terms, like Goodness, which are likely worked out by asking, 'what do all things that can be called 'good' have in common?'. From this question, a definition would follow which is comprised of a number of further terms. Definitions for each of these terms would be reached by the same method, and each definition would have to be consistent with what had been defined as 'good' previously.

This view seems to be inconsistent with what I have been arguing regarding the all-or-nothing assumption, however. I have argued that the all-or-nothing assumption is responsible for the MP and that this paradox is encouraged by a preoccupation with the objects of thought specifically. This concern, I have argued invites Plato to adopt this assumption because he believes that the mind must first be able to identify something, an object, to then go on and think something about it. To do so, that is to get the intended object in mind, the requirement is that I must know it completely for otherwise identification would be impossible. This had got the MP underway because forced to admit that all thinking is knowledge either we would have to say that inquiry is pointless, or fruitless because undirected. My argument regarding the all-or-nothing assumption is therefore unaffected by the suggestion of inferential knowledge because I do not argue that Plato believes that we do not make inferences in order to gain knowledge. Quite the contrary, everything about the elenchus suggests that we learn by drawing inferences from existing beliefs. The difficulty that Socrates is in follows from the all-or-nothing condition that he assumes for identifying an object of thought. In turn, because knowledge of a given object of thought would guarantee that all valid inferences render sound arguments, he got stuck in the MP. So inferential knowledge has not be ignored, overlooked or neglected since this has always been assumed and the impasse to fruitful inquiry had followed because of a confusion about the objects of thought and not with the actual process of thinking, or knowledge per se.[33]

The TR and Theoretical Groundwork

Socrates' account of the TR begins by considering the logical consequences implied by the Theory; he deduces that for this to be true either the slave boy acquired this knowledge he now has at some other time; or he always possessed it (85d-e5). Therefore, these two separable, yet presumably co-referential, 'levels of knowledge' or 'states of knowing' to which Socrates refers, require no further argumentation exactly because its truth necessarily follows from the TR. And since Socrates and Meno have both been satisfied by the Slave Boy Exercise that learning is recollecting—so that the antecedent of this conditional proposition is true—it is also true that there are indeed two levels of knowledge. There is Latent Knowledge (LK) and Current Knowledge (CK). Though Socrates ultimately opts for the latter view[34]—perhaps because the recollection of things learned in previous incarnations would commit him to an infinite regress—, his extremely vague treatment of the issue suggests that it is only secondarily important to his present objective. He says,

> And I, Meno, like what I am saying. Some things I
> have said which I am not altogether confident. But
> that we shall be better and braver and less helpless if
> we think that we ought to inquire than we should have
> been if we indulged in the idle fancy that there was no
> knowing and no use in seeking to know what we do
> not know—that is a theme upon which I am ready to

fight, in word and deed, to the utmost of my power
(86b-c).

So he is not interested in explaining why and how we came to possess this latent knowledge (LK);[35] rather he is interested in demonstrating how latent knowledge can remain unconscious, until [either] a catalytic question(s) [or object][36] intercedes causing recollection. Specifically, how, in fact, can the elenctic method be used for recollection without the aid of knowledge? As a result of this focused inquiry Socrates by-passes two vitally important epistemological questions regarding (1) the origin of knowledge, and (2) our initial acquisition of it. Though the origin of knowledge may raise an extraneous problem logically independent of the present debate, the acquisition of latent knowledge is in no way irrelevant. Shouldn't Socrates be required to say how this is possible if he is going to use it to show that the acquisition of knowledge in a state of ignorance is unproblematic? For the obvious point regarding latency is that it is because these true beliefs can be 'got in mind', that these currently recollected beliefs are necessarily true, and can be recognised as such. This claims that (1) latent and current beliefs are co-referential, that (2) it is possible to get these latent beliefs in mind by way of elenctic inquiry, and it assumes that (3) memory is infallible. Though the question of memory is nowhere considered in this dialogue, the TR seems to be hinging on its infallibility. The reason is fairly obvious: if it is possible to falsely recall some belief, then the MP would begin all over again; and Meno would ask, how is it possible in the absence of knowledge to recognise some recollected belief as true of the intended object of recollection, and so on.[37] It may be that this assumption is derived from the following invalid argument: because these beliefs are being recollected from the set of latent beliefs which are all necessarily true, it is impossible to get a false belief in mind since there are no false beliefs amongst them. It is invalid however, because this confuses the status of the intended belief with the method of attaining it; in other words, it overlooks the mental effort required to get that truth accurately in mind. The upshot of this assumption is that on the basis of the TR false belief is impossible; and now Socrates presumably can respond to condition (R1).

The claim regarding the co-referentiality of LK and CK says that if we are going to arrive at CK it will have to correspond to LK which may raise the question, 'how do we know that LK is, in fact, knowledge?', but is otherwise a straight forward point. However, regarding the ability of the elenctic method to deliver LK an important distinction must be made. Recollection proper does not occupy the process of knowledge acquisition until stage 3, and, in fact, does not proceed beyond this stage. For following recollection proper, Socrates says that at this stage the interlocutor has 'opinions which have a dreamlike quality..., so that a man who does not know has in himself true opinions on a subject without having knowledge'; and that these true opinions or beliefs can be turned into knowledge if the 'same questions are put to him on different occasions and in different ways' (85c-d). Hence, when Socrates speaks of latency, he is referring not to knowledge, but true beliefs; and when he refers to recollection proper he is again referring to the availability of these beliefs which are necessarily true, so that knowledge acquisition only follows when the arduous task of elenctic inquiry takes over. However, the method by which elenctic questioning turns these newly aroused yet true beliefs into knowledge is, as already mentioned in the previous section, vague. Again, since it is the elenctic method which is expected to convert true belief into knowledge the phrase 'tie down its truth by working out its cause' must have something to do with deductive inference. That is, the TR would guarantee a set of true beliefs, and the deductive method would incite answers to questions that would explicate the logical relations which validly govern them.

The Method of Hypothesis and the TR

The previous section has shown that the chief project of the TR was to guarantee the availability of true beliefs in the absence of knowledge; and that, in the absence of an explicit argument, it was surmised that the accessibility of latent truths counters the possibility of getting false beliefs in mind. But this confused the status or truth-value of the actual belief, with the ability of mentally getting them in mind correctly. It was also suggested in the section The TR and Knowledge-Acquisition that stage 3 is the most problematic because Socrates did not show how the mental state of the Slave Boy differed when he presumably had got hold of a true belief from his initial state of 'believing that some belief were true'; and how, in the later stage, he recognised it as being true. A criticism of the theoretical groundwork of the TR therefore seems to suggest that the paradox remains unresolved; but Socrates has one last argument up his sleeve called the Method of Hypothesis (MH).

Though it is the TR which is introduced to officially counter the paradox, and it is also true that Socrates treats the TR and the MH separately, the inception of the MH as a provisional method of inquiry when Meno and Socrates are finally ready to move their search for virtue to stage 3 is suggestive. That which had given Meno cause to introduce the paradox was the destructive stage of elenctic inquiry where his beliefs were shown to be internally inconsistent, and therefore comprised of both true and false beliefs. And what gave cause to Socrates to introduce the TR was to demonstrate that the destructivism of the method is temporary, and thereby prove the effectiveness of the inquiry, as well as convince Meno to re-submit himself to the method. Having accomplished this, Socrates' resignation to a provisional method of inquiry appears to be rather precariously imposed.

Meno is now convinced that fruitful inquiry is possible on Socrates' terms; but he nonetheless says he would rather pursue whether 'virtue is something that can be taught, or whether men have it as a gift of nature' (86c7-d). Were it not for Socrates' assent to this concession Meno's relapse could be the result of his misunderstanding; but Socrates accepts it and incorporates it into their method of inquiry, saying 'just grant me one small relaxation of your sway, and allow me, in considering whether or not it can be taught, to make use of a hypothesis...' (86e-87). Socrates clearly defines the logical structure of the method of hypothesis (87a-b), and in Vlastos' words:

> when faced with a problematic proposition p, to 'investigate it from hypothesis,' you hit on another proposition h (the 'hypothesis'), such that p is true if and only if h is true, and then shift your search from p to h, and investigate the truth of h, undertaking to determine what would follow (quite apart from p) if h were true and, alternatively, if it were false.[38]

Vlastos draws the obvious implication, namely, that this constitutes a shift away from peirastic to demonstrative argument.[39] No longer restricted by the belief-set of the interlocutor, and therefore dropping the doxastic constraint (R3); Socrates considers what can be gained by evaluating the logical relation that holds between variously proposed beliefs. In effect, Socrates is cashing in on what has already been described as part of the logical form of the elenchus: the hypothetical knowledge claim. In fact, if the MH is only some kind of more explicit exposition of the elenchus, which is taking on only a slightly different form in dropping (R3), Socrates would not have seen the need to make this into a full blown theory. Also, that (R3) is dropped is not a problematic omission since at this stage of elenctic inquiry it is no longer a requirement that the beliefs of the interlocutor be exclusively used, since the purpose of (R3) had been to assure (R2).

The contructivism of the method is, in fact, analogous to the destructivism of the elenchus: each involves the task of deducing the logical relations that hold between variously asserted beliefs as valid or invalid. However, the preliminary stage draws the negative conclusion, whereas the latter draws positive insight: the former that 'the interlocutor does not know what he thinks he knows'; and the latter, the understanding of what can not be the case.

The hypothetical knowledge claim being advanced is 'virtue is teachable', or {p}; and what Socrates draws as a logical pro-hypothesis or what is sometimes called the higher hypothesis, is 'virtue is knowledge', or {h}, because the only kind of thing that is teachable is knowledge (87b-c). Not much is made of this logical inference, instead attention is given to the conditional truth of the problematic proposition {p}. {p} is rendered true if and only if {h} is true. Therefore, the search shifts from {p} to {h}, and Meno and Socrates are left to discover whether, in fact, 'virtue is knowledge'. Taking their start from the postulated truth 'virtue is good', or {g}, Socrates renders the following syllogistic argument: if {virtue is knowledge} and {virtue is good}, then it must also be true that {knowledge is good}. According to the rules of deductive reasoning, for any valid argument that has a false conclusion, at least one of its premises must also be false. So the search is not even about {h} anymore, but rather about {g}; and Socrates and Meno predictably seek to discover some counter example to disprove {g}. Though Socrates does not use the words 'goodness itself', it is clear that the discussion which follows is subsumed under what is meant by goodness, from which it will be inferred that 'knowledge' does not belong to this class of things.

An understanding of whether 'knowledge is good' presupposes what is understood by 'goodness'. Curiously, Socrates does not allude to the problem originally raised by the priority of definition/knowledge, and precedes   by considering the distinctive feature which determines something as being good; and from each distinctive feature, the question is posed again, and so on and so forth. Good is advantageous; hence so too is virtue given that 'virtue is good'; advantageous things are health, wealth, etc.; but distinctively determined so only when accompanied by spiritual qualities themselves aided by wisdom. Despite the fact that these syllogistic arguments follow validly, and on the grounds of deductive reasoning preserve the truth of {p}, given what Socrates presents as a counter example, {p} can not be true. Socrates uses the invalidly argued counter-example regarding the absence of teachers of virtue, to prove that virtue can not be teachable because were 'virtue teachable' surely we would know of someone having this expertise. Socrates explains that what caused them to miss the mark was their failure to admit that true belief is as sufficiently able to guide action as knowledge is; hence knowledge is not a necessary condition at all.

What is the usefulness of the MH? Why does it not commit the mistake of the PD? and why does Socrates suddenly believe that virtue is not knowledge but true belief? Outside of the initially outlined logical structure of the MH, an answer to these first two questions must be derived from his illustration of the method. The structured movement from one hypothetical claim to a further hypothesis takes the form of syllogistic deductive reasoning; and each time the newly deduced conclusion supersedes the previously acknowledged object of inquiry. For instance, the original hypothetical knowledge claim had been {h}; and from there was inferred {p}; and then followed {g}; and finally a number of further syllogistic inferences derived from the properties which distinctively determine a thing as being good. What the initial starting point, as well as the latterly proposed arguments, suggest is that inquiry can render conclusive results because it is possible to logically infer with certainty certain distinctive qualities which we understand some general term as possessing. For instance, Socrates' original syllogistic argument obtained from the inference that 'only those things that comprise knowledge are teachable'; and the syllogistic argument regarding {g} obtained from the inference that 'virtue is good'. Each suggests the commonplace view that in order to apply general terms in at least a coherent fashion we must have an understanding of their meaning; we could not coherently communicate our beliefs if this were not the case. In fact, in the section Vlastos on the

Socratic Elenchus it was argued that the formulation of any propositional claim, that 'virtue is knowledge', in the absence of some understanding of the meaning of the terms would render all propositional claims gibberish or meaningless. Hence Socrates is assuming that the ability to employ and coherently communicate these terms to others presupposes the ability to render that understanding in words or an account or logos. Having accomplished the latter move, we have arrived at knowledge; though any time before, we only possess true beliefs, and are therefore at stage 3.

It has been previously mentioned that the problematic stage is not the fourth, but it is the third stage where true beliefs are got hold of rather than false beliefs, and all this in the state of ignorance. Socrates' concluding remarks again suggest that he acknowledges this point, for he says:

> ...true opinion is as good a guide as knowledge for the purpose of acting rightly...except that the man with knowledge will always be successful, and the man with right belief only sometimes... (97b9-c7).

This concession however commits Socrates to the priority of definition/knowledge, and the paradox all over again, for he finally admits, as he must given the search for the same terms they must employ, that this understanding which perpetuates the search and warrants these hypotheses are conditioned on our limited understanding of these terms, and therefore the possibility of getting hold of false beliefs rather than true beliefs. Does the deductively conclusive end of his original chain of hypothetical inferences, followed by the counter-example proving the falsehood of {p}, not make just this point? That the counter-example was used to discredit not the final conclusion of all those syllogistic arguments to prove the truth of {p}, but {p} itself, suggests that even having validly inferred the truth of {p} as a necessary consequent of all the above, still some premise may have falsely been admitted into the chain. Therefore the counter-example, and Socrates' commitment to it rather than the previously inferred conclusion, suggests, if nothing else, that the HM is presented as something that is only probable.

The *Meno* and False Belief

No where does the topic of false belief occupy the dialogue's explicit or immediate attention. False belief, Socrates surmises, is the consequent of the 'conceit of knowledge', and is interesting only as a serious objection to the peirastic method of reasoning where justified opinion is just a matter of presenting some point of view with persuasive reasons on your side; i.e. made believable to its listeners. Presumably, the possibility of false belief is important because it proposes that not all opinions are indistinguishably true just because someone happens to belief them so; and therefore, that there must be something extraneous to the psychological state of believing which makes something true. Protagoras had argued that 'something is true for the believer', yet the importance of the possibility of false belief here described undermines it at its very base since it denies that mere believing is enough to justify the truth of a given belief.

Can Socrates demonstrate when a given belief is, in fact, true? Or should we resign ourselves to the limitations of man's ability to derive knowledge, and submit to scepticism? At least such a state would have the advantage of making its listeners suspect all beliefs indiscriminately, and thereby counter the handicap which able-speaking sophists have over their impressionable conquests. The Socratic method presents mixed messages precisely because of its inadequacy to deal with the proposed Meno paradox. For on the one hand, (i) Socrates ardently opposes those who make claims to knowledge without having also worked out arguments to logically justify such a claim; and yet, on the other hand, (ii) his method seems to reveal either that (a) his criteria of knowledge are too strong and must somehow be amended; or, (b) knowledge is, in fact, beyond man's capacity to attain. The so-called Socratic Mission[40] would suggest the unlikelihood of (ii); and yet, the still unresolved Meno Paradox, would suggest the unlikelihood of (i).

The reasons why Plato was interested in the notion of false belief may certainly have involved his struggle against sophistic relativism, and if so, the most obvious, and classically acknowledged route, of his attack has been to set up a theory of truth, starting with falsehood. That is, given that the sophistic argument maintains that it is because there are no objective criteria according to which beliefs can be rendered either true or false, that knowledge is on par with belief, and consequently all beliefs are true so long as they are being believed, Plato need only have introduced a theory that could account for such criteria. Hence, as the classic argument goes, if false belief is possible then it must be distinguishable from true belief; and the criteria for distinguishing the two suggest 'the conscientious ability to work out the reasons for obtaining truth' and therefore, knowledge.

However, though this line of argument is certainly logically plausible, the nature of the epistemological puzzle that the MP involves; and the kind of resolution it requires suggests a more interesting alternative. The puzzle involves, as has often been voiced, confusing knowledge with belief. Put this way however, it seems an uninquisitive and irrelevant puzzle. However, Socrates' confusion concerned the ability to identify a belief, such that the ability of getting something in mind surely must require knowing it, for otherwise there could be no assurance in speaking of any belief. Put this way, belief looks very much like knowledge. In fact, it even looks like knowledge precedes belief, or that belief presupposes knowledge. So the question, 'What could be getting something falsely in mind?', or put another way, 'How can someone be mistaken about what he has in his mind?' becomes logically baffling. As the MP clearly points out, it is logically paradoxical to go through the procedure of getting some-specified-thing in mind, and then ask whether the specification of the given thing meets with the specified-object in mind, since the originally specified-thing must have already met the specification since you were able to identify it. So the problem with which Plato is toiling concerns thinking or getting into mind what is false.[41] In other words, it is more directly concerned with thinking a belief and judging the thinking to be false, rather than judging the content of the belief independent of believing it. Viewed this way the problem involves the formulation of a belief, which is significantly prior to establishing the truth-value of the content of that belief. Clearly, this is what is paradoxical about the MP; and, moreover, it is also what Socrates suggests is troubling; nonetheless, Socrates does not attend to this aspect of the puzzle, but instead seeks to accomplish what he set out to do from the outset, namely, to defend the elenchus from the accusation of sophism.

The *Meno* is limited to the task of establishing that the elenchus may be consistently applied, without weakening its conditions of pursuit, for the search for truth. The route Socrates chose to establish his task was to somehow show that all the beliefs that we have must be true because they are derived from the 'fountain of truth' which we must merely recall. That is, we 'know' that we have got hold of true beliefs rather than false ones because we are merely recalling beliefs which were known to us at a different time, and therefore, at stage 3 of the TR it can neither be argued by the sophist that in the absence of knowledge, and therefore the criteria to discriminate true from false beliefs, all beliefs are indiscriminately legitimate; nor can it be argued that the elenchus is unable to render knowledge without at the same time rejecting condition (R2). Because Socrates did not consider the possibility of falsely deriving these truths, and sought to counter the paradox by the first of the two latterly mentioned routes, he was blind to the deeper philosophical puzzle which the paradox involves. It is not, in fact, until the *Theaetetus* that Plato articulates his awareness of this deeper philosophic puzzle and attends to it in order to establish a theory of knowledge proper which could in retrospect be used to provide new insight to the solution of the paradox.

Conclusion

Two things have been going on concurrently throughout the *Meno*. At the centre of the debate has been the proposed difficulty set forth by the Meno Paradox by Meno and the invoked problematic regarding the relatedness of the elenctic method to the eristic method of the sophists. The dialogue is foreshadowed by Plato's concern that the conditions of the elenctic debate (R1)-(R3) make it impossible for the interlocutor to distinguish his true beliefs from his false beliefs without knowledge; thereby making it impossible to move beyond the acknowledged recognition of ignorance. The internal inconsistency of the interlocutor's belief set only demonstrates that he must possess both true and false beliefs and it was in this way that it was argued that the elenchus was inadvertently stung by its own tail; i.e. the objective of the elenchus is incompatible with its method of pursuit. Plainly both the TR and MH sought to justify the search for something somehow already known—this would make it possible to distinguish the true from the false—without that rendering the search pointless—why search for something already known? The TR failed because it could not explain the movement from ignorance to knowledge without begging the question; namely, it proposed that because we have innate or latent knowledge the elenchus works only to help us recall the truths which are stored somehow in our memory. Despite the obvious problems regarding both retention and requisition involving the TR, the TR begs the question that it was set up to resolve because latency is suppose to guarantee that only true beliefs could become part of the working belief set of any interlocutor, yet we want to know how to distinguish existing falsehoods from existing truths without at the same time undermining the pursuit for truth.

The MH is then introduced to demonstrate how to move from a hypothetical knowledge claim by deductively evaluating the relations between variously related beliefs. The point was that the elenchus shifts interest away from the original belief {p} to the proposed conditional hypothesis. This is not dissimilar to the elenctic logical form and seems only to serve to spell out how insufficient the elenchus is to obtain knowledge. In following the TR, and in overlapping with the elenctic form it has been argued that the MH is really just the continuation of the TR such that Socrates demonstrates unbeknownst to Meno that he has recalled knowledge of the nature of virtue at the end of this dialogue by hypothesis.[42] The argument which has been proposed is that the MH merely spells out the problem of the elenchus in that even having worked out the implications that would validly follow were the given hypothesis accepted or denied and thereby in taking the most tolerable alternative and consequently accepting or denying the antecedent of {h}, still there would be nothing to actually ensure that the more tolerable alternative was true. It is possible to see the MH as the continuation, or that which 'guarantees the continuity of the inquiry into the nature of virtue' as Bedu-Addo puts it, but still with this position intact it remains that knowledge acquisition via the elenchus is problematic; and that even were we to trust in the TR, its problems would still carry over to the MH. The working out of the cause, as it were, in order to move to the 3rd stage of elenctic progress by incessant questioning can not in the finale help to logically determine the true.

The epistemic assumption disclosed in Socrates' reformulation of Meno's paradox introduces a problematic for knowledge quite apart from the structural betrayal of the elenctic form. That is, quite apart from why the elenctic conditions betray its objective, there is a deeper epistemic puzzle looming here regarding the actual status of the so-called objects which comprise thought or belief claims. The Platonic Socrates says that 'something is either known or it is not known', there is no middle ground. The point, it had been argued, represents a strain of thought in early (Euthydemus, Cratylus) and later (Theaetetus, Sophist) Platonic thought regarding the assumption that for any propositional belief there must be a referent object, and that, in turn, the referent must be something that exists. Not knowing would consequently suggest the absence of an object to get in mind; whereas knowledge would imply exhaustive knowledge of the thing in question making the ability to get something in mind possible. This strain in Platonic thought will indeed dominate the debate throughout this thesis, but the elenctic puzzle remains intricately tied up in the debate as the setting in both the *Theaetetus* and *Sophist* reveals.

Notes

[1] Is there any evidence in the dialogues that supports the idea that the early Platonic dialogues are an expression of Socratic philosophy; and the later dialogues an expression of Platonic philosophy; or must we content ourselves that early and late refers to no more than respective periods in Plato's philosophical development? This is an issue that can be left to hermeneutic philosophers to unravel.

[2] '...anger...as Socrates declares (*Ap*. 21e, andc), often results from the elenchus; and if the elenchus really makes people hate you, surely this is bad teaching and a bad form of intercourse in general.' See Robinson's 'Elenchus', in G. Vlastos (1980) *The Philosophy of Socrates: A Collection of Critical Essays*, p. 79.

[3] The discussion on naming in the *Euthydemus* reflects this point as does the *Cratylus*. From the *Euthydemus* we get the idea that for any thought there must be a sentential subject that gets referred to and which must also exist; and in the *Cratylus* we get the suggestion that names acquire meaning neither by *convention*—for which a relativist view is proposed—or by the so-called *nature* of the named—for which a realist view is proposed. See M.M. Mackenzie (1986) 'Putting the *Cratylus* in its Place' in *Philosophical Quarterly 36*, pp. 124-150.

[4] Robinson has successfully argued that the elenchus can either be direct or indirect. In his 'Elenchus: Direct and Indirect', he says that 'To establish a thesis indirectly is to deduce a falsehood from the contradictory of that thesis; in other words, to show that its contradictory is false because it entails an intolerable consequent. ...Direct refutation is best defined as any refutation that is not indirect;...it reaches the conclusion of the refutand without at any time or in any way assuming the refutand'. See G. Vlastos ed. (1971) *The Philosophy of Socrates: A Collection of Critical Essays*, pp. 77-8. Also the elenchus varies greatly in complexity and length; that is, the chain of inferences from the original thesis or refutand proposed by the interlocutor, to the conjunct of its self-contradictory conclusion may be short or long. Nevertheless, there is agreement regarding the general pattern or form that the elenchus takes.

[5] G. Vlastos (1983) 'The Socratic Elenchus', *Phronesis*, p. 28.

[6] More often than not commentators (Vlastos, Brickhouse and Smith, Stokes, etc.) add that 'Socrates considers this thesis false, and targets it for refutation'. This seems an unnecessary addition at this point, and colours the purpose of the method, which is after all what we are attempting to discover. It also seems to suggest that irrespective of the content of the interlocutor's belief Socrates would want to refute it which has always been the job of the sophist. Should this also suggest that the interlocutors will necessarily have false beliefs, and/or that Socrates is infinitely wise, or that Socrates is a sophist after all?

[7] See H.H. Benson (1987) *Ancient Philosophy 7*, 'The Problem of the Elenchus Reconsidered'. This article is a response to the radical argument lucidly developed by Vlastos in his article 'The Socratic Elenchus' which maintained that the elenchus is not limited to the non-constructivist end of revealed inconsistency, but establishes that the refutand is, in fact, false. I have borrowed heavily from Benson's arguments; though others have also influenced the content of the arguments presented in this chapter.

[8] ibid., p. 70-72. Benson provides an excellent discussion of the three kinds of argumentative methods; (1) the personal or sophistic (irrespective of the content of the proposition, its purpose is to get someone to believe something); (2) the demonstrative or impersonal (irrespective of who can or does believe its conclusion, its purpose is to establish the truth of a proposition absolutely); and (3) the dialectic (which is interested in establishing the truth of a proposition to someone) which describes the elenctic method used by Socrates. Note that Socrates refers to this specifically at *Meno* 75d where he says 'I should not only speak the truth, but I should make use of premises which the person interrogated would be willing to admit'.

[9] That the interlocutor does not achieve all this on his own, but is sufficiently guided by the questions posed by Socrates, is certainly an interesting question but the argument here presented is unaffected by the answers to this question. For even if it is the case that Socrates directs the discussion, the fact that it is the beliefs of the interlocutor which lead to the contradictory conclusion of the counter-argument, and that he follows the logical consistency of the argument is all that this argument requires.

[10] G. Vlastos (1983) *Phronesis*, 'The Socratic Elenchus', pp. 27-70. Vlastos presents his views in this paper as refuting his previously argued views on the elenchus, recognising also its radical content. In his owns words, he says, '...I had maintained that Socrates never meant to go beyond (3)—that their objective was simply to reveal to his interlocutors muddles and inconsistencies within themselves, jarring their adherence to some confident dogma by bringing to their awareness its collision with other, no less confident, presumptions of theirs'. p. 45.

[11] See G. Vlastos (1985) *The Philosophical Quarterly*, 'Socrates' Disavowal of Knowledge', pp. 1-31.

[12] G. Vlastos (1983) *Phronesis*, 'The Socratic Elenchus', pp. 53-54.

[13] For a clear exposition of the argument regarding the circularity see T.C. Brickhouse and N.D. Smith (1984) *Oxford Studies in Ancient Philosophy*, 'Vlastos on the Elenchus', esp. pp. 188-189.

[14] Any introductory text on logic explains and verifies that this is the case. And further that validity can reveal only that the relationship between the propositions of the premise-set and conclusion do not logically follow.

[15] Note that the argument is more involved then is here suggested; it has been simplified in order show what the implication is of an invalid deductive argument.

[16] For an interesting discussion on the use of logical rules in the elenchus, which elenctic participants are expected to also be in a position to follow, see M.M. Mackenzie (1988) 'Socratic Ignorance' *Classical Quarterly 38*, pp. 331-350.

[17] Note that the priority of definition, as well as the requirement that all elenctic participants must have definitional knowledge of all the terms employed in their arguments is not a novel idea. It is also vigilantly expressed at the beginning of the *Meno*.

[18] G. Vlastos (1983) 'The Socratic Elenchus', p. 52. Note that this was the position that led Vlastos to assumption A; but, which he believed Socrates drew as an inductive inference from past elenctic experience.

[19] At *Meno* 72d Socrates attempts to clarify for Meno that he must first figure out what all possible instances of just acts/beliefs have in common, and then elucidate their commonality in the form of a definition. Obviously if we could provide an exhaustive list of common attributes for all possible just acts/beliefs, any stated belief regarding justice would thereby also be consistent. Note that this kind of advice is not unique to the *Meno*.

[20] Note Socratic conditions of knowledge is not the central issue at this point and for this reason will not be fully discussed. The objective is only to show that Socrates could have inferred deductively that for any belief its contradictory could be inferred and for this reason the elenctic method could not be viewed as having ambitions to render so-called positive constructivist knowledge claims.

[21] See M.M. Mackenzie (1983) 'Socratic Ignorance', *Classical Quarterly 38*. She discusses the latter situation which requires that all elenctic participants must be in a position to follow the logical implications drawn from the deductive elenchus, and thereby imply that they too must know something regarding the status or criteria of knowledge.

[22] For example, whiteness is not colour itself but a colour; and that there are other colours that are just as much colours as whiteness; and again straightness and roundness are equally shapes/figures without that suggesting that straightness is a

shape by somehow sharing in roundness and vice versa since this is the manner in which they are different and not the same, but just that they are the same in so far as they are shapes (74b-75a).

[23] Though commentators have usually paid sufficient notice to the word 'contentious', few have bothered to consider why Socrates would refer to the argument itself as contentious and nonetheless take it so seriously. In I.M. Crombie (1971) *An Examination of Plato's Doctrines*, Crombie writes, 'Socrates treats this [MP] as a well-known sophism, but takes it serious', p 532; and in J.T. Bedu-Addo (1984) 'Recollection and the Argument 'From a Hypothesis' in Plato's *Meno*', *Journal of Hellenic Studies*, Bedu-Addo writes ' Socrates describes this paradox as a piece of eristic, but he does not dismiss it', p. 1.

[24] H.H. Benson (1989) 'Meno, the Slave Boy and the Elenchus', *Phronesis*. Arguing against the new critics who say '...Plato does not go beyond Socrates in the sense of providing a substantive view about how knowledge is to be acquired, which Socrates previously failed to have. Rather he goes beyond Socrates only in the sense of substituting one substantive view about how knowledge is to be acquired with another;' Benson says 'A careful examination of the structure of the *Meno* suggests that Plato takes himself to be going beyond the Socratic method, not replacing or revising it.' p. 129. The view presented here is consistent with Benson.

[25] This is to make the point that even if Socrates could be shown to discern the truth-value of the executor's beliefs that would not satisfy the availability constraint of the elenchus.

[26] H.H. Benson (1989) 'Meno, the Slave Boy and the Elenchus', *Phronesis*. Benson refers to the sample elenchus as clearly divided into four stages of development; where the two parallel the early Socratic method; and the latter two comprise the addition that the TR makes to the elenchus which warrants a move beyond the early destructivism of Socrates, to the constructivism of Plato. The divisions are given as; Stage One 82b4-e4; Stage Two 82e4-84a2; Stage Three 84d3-85b7; Stage Four 85c20-d1 (not properly part of the conversation though). Benson's latter two stages correspond well to this addition of TR; though the first two stages do not clearly reveal the dialectic form of the method.

[27] Socrates emphasises this point when he says 'you say that the side of a double lengthed square renders a double sized figure' at 83a1-2.

[28] This suggests that at least Socrates knows the right answer, and therefore can distinguish true from false beliefs, which is inconsistent with the view of the elenctic method which has been elaborated here. Yet, it is my view that Socrates does this for reasons of expediency; it would be to arduous an affair to begin with some elenctic inquiry for which he and Meno were ignorant themselves. Also at this point the job of the elenchus is to show how it could be possible to know and not know at the same time; and on the basis of some kind of prior knowledge an a posteriori knowledge claim could be judged as being both valid and sound.

[29] Though I would not like to draw a parallel between the Socratic method and pragmatism, this sounds remarkably similar to what Peirce had said about inquiry, that it could only begin given genuine doubt.

[30] I. Kant (1985) *Prolegomena to Any Future Metaphysics that Will be Able to Come Forward as a Science*. Kant wrote that it was Hume's account of causality 'that first interrupted my dogmatic slumber and gave me a completely different direction to my inquiries...'.

[31] A great deal of literature has been written about whether Socrates' questions are leading; or somehow rhetorical; and whether he does, in effect, cheat. This subject will not however be treated here as it is a dissertation in itself.

[32] R.S Bluck (1961) *Plato's Meno*, p12.

[33] I find it interesting that D. Scott has argued that recollection does not involve *all* learning but is reserved for philosophical knowledge, and that Plato is unconcerned to explain the prior difficulty regarding how it is that beliefs (as opposed to knowledge) are formulated. Scott concedes that two distinct kinds of theories would be used to explain knowledge acquisition and belief acquisition. For the first, a rationalist theory is offered; and for the second an empiricist theory is offered, though not fully worked out. I do not disagree with a lot of this. However, I do believe, as I have argued here, that Plato is worried about belief acquisition even if this is not independently contrived. Specifically, Plato is concerned that to be able to *think* of an object (which has been derived from experience) that some kind of preceding conceptual framework must be available so that the mind can make sense of it. This is what I presume leads Plato to think that belief (should) presuppose(s) knowledge. An object must be known, so that it can be identified as such and such and consequently not arbitrarily mistaken for something else. Were this a threat, thinking and language more generally would become ridiculous. See D. Scott (1987) 'Platonic Anamnesis', *Classical Quarterly*, pp. 346-366.

[34] Socrates seems to, at least initially, opt for the former version, namely that these beliefs were somehow acquired at some other time (86a1); but he then adds that because at this prior time we were not in human shape (86a4-5), that knowledge must reside in our soul (86a6-9), in which case the soul must be immortal (86b). Apart from being an invalid and peculiar argument, it commits Socrates to the latter version; i.e. if the soul and knowledge have always co-existed, and the soul is immortal, so too must knowledge be. Since no interval is opened to account for a time when knowledge acquisition could have taken place, it simply must have always been. I have discovered that White made the same observation; see N.E. White (1976) *Plato On Knowledge and Reality*, p 49.

[35] These issues are the topic of debate in Plato's *Phaedo*. It is therefore unsurprising to find a rather different account of the TR, and the Method of Hypothesis (MH) there.

³⁶ Whether Socrates counts sense experience, as in the case of the diagram of the square that he uses in the Slave Boy Exercise, as triggering knowledge acquisition is still a controversial issue.

³⁷ N.E. White (1976) *Plato On Knowledge and Reality*; White also makes this point. He argues that the TR must be able to reckon with the fact that recollection is purposively directed at a particular thing in the same way that the aim of the elenchus was to acknowledge that which originally was the objective to recollect. For otherwise recollection would fall victim to a paradox of recollection analogous to the paradox of inquiry. White then concludes that if the TR is to meet the challenge of the paradox, Socrates must be able to show how 'it is possible to recognise a previously known but unrecollected belief in a way in which it is not possible to recognise the previously unknown', p 50. White advocates that the TR fails to counter the paradox, but argues that the more significant point is that 'it provides one with a way of beginning one's cognitive efforts short of their goal, while nevertheless being able to specify what that goal is and to recognise it when it is reached. ...It is a problem of clarifying what the starting point of an investigation is to be, how it attains its end, and how the attainment of its end is to be recognised', p 53. This, he argued, was the crucial point obscured by the TR.

³⁸ G. Vlastos (1991) *Socrates: Ironist and Moral Philosopher*, p 121.

³⁹ Vlastos' peirastic and demonstrative distinction may be paralleled to Benson's sophistic and demonstrative; see footnote 7. Of course, Benson also distinguished these two from what he called the dialectic argument which is interested in being able to persuade the interlocutor of the truth.

⁴⁰ See Brickhouse and Smith (1984) The Socratic Mission, *Phronesis*.

⁴¹ See Lyle E. Angene (1978) 'False Judgement in the *Theaetetus*', in *Philosophical Studies 33*, pp. 351-365.

⁴² See J.T. Bedu-Addo (1984) 'Recollection and the Argument 'From a Hypothesis' in Plato's *Meno*' in the *Journal of Hellenic Studies*, pp. 1-14.

2 The *Theaetetus* and False Belief

Introduction

Though a great number of Platonic dialogues involve some epistemological perspective it is not until the *Theaetetus* that Plato casts about for a theory of knowledge to show what differentiates a knowledge-claim from any other claim. Uncharacteristic of the later[1] Platonic dialogues,[2] the *Theaetetus* is non-constructivist in nature since for each proposed account of knowledge there is a corresponding refutation; and hence its aporetic end. Specifically, the dialogue is written in what could be divided into three distinct parts; (I) Part I sets up and refutes the Protagorean version of knowledge as perception; (II) Part II sets up the paradox of false belief; and (III) Part III sets up and refutes knowledge as justified true belief. Commentators have provided various versions of the belief/knowledge polemic to account for Parts I and III; yet, for the most part, Part II has been regarded as an interlude with little or no philosophical significance whatsoever.[3] It will be argued in this chapter that (i) the philosophical content of the *Theaetetus* resumes the problem of the *Meno* Paradox; (ii) that Part I coincides with the epistemological relativism of the sophist outlined in the *Introduction*, and encountered in the *Meno*;[4] (iii) for which a number of philosophically intriguing implications follow which enhance our understanding of the paradox. In turn, (iv) Part II plays a central role in the way that Plato understands the paradox; and finally (v) in chapter three (iv) alters the reading of Part III, and the *Sophist*, or his theory of knowledge.

Background Setting

The *Theaetetus* opens in a rather peculiar manner, and is followed by three further peculiarities which provide a preview to the philosophical perplexities of the dialogue and suggest its parallel to the *Meno*. The four peculiarities are: a) the dialogue is recounted third hand, b) the expert and his expertise c) the notion of learning and d) the problem of instances resumed.

Recounted Third Hand

The original dialogue, between Socrates, Theodorus, and Theaetetus took place some time before Euclid actually recorded it, until finally it is here being recounted to us by Euclid's servant in dialogue form as if to suggest that the conversation belonged to the present, or that it might as well have. The *Theaetetus* is therefore a dialogue that is being passed on to its readers at third hand, and as Euclid makes a point of mentioning, is the product of memory which is sometimes impaired.[5] That the final version of the *Theaetetus* reaches us third hand and is subject to *error* because the ability to recall something forgotten is not always accurate is strangely reminiscent of the criticism levied against the Theory of Recollection in the *Meno*. There it had been argued that because knowledge is latent it need only be recalled in our present state of ignorance in order to by-pass the Meno Paradox; but that Socrates must have been assuming that the ability to recall something is infallible, which Plato, as this passage in the *Theaetetus* suggests, would deny. After all, that memory lapse is commonplace, and often impaired is no surprise; Theodorus too had difficulty recalling the name of Theaetetus' father for Socrates moments before the elenchus was to begin (144a). It is peculiar that the literary form of the dialogue should highlight such an uninteresting notion as the prologue to their philosophic expedition, unless it is expected to somehow set the stage for what is to come.

The Expert and His Expertise

Immediately before setting out on their search for 'knowledge' Theodorus praises Theaetetus' noetic abilities, and likens his physical appearance to Socrates who asks whether he should take Theodorus at his word, or whether, as in the case of two lyres said to have been tuned alike, he should ask for the advice of the musician first. It is asserted that certainly an expert,[6] who presumably has knowledge, must first be sought out before passively submitting to any one belief. And of course, we would follow the advice, whatever it be, of the expert. The painter would advice us on their appearances; the elenchus on Theaetetus' noetic abilities. Though the elenctic method is well suited to the task of revealing when someone does *not* possess knowledge—exposed inconsistencies—it has thus far been shown that the elenchus can not obtain knowledge. And, in fact, that which remains conspicuously unanswered is how or wherefrom the expert derives his expertise or knowledge. Moreover, how is the expert apprehended.[7]

However, given that Socrates seeks to evaluate Theaetetus' noetic abilities by submitting him to the *elenchus*, it must be, according to its conditions (R1)-(R3), that the objective is for him to *learn*, or acquire the ability to discern truth from falsehood for himself. Hence their philosophic expedition requires that they simultaneously discover the truth (R3), and acquire the knowledge necessary for recognising it (R2). Put this way, their objective is equal to the paradox of the *Meno*; i.e. in the absence of the expert person who already possesses knowledge and could pass it on to others, the elenchus is *only a method of acquiring it in a state of homophonic ignorance*. Hence, the objective and the subject of elenctic inquiry is one and the same, knowledge. That is, the elenchus seeks to secure knowledge and simultaneously look for it, and that presumes the possibility of looking for something unknown but all along presupposing it. Certainly the paradox of setting up a search for the yet unspecified subject of that search coincides with the methodological-epistemological difficulty which all early Socratic dialogues encountered, and which culminated in the *Meno*, finding expression in the Meno Paradox. Yet, the search for an account of knowledge suggests not only the problem of determining the right answer to that search, but it also suggests that the required conditions or what would justify knowing the specified object is unknown. The implication is consistent with the novel reading provided in the previous chapter. That is, in the absence of what knowledge is, we neither know whether we know or do not know the thing in question. The problem boils down to the impossibility of distinguishing true from false beliefs; for I have beliefs (i.e. guaranteed by the doxastic constraint) about the topic in question, but I do not know whether those beliefs actually constitute knowing it, or not knowing it. The latter is a significant reminder of the arrogance of the elenctic interlocutors, and the elenctic objective to replace this conceit with perplexity. Or, put another way, the objective is to replace that state of 'not knowing that I do not know' with 'knowing that I do not know'. Immediately striking is the further implication that, if the elenchus has been shown to expose what knowledge is not; then, according to the all-or-nothing notion which had led Socrates to the elenctic deadlock, we must also know what knowledge is. Therefore, if the above implications are sound, Plato must be setting us up for the possibility of partial knowledge. It has been argued that were Plato *really* convinced that 'something is either known completely or not at all' he would be equally committed to its implication; namely, that the *elenchus* is impossible because it would be impossible to entertain belief [to get an object in mind to think of] short of knowledge. Clearly, Plato's aim is to reinstate the *elenchus* and Socrates but it is also true that the epistemic all-or-nothing assumption was introduced in the *Meno* and occupies Plato's philosophic thought considerably.

The Notion of Learning

The actual elenctic or primary question, 'What is knowledge?', is not posed however, until, as Socrates asserts, they first get over a little difficulty, 'What is learning?' (146a), which inevitably is identified as 'knowledge'. The point is here made explicit. For them to *learn* anything they must acquire knowledge, or be in the process of acquiring knowledge. This is where the curiosity transpires. Is the acquisition of knowledge something that is piecemeal as the 'process of acquiring' suggests it is, or is knowledge constant and eternal? The implication of the first is that there is an intermediary state before knowledge acquisition which conflicts with the 'all or nothing' notion of knowledge, whereas the latter implies that either you are in a state of knowledge or you are not at all. The naiveté of this so-called 'all or nothing' notion was brought to bare in the previous chapter. It was argued that the Meno Paradox was the outbirth of the conflicting conditions of the Socratic elenctic method, (R1) and (R3), which in turn suggested the assumption that to be able to think of something, *that thing* would have to be *known* in the strictest sense. That is, as far as Socrates was concerned, the ability to entertain a thought of something *everything* need be *known* of it, for otherwise one could not be sure that *the thing* to which one referred was not other than what it was supposed to be. This in turn would make a mockery of the whole process of thinking, and thus the paradox for inquiry. Namely, how is it possible on the view that any-thing entertained by thought, is also something that is necessarily *known* justify a search of any kind in its regard; and in the absence of *knowing* something, how could any-one ever get it into his/her head to inquiry about it? This comprises an 'all or nothing' approach to knowledge, which if nothing else, the Meno Paradox exemplifies, simply because for Socrates 'something is either known *completely* or not at all'. The effect of this position had also the consequent of the related Socratic Paradox regarding the possibility to learn piecemeal where the application or reference to examples, or instances, would for the Socratic method be a central theme.

It is argued that because 'learning is the process of growing wiser', and because wisdom is that which makes someone wise and someone is wise in that which he knows, it follows that 'wisdom is knowledge'. If, therefore, wisdom and knowledge are the same, it also follows that 'learning is the process of *growing or becoming knowledgeable*'. Therefore, knowledge is acquired piecemeal, and by implication knowledge can be partial, or it is possible to know some things and not others. Though Socrates does not argue for this conclusion it suggests that Plato wants to move away from the traditionally Platonic notion of knowledge as an 'all or nothing' affair, which had been responsible for the impasse to knowledge created by the Meno Paradox. The argument for the Meno Paradox was shown to be absolutely devastating to the elenctic method, for on the conditions set for knowledge, it would either be impossible to know anything, or impossible not to know everything. The reason that the 'all or nothing' condition had this devastating effect was because of the nature of the deductive arguments the elenchus was expected to impart. That is, because for each item involved in any propositional belief exhaustive knowledge was in turn required, for every complex definition previously defined expressions would have to be available for each term being employed; and this got the deductive regress going. Consequently, unless from the bottom up the terms of expression could be accounted for in the demanded way all subsequent definitions could not stand as knowledge. It is obvious, given that definition is always complex, that Socrates would have to be able to show that some things are known, specifically justified, non-inferentially. Since, for every inference there must be a preceding event or belief in virtue of which the one in question has been grasped, and inferences, when sound, provide the justification for believing that some belief, p, is true, the premises of these inferences will always in turn require justification in the same exhaustive way. That partial knowledge, that things can come to be known, rather than just believed, piecemeal would require that the means of ending this regress are now going to be made available, or at least that Plato acknowledges the need to. Indeed this may be anticipated to have a ripple-effect on his entire epistemological perspective.

The Problem of Instances Resumed

Theaetetus' first attempt to account for knowledge squarely misses its mark and demonstrates his affinity with Meno and other protagonists of the early Socratic dialogues who prematurely attend to first identifying instances of knowledge, before accounting for the specification of what constitutes knowledge, and justifies their referral to instances. That is, Theaetetus, perhaps misled by the previous argument, refers Socrates to a list of things that entail learning; for instance, the sciences, and crafts (146c). Living up to Theodorus' praise however, Theaetetus understands his mistake straightaway; Socrates does not want particular instances, but an account of what justifies classifying these instances as examples of knowledge. That this acknowledged understanding by Meno had originally introduced the Meno Paradox and the elenctic deadlock is here being repeated in a background of innuendoes calling attention to the problem of the paradox suggests at least that Plato recognises that a theory of knowledge will have to reckon with the paradox, thereby causing the suggested ripple effect; for after all, the Meno Paradox constitutes an impasse to knowledge acquisition, and otherwise puts it beyond human reckoning.

The Midwife Analogy

Though in the *Meno* Socrates is likened to a sting ray that catches and incapacitates its prey, in this brief interlude of the *Theaetetus* he is compared to a midwife. The former because the conditions of the elenchus created an impasse to its own prescribed end, knowledge; and in the latter, because the elenchus *induces* the birth of knowledge by sifting out and separating falsehood from truth.

The art of the elenchus under Socrates' device is

> to attend to the minds of men...and thoroughly examine whether the thought which the mind of the young man brings forth is a false idol or a noble true birth (150b-c),

but

> like the midwives, I am barren; and the reproach that is often made against me—that I ask questions of others and have not the wit to answer them myself—is very just; the reason is that the god compels me to be a midwife but does not allow me to bring forth. Therefore, I am not at all wise.

In which case, given that learning is knowledge, the job of the elenchus is to divulge the truth-value of the interlocutor's beliefs, but that Socrates, himself only the arbitrator of the method, does not have knowledge. Together these two points fulfil condition (R1)—the final objective of the method is to secure knowledge, but it seems to put condition (R2) into question. For if Socrates does not possess knowledge, by implication, he also can not teach, or rather, his interlocutors can not benefit or learn.[8] Presumably aware of this objection, which is after all commonly raised against Socrates,[9] he adds that

> those who do converse with me profit....they all make
> astonishing progress, [but] it is quite clear that they
> never learned [acquired knowledge] *from me*. The many
> admirable truths they bring to birth have been
> discovered by themselves from within (150d5-e).

Therefore, though Socrates himself does not teach them anything, they nonetheless do discover truths by submitting themselves to a joint search with Socrates. Socrates is clearly only the catalyst or the vehicle through which his pupils come to discover the status of their own knowledge-claims, and therefore, the doxastic constraint. That is, the elenchus works only with the existing beliefs of its participants, and introduces no extraneous beliefs that might instigate learning from some able expert, who would presumably have to possess knowledge, which would in turn conflict with 'the state of ignorance constraint'. Still it remains unclear how this is logically possible. How can one in a state of ignorance pass on knowledge to its would-be pursuers? Socrates only indirectly responds to this criticism. Those who fancied that their progress could thereby be achieved unaccompanied by the elenctic method, he says,

> suffered miscarriages of their thoughts through falling
> into bad company, and they have lost children of whom
> I have delivered them by bringing them up badly, caring
> more for false phantoms than for true (150e-151).

Socrates *ad hominem* argues that those who abandon the search prematurely, obviously before obtaining knowledge, become taken by the 'false phantoms' of Aristides who, adherent of the democratic and sophistic movement, also abandoned the search and comforted himself that there are not truths more true than what the circumstances permit. Clearly, Socrates is warning Theaetetus not to abandon the search prematurely, and disappointedly join the sophists; but stick it out through to the end where surely he will rejoice in the knowledge he has acquired.

Though this can not be taken as a serious argument in favour of accepting the merit of the elenchus and its ability to secure knowledge, it does manage to emphasise with great dramatic force what the previous section and its innuendoes could only murmur, namely, that now is the time that Plato must meet the criticism of the elenchus straight on; he must show how the elenchus, via Socrates, can benefit its pupils by providing the knowledge which they seek. For disappointed, they truly have no recourse but to submit themselves to some version of epistemological relativism or any of its corollaries.

Meeting the *Meno Paradox*

That the *Theaetetus* deliberates in search of knowledge against a background of alluring early Socratic props which initially sets-up the Meno Paradox when Theaetetus mistakenly refers to a list of instances of knowledge/learning rather than its account, confirms that Plato has not yet resolved it. And that Socrates resumes the problem of the absent expert when initiating the search, as well as commits himself to the promised elenctic end when referring to the midwife analogy, indicates that the resolution of the Meno Paradox occupies the project of the dialogue.

Moreover, Socrates has intimated that the all-or-nothing notion may be abandoned, and replaced by a 'partial' notion which was responsible for the Meno Paradox when he auspiciously introduced the preliminary debate on learning. There Socrates established the learning-knowledge identification, as well as the 'partial' notion. It has also been argued that the primary Socratic question, knowledge, when submitted to the elenctic debate suggests the 'partial' notion as well, since the elenchus professes to at least demonstrate what knowledge is not. The dialogic preview has therefore been determined as establishing a resumed interest in the Meno Paradox, as well as the reconsideration of the problematic assumption which had been responsible for the elenctic deadlock.

The *Meno* and the *Theaetetus* are philosophically related therefore, because both are immersed in the all-or-nothing condition which has rendered the pursuit of knowledge impossible and falsehood unthinkable.

In turn, the contentious character of the elenchus first insinuated in the *Meno* becomes, by implication of the impossibility of falsehood, unavoidable. For if falsehood is impossible, then all beliefs are true and the only thing that can be said of the sophists is that they more successfully affect the beliefs of others than anyone else. In the *Meno*, the TR and the MH tried to meet the implication of the all-or-nothing condition in order to reinstate the possibility of fruitful inquiry but failed; and in the *Theaetetus* the *Allodoxia Model*, the *Wax Tablet Model* and the *Aviary Model* will try to reconcile the all-or-nothing condition with the possibility of getting things wrong, but each will fail. Not only is the implication for the elenchus apparent therefore, but the same working assumption is responsible both for the MP and the impasse to falsehood; i.e. thinking requires the preceding ability to *identify* an object and this seems to require knowledge.

Part I of the Theaetetus

Knowledge is Perception

This empiricist definition of knowledge finds support from the Man-Measure Argument which Protagoras is famous for, and the Heraklitean theory of flux. It is an attempt to present a fair exposition of the arguments in favour of the relativism of the sophists which at the same time reveals important assumptions which are deeply lodged in commonplace beliefs about truth.

The Man-Measure argument states that 'man is the measure of all things that are, that they are, and all things that are not, that they are not'. In other words, all things are as they are to their observer, so that the wind itself is neither hot nor cold, but hot to you and cold to me. Consequently, truth can only be understood relatively. Serious consequences ensue from this standpoint: (a) falsehood becomes impossible because beliefs which are derived from experience will be as true as the appearances of the world are rendered by the experience for the percipient; (b) realism will be suspended so that truth would not be understood to correspond to physical objects or states of affairs in the world and a devastating kind of idealism gets inserted such that the mind would dictate the truths of the world independently; which (c) would in turn suggest that the truth-value of any belief is established in virtue of internal states of affairs; such that relativism would become only tautologically true. If the truth-value of beliefs are derived by experience *for* a particular percipient, then the truth-value of any belief is rendered in terms of what *S* believes s/he believes. Hence, *S*'s beliefs are no longer of the external world in *any* respect (we started off with empiricism which presumably assumes the existence of an external world) but are instead of his/her psychological state of mind. This would seem to be unintuitive because as communicators we expect that our beliefs are communicable to others, but these too would be experiential and rendered *for* the listener. Further complications follow because names are usually expected to uniquely name particulars or general groups of things (universal) which again would apply to particulars. Yet, were the same names for things used by all percipients we would falsely communicate the content of our beliefs unless all utterances were prefixed by the phrase, 'I believe that I believe that' which would in any event be interesting only to a psychologist. It does not seem obvious that the sophists would want to embrace the view that when speaking it is our intention only to communicate our psychological state of mind. If they are not willing to accept this implication, curiously they must accept that when *S* believes that s/he is conveying beliefs about *p*, s/he is really only conveying his/her belief that s/he believes *p*. Hence, *S* falsely believes.

The Heraklitean argument attempts to remedy some of these implications by demonstrating that the objects of perception *themselves* change at such a constant rate that different percipients actually view different things. In such a way, it is possible to resist the damaging idealism sketched above because the difference in appearances is explained not in terms of subjectivism, but in terms of changing external realities. Still damaging implications follow. The combined Protagorean-Heraklitean doctrine would establish the truth-value of any belief in terms of the circumstances, object and percipient subject involved in the rendering of an appearance such that for *each* experience there would seem to be a different object. Experience would have a pluralising effect that could not possibly match either our intuitive understanding of the world or our use of language. Looking back to the *Introduction* a connection with the Parmenidean Challenge is obvious. Parmenides' arguments on *being* had also been led to a pluralising effect which followed from the assumption that for every word there is a corresponding object in the world in virtue of which that word becomes meaningful. In both cases the trouble seems to concern the ontological status of the objects of thought and thoughts about them. Two issues are being intertwined into a single question here: rules about the physical world[10] and rules about thought (and language). The sophist who begins from the commonplace idea that different people have (and are entitled to) different beliefs about the same things, faced the troublesome premise which purported to support it, namely, that what *appears* corresponds to what, in fact, *is*. That is, perception had been haphazardly illustrated as an encounter between a percipient and the world and the rendering of perceptions thereby into beliefs. The assumption presumably had been that perception and beliefs necessarily and naturally correspond. This clearly leaves the articulation and thought about the perceived object, not to mention the distance of the sense-object from the sense-data rendered, out of the picture.[11]

Our understanding of the Meno Paradox when originally considered in the *Meno* had two arresting consequences which followed from the ineptitude of the elenchus to produce knowledge. The first, was the revealed contentiousness of the method. The elenchus always did get underway, and it always did end destructively, so that one was always left without the means to acquire anything beyond the consistency of one's own belief-set from which knowledge could not obtain since knowledge requires truth. The second, followed from the all-or-nothing assumption which Socrates inserted regarding the ability to get something in mind to think. The point had been that it is impossible to think of something unless you already know that thing. Consequently inquiry should have been stumped from the outset. Yet, the contentiousness of the method would have us accept the possibility of embarking on inquiry and found fault with the elenchus because there seemed nothing to differentiate it from the eristic method of the sophists. There is an obvious incongruity between the expected implication of the Meno Paradox proper therefore, and what Plato was willing to accept for the elenchus. The all-or-nothing notion is now successfully shown to have a wider audience then perhaps initially expected and this seems to be the result of certain misconceptions about how we (the layman, the sophists, Socrates, Plato probably) expect the mind to work. Both the sophists and Socrates have confused the *process of thinking* with the knowledge of the objects which furnish the mind with things to think about. In the *Meno*, Meno was led to the Meno Paradox as a result of Socrates' insistence that he first elucidate the definition/meaning of the term in question prior to referring to rightful instances of it, so that it seemed that one could not arrive at the meanings of things through experience. Instead, there had to be prior knowledge which would provide the means for successfully interpreting the world. The discussion of this first definition of knowledge as perception helps us understand that thinking is a separate topic. That is, even if we were to work out where the objects of thought come from and how, or if, these are accurately derived, still this would not guarantee that thinking would follow truthfully. The topic of false belief will be treated as a problem for thought and will be shown to follow from blurring an interest in truth with thinking meaningfully. This insistent interest in the actual objects of thought and their employment in thought will take us a long ways into ontology until finally in the *Sophist* Plato will take on board that which was already before us since the *Meno*. That is, thinking is possible without knowledge. Remember the all-or-nothing condition should have stumped the elenchus from the start, but the first argument rendering the elenctic method contentious was willing to accept the possibility of inquiry; hence the possibility of belief short of knowledge.

The all-or-nothing condition poses a problem therefore, because its adherent is a realist who wants to nonetheless be able to explain how falsehood is nonetheless a possibility. The kind of realist he is had led him to believe that there must be a sure fire way for the objects of thought to actually and accurately correspond to the objects they are of. These perfect objects of thought unaltered by experiences had been called *forms*[12] and this seemed to make sense of the ability to recognise things as such-and-such when experienced for the first time (for how else could a percipient know what some thing was) as well as bring them to mind for contemplation thereafter successfully. The first telling implication of such a view shows that if all objects which furnish the mind to contemplate are known completely, then it must be impossible for the mind to ever be mistaken about its thoughts. Such is the problem that will concern us for the remainder of this dialogue, but it should already be clear from the opening paragraphs to this section that this involves a misunderstanding regarding the *thinking process* per se and that it would seem to liken thinking to perceiving.

Part II of the Theaetetus

The refutative arguments raised against relativism clearly discredited the assumed word-object correspondence in two essential ways. The first involves a distinction between sense object and sense data; the second, the incongruity discovered between the *act* of judging or thinking and the *contents* or *objects* of judging or thinking. The object/sense datum distinction unfortunately plagues all epistemological theories that want to hold on to however watered down a version of empiricism, that at the very least the mind is furnished with things to think on through experience. In turn, the correspondence theory of truth—that for every thought there is an object [event or state of affairs] in the world to which it corresponds—would be infected in the same way. The latter distinction drawn between the *act* and *contents* of judging or thinking has a modern ring. Frege had been concerned to distinguish what we call psychologism from logic in this way.[13] Yet, for Socrates this entailed the significant recognition that the incongruous word-object correspondence had overlooked the process of *thinking*. Namely, how these things are worked on once concatenated by the mind. This is not just the problematic Heraklitean-Protagorean doctrine which toiled with the idea of *how* the world and its objects are viewed, interpreted or taken in by a subjective onlooker. Rather, this observation is meant to provide important insight to *knowledge* as such (187a-b) independent of the partiality and faltering of this doctrine. That however the mind concatenates, *how* or the process by which the mind is occupied 'with things by itself' suggests the means for determining truth independently.

The ontological status of the objects of thought as first explicitly made problematic by Parmenides will reflect the manner in which the impasse to false belief is set up forthwith in the subsequent puzzles. These puzzles are derived from the yet unrevealed erring assumption of Socratic epistemological principles. Notwithstanding, the models suggesting various explanations of false thought will exploit the second distinction involving thought and its contents for thinking specifically. The three models are all attempts to dispel the faulty reasoning that has given rise to these paradoxes. Each attempt to reconcile knowledge with the possibility of false belief fails; but not without exposing a number of assumptions along the way; and at the same time, instructing what knowledge can not be taken to involve. The *Allodoxia Model* exploits the assumption being made about the objects of thought, and introduces a semantic distinction between what the modern debate refers to as *opaque* and *transparent* beliefs; i.e. sometimes a word in a sentence stands in for the object it is of, other times it stands in for the *meaning* of the *word* named. This semantic distinction which would require a fundamental analysis of language is raised and dropped until the *Sophist*. The next attempt to resolve this enigma, the *Wax Tablet Model*, returns attention to the problem of memory because Socrates understands that if *thinking* or *judging* can go wrong, then there must be something that happens when the mind 'by itself' thinks of the objects with which it is furnished that causes falsehood. After all the so-called enigma of falsehood concerns the possibility to actually think of something— which until now requires knowledge following from the assumption in use since the *Meno*—and then go on to think *about* that extant thing what is not the case. The opaque/transparent rendering or function of an object for thought will be flushed out because of its inability to respect the problem as cited. That is, opacity will reduce to a problem of transparency because the so-called identified object must be what is falsely thought of. The *Wax Tablet Model* is therefore not only an attempt to describe two alternative ways of getting hold of an object for thought in order to then go on to show how *mis-matching*—[actively] taking one object [perceived] for [passively] another [remembered]—occurs; it also effectively highlights that such a distinction could not do justice to the problem under discussion since it could not explain how *S* could not know *x* before taking it into his/her head to think it. In effect, troubles persist because for Socrates thought must be full, and consequently, every thought or judgement must ultimately be of something. In turn, knowledge presupposes the ability to identify something to think of. The final try, the *Aviary Model*, introduces the notion of *understanding* as opposed to simple identification with which the two previous models were occupied as the locale of falsehood in an attempt to amend the series of steps just outlined.

The Role of False Belief in the *Theaetetus*

At the end of Part I Theaetetus' first born is delivered still-born and forced to admit that the definition 'knowledge is perception' cannot be consistently supported, falsehood is already in our midst. It would not be a mistake to argue that because Theaetetus' first attempt to define knowledge turns out to be false, the ensuing arguments rendering the impossibility of false belief must somehow be amiss. Yet, this should come as no surprise, the possibility of false belief is commonplace, and Socrates makes no secret of the endorsement of its truth. In fact, we see Socrates arguing in Protagoras' Defence that the combined empiricist view must somehow be reconciled with its possibility if it is correct.[14] Though Socrates has not yet proved the contrary, namely that there is [objective] knowledge, and that knowledge is somehow attainable, evidence suggests that it has been accepted as true because of the intolerable nature of the consequences which follow from the elimination of this epistemological possibility; i.e. the arbitrariness of our beliefs, and the consequent faltering endorsement of our beliefs. Still, this does not prove anything. It may very well be that the consequences of relativism or scepticism are undesirable, but the sophistic method may, after all, be the best possible means of meeting these consequences. Socrates must therefore do more than just discredit the logical implications which follow from taking relativism seriously, he must *prove* that knowledge involves true belief, that it is distinguishable from false belief, and that it is attainable. What role is false belief to play in this proof? And specifically, why is the problem of false belief sandwiched between the recommendation and refutation of knowledge as true belief? Or as Benson puts it, 'Why are the problems associated with false belief raised between Theaetetus' proposal that knowledge is true belief (187b-c) and Socrates' refutation of that proposal (200-201c)? What role, that is, do these thirteen pages (187c-200d) play in the structure of the dialogue's argument?'[15]

An obvious reading would be that Socrates is fishing for a theory of truth. This independent discussion of false belief involves not the logical implications of accepting its possibility, or the problems associated with it generally, but rather the very specific task of *proving*—what has already been assumed—that falsehood is possible. The curiosity is then, 'what does Socrates in his attempt to provide a definition of knowledge have to gain by *proving* the possibility of false belief?' One thing he stands to gain is the justification for the search for knowledge. Let us not forget that the topic of investigation is in the *Theaetetus* not just any inquiry, but it is what Socrates' acquittal would have been hinging on. That is, if we are willing to assume that the actual indictment brought against Socrates for introducing new gods, and corrupting the youth hid his real offence from view, namely his insolent ambition to engage influential persons in conversation only to make a mockery of them. Were the elenctic method not purely destructive, these men could have taken leave of Socrates at least with the feeling that Socrates' intentions were noble. However, the problem which the MP touched upon, namely the Socratic elenctic search for truth in the absence of knowledge, is a significant reminder that Socrates had been convicted, and executed because in the finale he could not disassociate the elenchus from sophistic inquiry. Proof for Socrates' unwavering assail of the elenchus against sophistic attack required proving that knowledge acquisition is logically possible. *Proof* that false belief is possible would be a round about way to also prove the possibility of knowledge, even in our present ignorance of what it is. For the ability to distinguish between truth and falsehood implies that there are criteria in virtue of which it must be logically possible to discriminate between a belief which is true, and another which is false; thus opening the door to knowledge. That would place Socrates' interest in rendering the conditions by which some beliefs are discriminately true and others false; i.e. a theory of truth.

This reading can account for why Socrates could have wanted to take this route, but it does not conform to the text. The challenge is to determine *the* false belief which makes it appear that false belief is impossible. It also seems to follow that what has given rise to this false belief is some misappropriated belief regarding *knowledge*. Not only does Socrates tell us as much at 200c when he argues that 'we should not have entertained the problem of false belief until we understood what knowledge is'; but the preceding section confirms it. It was the Protagorean-Heraklitean misplaced understanding of what knowledge is, which caused them to also adopt the view that falsehood is impossible. The text therefore indicates that falsehood is under discussion not to indirectly prove that knowledge is attainable; but rather, because this will dispel the assumption about knowledge which the Socratic method has been making, and thereby provide the means of disentangling the problem which the MP poses for the method. The importance is in recognising that Socrates has already argued against the impossibility of false belief in his refutation of Protagoras, and that therefore, his interest in false belief is directly determined by what this can teach us about knowledge. The Socratic method does not stand against the *possibility* of false belief—for the elenctic rendering of contradiction exposes its possibility—but that *the Socratic theory of knowledge gives the appearance that it is indeterminable.* That is, the elenchus has derived the conclusion that there must be falsehood because of the rendering of contradiction (of course, the sophist would argue that it is only because we lack the understanding of what we are really asserting that we are led to believe that there are logical contradictions), but the elenctic method has been incapacitated by some, obviously false, assumptions regarding knowledge, to thereby determine which of the contradictory beliefs is, in fact, false.[16] A consideration of the problems associated with false belief will expose the mistakenly adopted assumption about knowledge, therefore.

In the prelude to the sequel Socrates sets the reader up for what is to follow. 'When we began our talk', he says, 'it was certainly not our object to find out what knowledge is not, but what it is. Still, we have advanced so far as to see that we must not look for it in sense perception at all, but in what goes on when the mind is occupied with things by itself...'. And, he continues, 'how there can be false belief—that difficulty still troubles *the eye of my mind...*' (187a-b). In other words, having discovered that it is wrong to believe that 'knowledge is perception', and having derived this conclusion from the argument that knowledge is meaningless when confined to the appearances depicting sense objects unless something truthful can be said about the given object, knowledge must consequently 'involve what goes on when the mind is occupied with things by itself'. Or it must involve the mind when it thinks 'thoughts about things', or asserts something as being true of some object. That being the case, falsehood seems a perplexing idea, or, 'the thinking of something false' is puzzling for it is unclear what the *origin* of this mental experience would be (187d3-4). Where does this false thought come from? Socrates is not arguing against the view that knowledge is somehow derived from sense perceptions, he is merely arguing that knowledge is not that which is perceived unattended by the mind. In fact, Socrates' difficulty seems to be what the mind's eye will be occupied with when it is attending upon 'false thinking'. That is, resuming the place where we took leave of the first definition of knowledge, Socrates is concerned with the ontological status of the objects of thought, or what the preceding section cast in terms of a choice between (a) and (b). Must all thoughts attend upon an existent object; or do all thoughts have to be of something which exists? In other words, if thought necessarily involves some existent object, what will the object of thought be when that thought is false, or put another way, what is to be the *object* of the thought of *what is not the case*?

Puzzle One

Socrates renders the logical form that a false belief must take as four exhaustive possibilities (188c7-9): (i) someone judges that something he knows, is something else he also knows; (ii) someone judges that something he does not know, is something else he does not know; (iii) someone judges that something he knows, is something else that he does not know; (iv) someone judges that something he does not know, is something else that he knows. What reasons does Socrates give to suggest that these are the only logically possible forms that falsehood can take? For, given that (i)-(iv) are going to paradoxically prove that falsehood is impossible, how Socrates has come to hold (i)-(iv) will expose the faulty reasoning from which these paradoxes are derived. Given that the argument provided for (i)-(iv) involves 'knowledge', it follows that Socrates is assuming its truth throughout; and that it will be the job of the following three models (Allodoxia, Wax Tablet, Aviary) to explain how false belief is to be understood; thus, consequently exposing what has gone wrong in his thinking.

Socrates argues that {p} for all possible propositional claims[17] there is always the possibility of both false belief and true belief; and {q} that for each and every possible case, it is possible to either know or not know something; in which case, {r} when one is thinking, he is either thinking something he knows, or something he does not know (187e5-188b). So that by implication, {s} it would be impossible for someone knowing something not to know that thing; and conversely, it would be impossible for someone not knowing something to know that thing. In other words, if {p} and {q}, then {r}; and if {r}, then {s}.

The importance of {p} is that it asserts that the consequences of this argument extend to *all* propositional beliefs alike; whereas {q} then goes on to restrict what these propositional claims can be about. Beliefs can *only* concern things already known, or unknown, suggesting therefore that there is no middle ground for the *thinking* of some object. Either you have that thing in mind and can think it, or you do not. It is because {p} is logically restricted to {q} which involves a metaphysical claim about the objects of thought that it is unclear how Lewis and Benson could have argued that the scope of knowledge in play, given at {q}, is anything less than exhaustive knowledge.[18] For {q} just says that beliefs can either be true or false; *but* the objects of thought, which they are about, are either known—thus providing the necessary criteria for getting some intended object in mind—or not. So that, consequently knowing everything regarding some object of thought counters the possibility of believing anything falsely about that object. The point being that if falsehood were possible, the object of thought could not have been known. Or as Burnyeat put it, the necessary conditions for knowing are also sufficient conditions for not getting anything wrong. Knowledge is, therefore provided as a necessary condition for any kind of thinking; and the impossibility of falsehood follows as a consequent of that.

The obvious exhaustive choice between thinking or judging something either *known* or *unknown* is striking. It is also familiar. This bridges a recurring theme since the *Meno* which had introduced the paradox of inquiry. The problem for knowledge is actually a problem for *thinking*. The issue concerns specifically the object of thought, where as Socrates understands the matter, the ability to identify—to *know what* you are talking or thinking of so to speak—something or object requires knowledge of that thing. Were it possible, as most would likely support today, to know only *some* things about this identified object or that some things believed in its regard were *false*, there would also be room for not actually thinking of the given object. This would introduce insurmountable and for Socrates intolerable difficulties. For were it not at least certain that when an object was called upon or apprehended for thought, x, that it was indeed that intended object x, no kind of communication whether to oneself or others would be possible. The counter intuitive position being postulated here holds that, for instance, even when acquainted with someone or thing, still there are many things that are unknown with his/her regard, in which case, when in the future there is occasion to meet him/her again, or need to bring him/her to mind, there would be no guarantee that such an attempt would be successful. That is, rather than identifying Socrates, Theaetetus is taken in his stead. That this is the case is confirmed by Socrates' conviction that the exhaustive choice provided at the outset rules out the possibility of false belief.[19] This is especially clear with respect to the negative case of an *unknown*. This would be impossible, as the Meno Paradox also verifies, because as far as the thinking subject is concerned it just *does not exist* for thinking to ascertain. The choice between the 'known or unknown' comes down to knowing everything—'all'—or absolutely nothing—'or nothing' in which case the first couldn't warrant the need for inquiry with its regard, whereas the second could not register in the mind of the inquiring subject for questioning at all—the Meno Paradox. The upshot is that Socrates is still toiling with the idea that knowledge, or more accurately, grabbing hold of an object for knowledge or thought to be of, is an 'all or nothing' affair: thinking x presupposes knowing *everything* about x, the only other alternative is that the object x does not even *exist for* the thinking subject.

The question which remains unanswered is, *why* does the ability to get something in mind, and consequently the ability to think it, necessarily imply knowing that thing *completely*? The latter is a consequent of the former; that much is clear. The problem lies, therefore, with *thinking*, specifically with the content of thinking. It is important to make this point clear: Socrates is arguing *from* the conditions of *thought* not knowledge. Thought must be of something; and that thing, as a condition of thought, must either be known completely or not known at all. This is why it was said that false belief is impossible, because thought presupposes knowledge. Consequently, false belief would be tantamount to a non-thought; empty. There could be no middle way between knowing and not knowing then, because thought must be full, it must attend upon a given object. But, the argument goes, in order to attend upon an object it must already be known. That thought presupposes knowledge is not an anomaly; in fact, the previous chapters have argued that for Socrates thinking must be of something, or x, and that the 'articulation of thought' thereby requires the acknowledged ability to identify x. But the ability to identify x then requires the knowledge of all the properties which are truthfully attributable to x (i.e. x is F). Briefly, Socrates is committed to this exhaustive choice because he is also committed to the view intimated in the previous paragraph, that when only some things are known regarding x there may be some occasion at some time when the required missing or wrong information in its regard would be necessary for correctly identifying him/her. The point is that this occasion could never be foreseen, that unless one had a complete set of true beliefs attributable to the object in question, there would always on some occasion be some other thing, y, which shares all of the only partially 'known' truths about this thing, so that consequently when thinking x one could not be certain that he was not actually thinking y in its stead. To admit, therefore anything less than complete knowledge would compromise the ability to identify some object x as *uniquely* and absolutely unmistakably not anything other than itself.

The ability to recognise an object for thought is, in effect, an ability to recognise its uniquely telling conditions [necessary and sufficient conditions] in order to counter the threat of mistakenly thinking some other thing instead.

If it is true that puzzle one accurately coincides with the assumptions of the elenctic method, why does Socrates discredit the truth of {q}; i.e. the impossibility of some middle way? Immediately prior to expounding {q}, which we have said has the peculiarity of restricting the logical possibilities that false belief can take given this reading, two counter-examples, namely, memory and learning, are introduced to illustrate the possibility of the middle way between knowing and not-knowing. Acknowledging the falsehood of {q} by way of example, Socrates goes on to say, 'but this takes us outside of our present debate'. Why does this take us outside of the present debate? And why are these examples important enough nonetheless that Socrates would point them out? The scope of the present debate is restricted to the prescribed task of the puzzles. These puzzles, mentioned earlier, are not arguments as such; that is, Socrates has not set out to prove the possibility of false belief. Rather, the puzzles seek to isolate the working assumptions of the elenchus which render false belief impossible. Consequently, the puzzle must not work outside of the assumptions or consequences of the elenctic method; so that, because memory and knowledge acquisition are incompatible with the elenchus, they do not belong to the present debate. Why mention them, therefore? Just because they are incompatible with the elenchus. That is, the elenchus has been described as a method for the acquisition of knowledge, and yet, conditions (R1)-(R3) discredit (Meno Paradox) this objective and must involve the faulty assumption which these puzzles seek to expose. That is, the false belief which has rendered false belief impossible, must be able to account for both memory and knowledge acquisition.

Puzzle Two

The impossibility of false belief hinged on an exhaustive understanding of knowledge; but it was argued, this understanding followed as a condition for thought. Namely, if S thinks x, x has been identified as the object of S's thought; and the identification of x, requires knowing x completely. The problem of false belief therefore, was hinging on this assumption, introduced as $\{q\}$; and acknowledging this Socrates now argues that thought must not be cast in terms of 'knowing and not-knowing', but in terms of 'being and not-being'.

The argument itself contains three premises, followed by a further six premises taken from an argument from analogy. False belief is cast in terms of thinking 'what is not' about anything; such that, if S thinks 'what is not', either (i) S is thinking 'what is not' *about* something that *is*, or (ii) 'what is not' *absolutely*; but, (iii) something, or again the object of thinking, must be reckoned among the things that *are*. The second premise is commonly interpreted as working up to a distinction between beliefs of different contextual order; in the language of modern philosophy, the first would be a case of opacity, and the second, transparency. It is slightly premature to talk in terms of semantics, yet Socrates' reformulation of the problem of falsehood in terms of *being* and *not-being* certainly introduces an interest in the ontological import of words for thought and speech. Moreover, the distinction between (i) and (ii) (188d4, 188d9) seems only apropos in the case that Plato is intimating that words may not necessarily be of absolutely *no-thing* (ii) when occupied by thoughts of 'what is not'. Perhaps, (i) false thinking involves thinking 'what is not' *about* something else that *is*. In this case, the status of *not-being* would, in a way, derive existential import from the *object* it is *about* (188d4), and consequently the 'what is not' bit need not itself also stand in for its own existent object. Leaving the modern philosophic debate for a discussion of the *Allodoxia Model*, it suffices to say that though Socrates has identified two kinds of propositional beliefs (remember p1 in puzzle one extends to all propositional beliefs), the third premise reduces each to like paradoxes. Propositional beliefs either assert that some object of thought has certain identifiable properties, or that x is F; or that thought merely identifies some object *x*, that it is *y*. All thoughts of some identifiable object, or something, must exist, however; so that, when cast in terms of 'what is not' the ontological status of the thing thought (*F*) and attributed to something else (*x*), must be something that is not [existent]. But that is impossible, so false belief too is impossible.[20] The paradox arises because premise three confounds the initial semantic distinction with an empiricist conception of knowledge. That is, as the argument from analogy expounds, it is assumed that there is a direct causal relation between thought and the object it is about, in the same way that perception is causally related to its sense-object.

The analogy between *thinking* 'what is not' and *perceiving* 'what is not' is given as follows: if *S* sees, hears, etc. something, then *S* sees, hears etc., something that is; if *S* thinks something, then *S* must necessarily think something that is; and conversely, if *S* thinks 'what is not', then *S* thinks nothing; for if *S* thinks 'nothing', *S* is not thinking at all; because it is impossible to think 'what is not', either about something that is, or absolutely; therefore, thinking falsely must be something different from thinking 'what is not'. Though this argument differs from the false belief adopted in Part I, namely that perception and knowledge naturally and necessarily correspond; it does endorse an affinity between the processes of *thinking* and *perceiving*. That is, this argument is valid only on the assumption that thinking something and perceiving something involve parallel processes (the ambiguity of the process of getting something in mind may be responsible for this rendering). In fact, the process of perceiving something requires a corresponding sense-object just because that is what it is of; i.e. it is the object with which *S* is acquainted that actually causes him to see *x*. In the case of perceiving it would therefore make sense to say that in the absence of a sense object there is nothing to be seen, and consequently no perceiving is going on. Yet, thoughts are not just of things, they are also *about* things. This was, in fact, the point of the distinction made in the second premise; but because the working belief throughout was that something must necessarily be existent; (ii) was reduced to a special case of (i). Therefore, Socrates invalidly adopts this analogy to prove something about thinking and its objects. It must therefore be, as the conclusion confesses, that thinking falsely (in fact, all thinking) must be different from thinking 'what is not' (and in the case of thinking truly, different from thinking 'what is'). Thought must be full, but the things that occupy thought need not correspond to the objects it entails in the same way perception does.

The Allodoxia Model (M1)

Because of the similarities of this *Model of Allodoxia* with the first puzzle, it is tempting to simply reiterate that puzzle. But there are two significant additions attached to the model: first, the mismatching taking place here does not concern particulars, like Theaetetus and Socrates (188b9-11), but mis-taking universal terms, like beautiful for ugly (188c-d); and second, an analogy is presented to link *thought* and *speech*. A bit of terminology would be useful at this point: puzzle one framed the logical form of false belief in terms of misidentification; whereas, the second puzzle, introduced the possibility of falsely describing an identified object as such and such. Exhaustive knowledge of the objects of thought was prescribed as a condition of thought because it would otherwise be impossible to identify the object in question; and later, this condition was to reduce *mistakes of description* to *mistakes of identity*, because descriptive mistakes involved the attribution of *what is not*, and therefore of what does not exist, for which consequently, there could be no thought of (i.e. *S* must also be able to identify these attributes which must also be something). This model now has us worried about mis-matching not just particulars but also the universal concepts usually used to *describe* those particulars. Still there is insufficient evidence in the text to support the claim that Socrates sought to draw a distinction between the function of a sentential subject term (often a particular, or at least denotative) from a predicative term. Instead, it will be argued that the *Allodoxia Model* looks or prepares the way to the *Sophist*, but that Socrates is still concerned with the specific problem of *identification* for thought, as an epistemological enigma. Hence, the model must either pertain to the ability to think *x* without *identifying x* as such; or *identifying x* without *knowing x* as its solution. Still, *universals* are nonetheless different from *particulars*, and this will introduce, if only implicitly, that for instance, 'the beautiful' has a meaning which is independent of the things to which it can be applied or the things that can be called by its name (196a2-3).[21] In fact, the *Allodoxia Model* does seem to try to cash in on the separability of descriptive properties or universals and the objects or particulars that they describe; however, the strict understanding of 'what knowledge is' again will demand that the ability to entertain a thought involving something—whether particular or universal— requires at least being certain that the given thing is the intended one. So far, certainty requires exhaustive knowledge. Nonetheless, the knowledge of particulars involves *acquaintance* in a way that the knowledge of universals clearly does not.[22] Knowledge acquisition or *how* we obtain knowledge is the paradoxical starting point which has made the project of determining falsehood personally important to the elenctic method, and by implication to Socrates. For the sophists and the empiricist rendering of knowledge, there need be no method of inquiry at all, for all thought just is knowledge. 'Why seek to find that which you already possess?' formed half of the paradox of inquiry; the search for something unknown formed its latter half. Socrates must show how we can entertain beliefs without knowing [the objects they are about], and this distinction between the knowledge of universals and the knowledge of particulars comprises, in foetal form, that argument which will attempt to resolve this paradox. However similar to puzzle one therefore, identity and descriptive statements are being treated as different and separable kinds of mistakes. Puzzle two reduced descriptive mistakes to mistakes of identity and this rendered the semantic distinction redundant. But do they involve the same epistemological principle?

The *Model of Allodoxia*, or other-judging, formulates false belief in terms of some sort of misjudgement that occurs when a person *interchanges in his mind* two things, both of which are/exist, and asserts that the one is the other (189c1-4), so that, he comes to falsely think that x is y. Mistakes do not arise because something has gone wrong in the causal movement from object to thought; rather, false belief is the result of some confusion of thought by itself (189c7, 189d6). This marks a difference between misidentifying and misunderstanding. The example used to illustrate this difference is particularly successful because it manages to draw out an equally significant distinction between *thinking* and *judging*, *discourse* and *statement*. Notably, *thoughts* and *discourse* do not involve asserting any claims to truth or falsehood; whereas *judgements* and *statements* both do. Thoughts have thus far been assumed to involve truth because otherwise there could be no identifiable object. Yet, this distinction would suggest that this troublesome assumption regarding thinking need not apply in the case where there is no judgement. Thinking is described,

> As a discourse that the mind carries on with itself about any subject it is considering. ...when the mind is thinking, it is simply talking to itself, asking questions and answering them, and saying yes or no. When it reaches a decision—which may come slowly or in a sudden rush—when doubt is over and two voices affirm the same thing, then we call that its 'judgement'. So I should *describe thinking as discourse* and *judgement as a statement* pronounced, not aloud to someone else, but silently to oneself (189e8-190a6).

Thinking, therefore, *resembles* discourse, yet it is not discourse itself; and judgement *resembles* a statement, but it is not the same as a statement. This excessively lengthy description of thought, and the obvious use of words particular to the distinctiveness of the *Model of Allodoxia*—thinking of *x* as *y*—must carry some significant message. That *thought* and *discourse* is the actual seat of the ongoing debate calls out for special recognition. The brief dialogue makes the distinctiveness of thought and judgement, discourse and statement clear: the first of either two pairs—thinking and discourse— do not involve claims to truth, whereas their counterparts—judging and stating—do; moreover, the former pair is covert, and the latter, overt in nature. The mistake of *Allodoxia* that we would commit in this case would be to think that when thinking or inquiring, we were really judging or stating; i.e. that when thinking of thought *as* judgement, thought then is taken to *be* judgement. Thus far thinking and judging, inquiring and stating have been considered interchangeably; and, in fact, no essential reason has presented itself to suggest an alternative treatment of these. Indeed, the conditions which apply to knowledge have, in fact, been derived from the *act of thinking*. Looking forward to the *Sophist* there will be reason to differentiate thought from the act of judgement. However, the *Theaetetus* is not yet in a position to take this valuable point on board because that which is currently under discussion is why anyone in their right mind would *think* something [known] and then go on to think that [what it has been identified as] it is not what it is. It is looking to clarify, therefore, the cognitive justification for such a move; the *Sophist* will later be in a position to exploit this dialogue because by then Plato will be concerned to show how falsehood can be explained. In other words, currently the query is why one would 'believe what is false', later the inquiry will seek to say 'what falsehood is'.

Still the example also illustrates what the *Model of Allodoxia* claims falsehood entails where again the emphasis placed on the act of thinking is important. The likeness of the two pairs lies in the dialogue form of questions and answers; and in dialogue resolving itself in agreement, respectively. That is, thinking and discourse, judgements and statements, resemble each other because they share a common property; each can, in virtue of their likeness, be *described* in the same way. But could someone, given these likenesses then take it into his head that *thinking is discourse*; and *judgement is statement*? This is what *Allodoxia* affirms, namely, false belief occurs because when '*S* is *thinking* of one thing *as* another; he then goes on to *affirm* to himself that the one *is* the other (190a8-9)'. Things may share at least one descriptive property and thereby be *similar* in terms of that description; but to assert that the one *is* the other means that there are no properties that can be attributed to the one that can not be attributed to the other. Socrates adopts this reasoning when he argues that *Allodoxia* is impossible. With the 'all or nothing' notion in play or the condition of exhaustive knowledge regarding the objects of thought for their subsequent identification makes it once again perplexing how *S* could not recognise that one thing *is* not another thing, when thinking of the one *as* the other. Yet, this would miss the point. As the example in the case of the opposed universals, *the beautiful* and *the ugly*, illustrates *S* would not describe *the beautiful as ugly*, because *S* already knows *what beautiful is.* Misidentification in thought is taken as a necessary condition for misdescription. This had already been explicated by the end of puzzle two; so what's new? The point is in *how* the beautiful or ugly is *being thought* or rather, *how* something *is* for thought. Notice, that entertaining the thought that '*x is y*' does not necessarily involve *judging* that it is the case or true that these are the same thing. Common sense condones the ability to entertain the thought 'My father is Plato'; but were you to *state* this you might find yourself amongst a number of other people making similar claims to 'being Jesus Christ', 'Napoleon' and so on. Also, previously the causal connection between the mind and its objects imposed a transparent context where the meaning of some belief was determined by what was being referred to, namely the objects(s), so that belief was given as representations of reality. Hence, a belief for which there is no referent or corresponding object would be impossible. This has been the problem that Socrates and Theaetetus have been grappling with; for thought of *what is not* just doesn't refer to anything. Yet the freshly formulated understanding of false thinking would seem to suggest an alternative *context* of thought, a context where the meaning and truth of thought is not established transparently. False thinking now described as a case of *mis-matching*, is reformulated as 'thinking *of x as y*'. Socrates argues that what makes false thinking impossible is the presence of two identified objects of thought; option (i) from puzzle one—*S* judges that something s/he knows, is something else s/he also knows (190c5-8). A quasi kind of opacity is ushered in as an alternative, it would seem, when Socrates suggests that thinking '*of x as y*' may not necessarily involve thinking of both *x* and *y*, but only *x*. It would make sense to argue on the grounds that *y* is not being identified, and hence not known as such, that it is falsely or wrongly applied—option (ii) from puzzle one which is what Socrates will, in fact, opt for.[23]

There is some question regarding the actual proposal that this *as* condition seems to be expected to explain. Socrates may be arguing that for any thought there is only one referent object, and that mistakes occur with regards to what is asserted or stated *about* it. So that, the formulation of falsehood really concerns typically predicative statements, '*x is F*', where *F* is mistaken for something else, *G*. So while getting hold of the right object, and thus leaving the condition for identification uncompromised, the predicative term is mistaken for another. Socrates may also be arguing that there is only one referent object, and that falsehood occurs as a result of taking the object x for the object y, such that when plugged into the statement 'Socrates is beautiful'; it would involve thinking of, for instance, Socrates *as* Alcibiades; and hence mis-taking Socrates for Alcibiades.[24] There is not much to go on to resolve this ambiguity. However, this second alternative does seem to be what Socrates intends since it conforms to the refutation of *Allodoxia* at the end. *Allodoxia* fails because confusing or mis-taking one object, x, for another object, y, would require the patently impossible thought that the referent object identified *is* something else. This feeds into the following *Wax Tablet Model* as well, since it picks up the issue by trying to determine how two things could be before the mind without that involving the *act of identification* as such (i.e. passively via perception). Moreover, the alternative reading would require an overstatement of the thought versus judgement polemic, as well as a thorough going semantic analysis of what a statement involves which is only explicitly discussed towards the end of the *Sophist* (with the discussion of *onomata* and *rhemata*). There is no explicit recognition of predication anywhere in the dialogue to justify therefore, that Socrates is for the time being interested in anything other than the referent or identifiable object of thought. Hence, the locale of falsehood is not yet recognised as residing with that part of any thought which gets something said about the subject term, as it were, namely with the predicative. When Socrates goes about exposing the weaknesses of *Allodoxia*, he says, that 'so long as one is making a statement or judgement *about* both things at once and *his mind has hold of both*, he cannot say or judge that the one is the other'. Confusing an ox for a horse then follows as an instance of *Allodoxia*. The application of particulars in this example again reinforces the view that Socrates is talking about a confusion of *identification* regarding the subject term. The *as* condition, is consequently rendered redundant because Socrates is still unable to satisfactorily explain how it is possible to simultaneously think of two distinct things, x and y, and not recognise that the one is taken *for* or thought of *as* the other. So that consequently, getting stuck with the wrong subject term results in talking about it *as if* it was something else, and falsely thinking about [here predicates] it *as* the other thing.

In case that mis-taking takes place with the referent or subject term of a statement or judgement, there would be nothing to distinguish what is claimed here from the first puzzle. Mistakes have from the beginning of *Allodoxia* been identified as *occurring* when 'thought contemplates by itself', and the elucidation of statements and judgements, though yet unanalysed, must be expected to at least recommend their distinctiveness from thought and discourse as such, and hence a claim that something (*x*) is something else (*y*) when plugged in for a judgement. That which comes through following the refutation of this model is that were it possible to make a statement or judgement where only *one of the two terms* need be identified or thought of as such, false belief could be explained. However, as the closing argument explicates, 'if he is *thinking* of one only and not the other *at all*, he will never think that the one is the other' (190d6-7). In other words, falsehood is described as cognitively perplexing *because* it requires thinking 'of something, *x*, that it is something else, *y*'. The ability to make such a claim requires having *both* in mind, since were *y* not also before the mind, it could not be a part of this complex thought. Still, this being a debate on knowledge, and falsehood being interesting only as relevant to the cognitive apparatus making knowledge attainable; this so-called locale is rendered fruitless because Socrates will not be able to explain how when both objects are, as the puzzle requires, before the mind it is possible to think of the one as the other. It is interesting, with a look ahead to the rich semantic material in the *Sophist*, that were the second reading regarding predicative statements accepted (so mis-taking would involve not the subject or denotative term, but one predicative term for another), it is likely that Socrates would once again, in similar vain, protest that the predicative component of a thought could not be efficiently used unless the thinking subject was acquainted with 'what it is'. Consequently in either case, the problems founded at the end of puzzle two begin all over again. Indeed this is how Parmenides has set up the problem in his poem: advocating semantic atomism each element of a propositional statement was expected to refer to corresponding bits or elements in the world such that thinking *x* and then going on to assert the statement '*x* is *F*' would involve thinking the referent object x is the other referent object F; so that, in effect, this would involve the perplexing thought that x *is both x and not-x at the same time*.

However for now the puzzle is still hinging on how the mind gets hold of something, where the condition for grabbing hold of something is a sufficient condition for not mis-taking one thing brought to mind with another. Again the point is made explicit, 'if one is thinking only of *one* thing and not *at all* of the other, he would never think that the one is the other'. Mistaking necessarily requires having two things before the mind such that the one is, in fact, taken for the other. In this case, there would be nothing to confuse the given object with. This is a rare occasion when Socrates explicitly spells out the assumption: because thought is full, namely it involves an object(s) of thought, the mind must be attending upon the object(s) of which his thought is about. Unwavering, Socrates adopts the view that the mind either grabs hold of an object of thought completely or not at all. The much anticipated framework toward an alternative context of thinking, opacity, consequently finds itself subsumed by the context of transparency because mis-taking *must* involve actually thinking of one thing, and *taking* it for something else which is also being thought of in its stead. The function of either the subject or predicate name formulated thus would be to bring the corresponding object or thing to mind for thinking; it would be purely referential, therefore.

Clues From the Modern Debate

Any philosopher convinced by some version of empiricism, namely that the mind is occupied with thoughts furnished, one way or another, by experiencing the world, will also want to hold on to some version of the word-world analysis of language. That would mean that for every thought there is some kind of corresponding experience; and that for everything named for thought there is a corresponding object or extension of that name, from which its understanding or meaning is derived; i.e. denotation establishes connotation. A number of problems plague this approach; firstly, experience not being objective could not guarantee that the meaning accompanied by any referent sense-object would be the same for any two persons; secondly, this would terribly stunt the number of names or referential expressions that would be meaningful to any one person; thirdly, nonexistential expressions, or names for which there are no corresponding referent objects (egs. unicorns [imaginative objects], Homer [historical figure], Ms. x's daughter [where Ms. x has no daughter]) could have no meaning whatsoever, and fourthly, a respective problem of modality would also emerge.

In his article 'Reference and Modality',[25] Quine argues that the reason why for two coextensional expressions substitutivity fails (i.e. two names refer to or stand for the same person or thing; but when one expression is supplanted by the other in some assertion a different truth-value obtains) is because there are two distinct contexts of reference—the *referentially transparent context* and the *referentially opaque context*. Loosely the opaque context is defined by the failure of substitutivity, but this doesn't say much until we understand transparent reference, and especially why substitutivity fails because of this difference in context. Basically the point is that when a name is used to *stand-in for* the object being named, so as to *denote* that object, the context is transparent. Whereas, when the name is used only to say something about the sentential subject, then the context is opaque. For instance, Ms P. may also be called or referred to by her students as 'The little Buddha' (because she assumes the Buddha position before the class while teaching), and either names could pick out the teacher in question (i.e. 'Ms. P' and 'the little Buddha' are coextensional expressions) with equal success, at least for those familiar with her alias. But, the statement ''The little Buddha' is so-called because she assumes the Buddha position before the class while teaching' is true; yet when the coextensional name 'Ms. P' is substituted for 'the Little Buddha' it is false. The failure of substitutivity follows because the context of this statement is opaque, which just means that the name 'the Little Buddha' does not refer simply to its object. In other words, the statement does not depend upon, or in effect, what gets *said* by the statement does not depend upon the *object* denoted by the name, but on the *name* itself.[26] Two distinct contexts of referring expressions provided Quine with an answer to the aforementioned third problem regarding nonexistential expressions which is also at the forefront of the present debate on falsehood. Returning to the explicit epistemological puzzle at hand, the question which this semantic distinction must be able to answer is, when the name for an object functions in an opaque context, does this in any way change the *kind* of knowledge that is involved when thought is occupied by the same object, whether as 'Ms P' or 'the Little Buddha'? The point which must be emphasised is that it is not the *name* which marks its contextual use, since both 'Ms P' and 'the Little Buddha' could be used transparently; rather it is *what is getting said or thought that decides the function of a name* [whether it stands in for its object or not]. Socrates' stock response would address the ability to efficiently and successfully use these names; namely, unless there were prior knowledge of *what* these names *denote* or *refer* to irrespective of *how* these are actually being used presently any statement employing them would be meaningless. That is, no one could get it into his/her head to say or think 'Little Buddha is a good teacher' unless s/he was an efficient user of the name 'the Little Buddha'. When, s/he is not even aware that his/her 'teacher of ethics' is also known by the alias 'the Little Buddha, s/he could have [falsely?] claimed, 'I don't know the Little Buddha'.

There is a strain in the *Allodoxia Model* which opens the door to semantic considerations which are picked up in the *Sophist*. The intention of the *Allodoxia Model* has been to suggest that it is possible to think of one thing known as, or in the place of another thing known. We know from the modern debate that names can be put to alternative uses so that we do not always expect names to denote an object and can thereby avoid the obvious implications here being discussed. In the stretch of argumentation, the gist had been that the mind can be furnished with known objects but that when thinking takes over one thing could be taken for another thing. Consequently, falsehood would follow as a result of thinking of *x as y*. The suggested break between the known objects of thought and the actual act of thinking is responsible for opening the door to language, however implicitly, because when the object-*x* is thought of in place of the object-*y*, what happens is that the wrong name gets inserted for the given thought without that at the same time rendering it meaningless. Of course, this suggestion is dropped because Socrates is still   confused about the move from the known objects of thought to the thoughts about these, and rejects this as a possible explanation of falsehood because he still seems convinced that the knowledge of the given objects would guarantee bringing the right objects to the forefront of thought, thus guaranteeing truth. The modern clues thus suggest that the *Theaetetus* looks forward to the *Sophist* and at the same time show that even from a purely epistemological perspective, an understanding of the move from the objects of thought to the act of thinking would have to first be clear on how thinking and inquiring differ from stating and judging. It would suggest that the objects which furnish the mind with things to think about is not responsible for making thinking either meaningful or interesting. It is wrong to look therefore, to theories regarding the acquisition of knowledge for an answer to how and where thinking goes wrong. Socrates could be described therefore, as groping for something like the modern distinction between opacity and transparency to explain the on-going enigma on falsehood but remains presently unable to do so because the current discussion has taken him into the delves of the mind which does not seem to properly involve a discussion of language.

The Wax Tablet Model

The *Wax Tablet Model* is the first attempt to resolve the problem of false belief; it is an attempt to show why getting some thing in mind is not a sufficient condition for not making mistakes. So far, exhaustive knowledge was given as a condition for getting something in mind because for Socrates it would otherwise just be impossible. This condition is at the heart of the *Allodoxia Model* since it exploits the interplay between *getting some object in mind* and *thinking it*. Basically the difficulty encountered previously pertained to the 'all or nothing' or exhaustive condition of knowledge regarding the identifiability of something to think of. In turn, the attempted suspension of *identification* for one of the two terms comprising a complex statement was shown to fail. That is, even the intuition (this will be picked up in the *Sophist*) that complex statements are comprised of only a single subject term which requires *identification* as such, and a predicate term which merely says something *about* the subject term, confusion or mistaking only makes sense when both terms are independently meaningful, and when in truth one is literally taken for the other by thought. The attempt of the *Wax Tablet Model* must be to show how two things—names of things—can be brought before the mind for thought simultaneously without their identifiability thereby frustrating the possibility of taking the one for the other. The *Wax Tablet Model* is an epistemological argument which tries to come to grips with the origin of the objects of thought, and how we come to know these things, which will involve an account of how the mind gets hold of some thing for thinking. For the *Allodoxia Model* may have introduced an interesting semantic distinction between beliefs of differing order, but if the condition for thought applies to both referential and opaque beliefs, entertaining a belief about some object which is other than the object being thought wouldn't be any less problematic. Again, how is it possible to think anything other than what you are thinking? First perception, then memory will be discussed as the locale of false thinking.

The *Wax Tablet Model* likens the mind to a wax tablet, and likens knowledge acquisition to memory retention. Yet, no attempt is made to account for the process by which impressions are cast onto this block, nor is there any mention of the origin of the stock of impressions.[27] Perception, which we know from Part I, is not equal to knowledge, may bring something never seen before to mind, and this may cause false thinking when this sense perception is taken for something else known. Memory is then isolated as the locale of false thinking since it can be argued that something already known, but not actively before the mind, can be wrongly identified or recalled from the stock impressions of things imprinted on the mind/wax at another time. So that, when seeing someone from a distance, *this actual stranger*, the sense impression depicted is mistaken for the sense datum of someone else previously known. Consequently, confusing this sense impression with an old sense datum will result in unbeknownst plugging the wrong subject term in the statement of choice. The mistake will involve naming Socrates, and going on to say of the stranger that 'Socrates is snub nosed'. This corresponds to the case which Socrates at 191b concedes is a legitimate case of false thinking, namely *it is possible to think that things you know are things you do not know*; i.e. case (iii) of puzzle one. Moreover, all of the assumptions would appear to be accounted for: the identifiable object is something known and retractable from a stock of impressions stamped upon the mind, and recalled at will by memory; these impressions are also the kinds of things that can be *described*, though through the alternative epistemic route, perception, this is impossible. This is what should be expected since the case of memory involves knowledge, whereas perception passively casts things unto the mind's eye and does not involve knowledge. The original exhaustive list of false thought is now amended: for any case where (i) x and y are known but not perceived; or (ii) x is known but y is neither known nor perceived; or (iii) x and y are neither known nor perceived, false belief would be impossible because retrieving some object via thought presupposes knowledge (cases (i)-(ii)), whereas, when neither route holds there just is nothing for thought to be of whatsoever. However, when for either x or y, or both, perception brings that object to mind, then false belief is possible. False belief is once again cast in terms of *misidentification*; where the perception of y does not bring the correct sense datum to mind from the stock impressions; and hence identifies x as the object of thought for judgement. Consequently, the judgement will involve descriptions which really belong to Socrates, rather than the stranger.

The memory-perception dynamic is an obvious case of falsehood; yet, it is curiously incongruous with what has preceded its recommendation. An analysis of the *Allodoxia Model* revealed that the kinds of mistakes that are under discussion concerns typically predicative statements. Moreover, the *kind* of mistake committed does not involve the identified subject term itself, because it was argued that that would require knowing and not knowing the identified object at the same time which is impossible. Further, this rendering can not respect the *as* condition as a case which inhibits right thinking. At most it can be argued on this account that thought is not responsible for bringing the faulty object to mind, and hence the condition for identification for an object of *thought* does not apply. Hence, where perception is involved there is no problem explaining falsehood. Unfortunately, this only explains the obvious, and leaves many other questions unanswered. Socrates must intend more than the suggestion of two alternative and independent epistemic routes—perception and memory—for getting hold of something for thought to be about. To begin, this does not square with the perplexity of falsehood, after all there is nothing paradoxical about confusing something seen with something remembered. The perplexity with which the dialogue is involved concerns the problem of *thinking per se*; particularly with how *once* thought is occupied by some identifiable object, it can then go on to think *about* it something which is not [the case]. Or as Angene puts is, 'a suitable subject is one such that we can think about it *what is false* of it';[28] i.e. the false belief must involve that thing occupying thought. To go on to argue that the mis-take does not involve *thinking* some *identifiable* object, only perceiving one, is commonplace, but disappointing therefore. In fact, from 195c-196c Socrates gets Theaetetus to acknowledge that the *Allodoxia Model* does not apply to cases where two things are being *thought* of simultaneously by the same man (195e-196). Moreover, were falsehood properly addressed in terms of *thinking* per se, then we will have come full circle to the original paradox, and affirm that (i) something known is taken for something else also known which is impossible because this would require that something be known and not known at the same time (196b-c4); i.e. when something is known [completely] mistakes are rendered impossible.

Exploiting the distinction drawn previously between thought and judgement, Socrates now admits that if falsehood is possible it must have something to do with the actual *act of judgement* which will introduce *competency in thinking or deliberating*. Much ado is made of the quality of the stock impressions from 197c7-8. Socrates' description of *impressions* includes the quality of the wax, or mind, and its competency to accurately and permanently seal sense impressions (esp. 191d-e, 194c-e). Impressions come through the senses and are stamped onto the wax slabs. Those with good slabs learn quickly, have good memories and do not interchange the imprints of their perceptions (194d-e). This takes care of the cognitive side of the puzzle: namely, the reason why some people are prone to making mistakes is because of the manner in which they ascertain their experiences. 'When they see or hear or think of something, they cannot quickly assign things to their several imprints.' Hence, the misfitting of thought to perception. Yet, already this requires *judgement*. Clearly there should be no surprise that things imprinted unto the waxen block via perception is not also equal to knowledge. Again, unsatisfied that the *Wax Tablet Model* has not resolved the problem as stated, Socrates reverts to the originally baffling puzzle regarding the ability to *think* two things at the same time and take the one for the other. Theaetetus astutely responds that though mistakes can be made when counting the number of objects before one, so that instead of eleven, twelve are counted; it is impossible when thinking the *number* eleven *and* twelve to *judge* that the one is the other. Once more Socrates confirms that, the number, not their instances, once cast unto the waxen block can not in any way permit false judgement. The compelling implication invited by this excessive scenario is that a vacuum has been created for the actual application of thought. Still, the objects identified by thought can never in any way be mistaken; yet, when applying this knowledge to the world *judgement* becomes impregnated with the prospect of falsehood. The following *Aviary Model* turns on a distinction between two distinct levels of knowledge: latent and current. This is a much more illuminating and relevant description of the problem at hand since this will necessarily involve, what perception cannot, 'the mistake of contemplating by itself'.

The Aviary Model

Left with the possibility of falsely 'believing that something known is something else also known', and the prescribed problem of accounting for falsehood in thought, the Aviary Model presents two alternative ways by which an object can be presented to mind. The problem still awaiting response is how it is possible to make mistakes when beliefs of description depend upon beliefs of identity. That is, if it is impossible to get something in mind unless it is identifiable, then, because beliefs of identity are exhaustive, descriptive beliefs would necessarily follow truthfully, thus drawing an impasse to false belief. It is the mental mechanism that moves from beliefs of identity to beliefs of description that requires elaboration, and it is this that the Aviary seeks to somehow clarify. For the Aviary Model does not, as the previous model did not, involve providing an epistemological theory to explain *how some object comes to mind for identification* (see p. 55, esp. p. 56).[29] Rather it starts from the moment that some object is presented to mind, and proceeds to determine *how the mind works on these or thinks about them,* such that something may ensue falsely. We should be justified therefore, to criticise the argument only with respect to the latter, but not with the former. Nonetheless, that Socrates has channelled the pursuit for the falsification of the impossibility of falsehood to the latter does suggest what might be called two levels of knowledge: it may be possible to know that some object *is x,* but not know why it is *x,* or what *x*hood encompasses. This would be incompatible with the condition of thought so-far attributed to Socrates, but it would be compatible with the typical Socratic use of examples when in pursuit of something yet unknown. Of course, it is common knowledge that Socrates reprimands himself for doing so; and now is no exception; i.e. just before setting up the Aviary Model he says that they should not have been applying the term 'knowledge' when 'what it is' remains unknown. Once more, Socrates wants to amend that part of his theory of knowledge always in play to accommodate the latter difficulty.

The Aviary Model proceeds to account for falsehood from the point where there is already an identi*fied* object, what is described as *knowledge as possession*; and, goes on to distinguish this from, the act of seizing an identi*fiable* object, what is described as *knowledge as having.* In terms of the aviary, the mind is likened to a birdcage, and the birds we put into the cage are pieces of knowledge. When enclaved there is *knowledge as possession*; and when retrieved from the enclave there is *knowledge as having.* So that, what Socrates is reaching for is the possibility of possessing the knowledge of something such that it has been identified; but still, not either *actively* or *correctly* using or retrieving that knowledge. This way, he says, 'we agree that it is impossible to possess what one does not possess [i.e. you either (possess) knowledge or you do not at all], and so we avoid the result that a man should not know what he does know [the original contradiction 'knowing and not knowing the same thing'] but we say that it is possible for him to get hold of a false *judgement* about it' (198a-b). Were falsehood understood as a mistake of not activating the right bird, it would constitute grabbing hold of the wrong thought-object or bird, but were it a problem of correct application, it would constitute misunderstanding or thinking about the right object or bird but in the wrong way.

This first rendering would closely echo the Wax Tablet Model, but instead of perception causing the recollection of the wrong object, here it would be thought. Falsehood would involve retrieving the wrong thought-object or bird, and then going on to plug the wrongly retrieved thought-object into a belief claim that involved the intended thought-object. The reference to the Wax Tablet Model at 197e2, and the analogous method of recollection indeed strengthens the credibility of this reading. Yet, to begin it would not meet the left-over problem which Socrates himself raised against the Wax Tablet Model, namely that the object responsible for inciting the false belief was not actively in play. Moreover, the example provided to illustrate the application of the model does not support this interpretation. After all the objective has been given as an attempt to show how one can have knowledge of identity (as possession) and yet get knowledge of description (as having) wrong. The first case involves a problem of identity alone; i.e. getting or identifying the wrong bird from a host of birds. Furthermore, all references to the Wax Tablet Model are restricted to their common point of departure—when the mind is already stocked with wax imprints or birds—and therefore, to their shared interest in the process of recollection.

The example belongs to the class of abstract thought for which there is no identifiable object as such, it is about numbers. By what process of thinking could someone mistakenly judge that 5+7 is 11? Of course, we know that 5+7 is equal to 12; but the problem should not be recast in terms of mismatching 11 and 12, since 5+7 must be actively involved in getting the *answer* wrong. Hence, it must show how 5+7 is taken for 11, or how someone knowing his numbers could get this sum wrong. Recollection or the process by which something is retrieved is responsible for falsehood. The movement proceeds from the aviary, and for this reason Socrates is rightly concerned with the general state of this mental apparatus. The aviary, like the wax tablet, is stocked with birds [or imprints]; and somewhat similarly, these birds or *pieces of knowledge* are variously described. Though imprints were said to vary according to the original quality of the wax, here emphasis is given to a more general description defining the state of any birdcage:

> Let us suppose that every mind contains a kind of aviary stocked with birds of every sort, some flying apart from the rest, some in small groups, and some solitary, flying in any direction among them all (197e1-6).

The mind is filled with pieces of knowledge, but these pieces are diverse and variously situated; or unorganised. Not only does *knowledge as possession* not tell me where to look for some intended thought-object; but more importantly, it does not tell me how the host of identified thought-objects are related to each other. Therefore, though the condition for thought is satisfied, this condition does not tell me how to think about these things. This is why Socrates describes recollection as a process by which 'a man knows his numbers, but is trying to find out what he knows as if he had no knowledge of it (198c)'. Burnyeat has argued that this qualification is important because it implies a third epistemic route by which an object can come before the mind for thinking. The reason why someone can mistake 5+7 for 11, without entertaining the obviously contradictory notion, 11 is 12, is because it is possible to be thinking of 12 without recognising it *as* 12. It is in the asking, 'what is five and seven?' that Burnyeat believes someone must be unknowingly thinking of the number 12.[30] This botches the point that the aviary is trying to make. The search for the answer to this arithmetic problem involves, not looking for 12 knowingly or otherwise, but in the understanding of how 'five' and 'seven' relate for addition. Unless 'the pursuit for 12 unknowingly' means '12 is not recognised as the answer to 5+7', it incorrectly places the emphasis on the so-called 12-bird. But surely the force of the example resides with the arithmetic problem itself, '5+7', and the search for its reference, such that a mistake involves misconstruing the relation between these numbers and not the capacity to recognise 12 as such. Nowhere does Socrates argue that the mistake is one of recognising 12; but rather, the mistake is initiated by the pursuit for the unrehearsed answer to what five plus seven amounts to. He is interested not in the precision of memory; rather second level knowledge takes for granted that first level knowledge is accessible, and that it is in virtue of this knowledge that learning is possible. Learning here is depicted as *new* knowledge or higher order knowledge, so that something previously unknown comes to be known. Trouble begins when Socrates and Theaetetus try to come to grips with *this* 'something' of further learning.31 Identifiable object? Hence something already known, or a newly identified object previously unknown? How is knowledge acquisition or learning defined at both levels?

> When we are babies we must suppose this receptacle empty [the aviary], and take the birds to stand for pieces of knowledge. Whenever a person acquires any piece of knowledge and shuts it up in his enclosure, we must say that he has learned or discovered *the thing of which this is the knowledge*, and that is what 'knowing' means (197e-198).

So first level knowledge is acquired by some, yet unspecified, method of learning; but which constitutes 'knowing' the *thing* or object of thought; hence an identified object for thinking. Second level knowledge is also described as learning.

> Now we think of him as hunting once more for any piece of knowledge he wants, catching and holding it, and letting it go again. In what terms are we to describe that—the same that we used of the original process [for first level knowledge] of acquisition, or different ones?

In answering, he says, that for numbers, the mathematician (the numbers expert) who knows all his numbers, would for second level knowledge acquisition be interested in figuring out what some number amounts to. This would constitute counting 'numbers themselves [abstract mathematical problems] or some set of external things [counting what some set of things amounts to]' (198c) and is compared to a literate man who knows his letters, and sets out to read (198d). Obviously there is more to maths and reading than 'knowing' your numbers and letters, and this is what the aviary fails to recommend, but which the following section will endorse. For now knowledge acquisition for first and second level knowledge is given as follows:

> our illustration from hunting pigeons and getting possession of them enables us to explain that the hunting occurs in two ways—first, before you possess your pigeon in order to have possession of it; second, after getting possession of it, in order to catch hold in your hand what you have already possessed for some time. In the same way, if you have long possessed pieces of knowledge about things you have learned and know, it is still possible to get to know the same things again, by the process of recovering the knowledge of some particular thing and getting hold of it. It is knowledge that you have possessed for some time, but you had not got it handy in your mind (198c).

The Aviary Model distinguishes between two separate and distinct epistemic routes, so for good reason Socrates places considerable importance on what is involved at either level of knowledge acquisition. Learning, though somehow different because for first level knowledge memory is not involved; but nonetheless *what* is being learned seems to unnecessarily overlap, and consequently lead to the Aviary's rebuttal. Because the same terms describe learning at both levels of knowledge acquisition, they are stuck with the familiar paradox: either say, in the case of second level knowledge, 'the man is setting about learning again for himself what he already knew', which sounds odd; or 'he is going to read or count something he does not know, when we have already granted that he knows all the letters or all the numbers', which is absurd (199a). The oddity consists of searching for something already known; whilst the absurdity resides in searching for [the answer to] something unknown when at the same time the pieces [which comprise the question] are known. This is strangely a re-enactment of the MP: if you either know or do not know something, then inquiry is either meaningless, because you already possess the knowledge you seek; or it is absurd, because you must have an identifiable object for thinking.[32]

Knowledge as possession grants an identifiable object; but when Socrates applies the same terms to both levels of knowledge he comes to confuse *what* is being learned, so that in either case the objective focuses on determining the referent object for any thought, when clearly it is arguable that '12' and '5+7' have a different sense. Or in epistemological terms, there is a different mental process which is required in each case to bring the common referent, 12, before the mind. Having set us up for falsehood as a mistake of understanding, he subsumes it under a mistake of identity. That is, when searching for the answer to 5+7, namely 12, the 11-bird is grabbed hold of instead. But this interchange of pieces [parts] of knowledge is a strict case of misidentification and does not involve the original question about how five and seven relate for addition. Such a mistake of identity would entertain knowledge only at the first level, and according to Socrates should involve a contradiction, but he says; 'it does not seem reasonable to say that when a piece of knowledge presents itself that it should be unrecognisable' since that is the meaning of 'identifiable'; i.e. that the knowledge necessary for identification has been satisfied. Yet, were Socrates still talking about strict identity mistakes in place of 'unreasonable' above, he should have said 'contradictory'. Instead, the argument seems to involve *reason* in a more serious way. For falsehood is not the failure to recognise *the thing* for which there is knowledge [or for want of knowing that thing], but it is the failure to recognise *that thing as the answer* to the given question *by reason of this knowledge* (199d). Knowledge is going to be held accountable for false belief, which is why Theaetetus is then going to recommend that any aviary is stocked both with pieces of knowledge and pieces of ignorance.[33]

What justifies this move from knowing to false belief? Somehow it is unreasonable that from the knowledge of numbers, of 5, 7, 11, and 12, that 11 is taken for 12, since part of knowing 12 must be knowing what numbers amount to 12. For how else is any number identified if not in virtue of what it amounts to. Of course, for the case of addition this straightforwardly follows since counting does seem to comprise an essential understanding of [what] 12 [is]. But what of more complex mathematical problems? Surely, knowing the answer could not be cast in terms of counting.[34] The failure to assign learning of a different kind to the operation or function of addition accounts for the reduction of second level knowledge to first level knowledge. Just as the failure to read a new novel [where recognisable letters are variously arranged] happens because the rules arranging these letters into words, and words into sentence are unknown; so too, is the failure to solve mathematical problems the result of misunderstanding the rules which render the correct answer. Learning at this level resides in coming to grips with *how* pieces of knowledge come together to provide greater insight rather than recognising and founding new objects for thought.

Recollection in the *Meno* and the Aviary

Though it has been argued by McDowell that the Theory of Recollection in the *Theaetetus* (TRT) is reminiscent of the TR found in the *Meno* (TRM), I do not support this view. To begin with the TRM is intended to respond to the Meno Paradox. The paradox, I have argued, is complex. It involves two distinct, though related problems. The first, involves the movement from belief to knowledge. This, I have argued is the intention of the elenchus which sets it apart from sophistry. The latter is peirastic; it only seeks conviction. The problem Meno raised caused us to question whether the elenctic conditions could live up to its feat. Because the problematic condition involved the doxastic constraint, it was no surprise to find that the TRM argued that the aviary is full at birth; and that the transition from belief (which we all have) to knowledge (which few will ever have) occurred when the elenchus, by frequently asking the right questions, invoked these innate pieces of knowledge (probably, knowledge of things) to be recalled. Responding to the elenctic exercise which first casts its interlocutor in aporia, again it is not surprising to find that the choice between explaining this movement as a case of 'knowing and inquiring' and 'not knowing and inquiring', the latter is adopted. Here recollection is developed as a theory of innate knowledge.

The second half of this complex puzzle, I have argued is inserted by Socrates when he casts the above in terms of justifying *inquiry*. Remember the above is about *knowledge acquisition*. Socrates argues that either 'the object of inquiry in known, and therefore it is pointless to search for it', or 'the object of inquiry is not known, and therefore there can be nothing in mind for the search to proceed'. This overlaps in interest with the present difficulty encountered here in the *Theaetetus*. Again it is the all-or-nothing assumption regarding the ability to identify something for thought which is at issue. This was dropped in the *Meno* and picked up here as a problem for false thinking. The TRA is different from the TRM therefore, because its objective is to explain how it is possible to identify something known, and then go on to think something falsely of it. Notice here, the staring point is knowledge, where previously it had been ignorance (innate knowledge is latent, so that one possesses it but is otherwise ignorant of it [until it is recalled and becomes current]). This being so, the TRA begins with an aviary which is empty at birth and which through the process of living and experiencing is filled. This means that the TRA is not interested in the narrower question about how belief is converted into knowledge for the select few. It is the broader question which occupies the *Theaetetus* regarding how thought, short of knowledge, is possible. Indeed, it is possible; all men in sound mind (and with no cognitive handicaps impeding thought) think, have beliefs, and contemplate. Though, not all men are right in what they think, etc., all of the time. Sometimes we think falsely. Since the TRA asks a different question, the answer, namely the TR, should be different somehow. We have already seen that its aviary is empty at birth; but the additional distinction is that *knowledge as possession* versus *knowledge as having* reflect to distinct *states* of knowing rather than different levels of knowing corresponding to latency and currency.

Conclusion

It requires little effort to foresee the sequel to Part II given that it has in its entirety been bogged down and failed to explain *how* false thinking occurs as a result of the flagrant condition endorsed for thought. Thought is impossible unless *knowledge* of the thing in question precedes it. Hence, so long as the puzzle of falsehood is understood in terms of mis-taking one thing for another, such that both must comprise that thought, there seems no obvious way to suspend the condition. To opt, in other words for the argument which attempts to suspend the need to identify one of the two objects as such; i.e. to think of that thing *as* equal to itself. The *Allodoxia Model* first introduced this possibility, and with it the transparent-opaque distinction followed, as well as the implicit suggestion that *thinking* is not the same as *judgement*, such that the stringent conditions which apply to the latter may not actually apply to the former. The subsequent models, the *Wax Tablet Model* and the *Aviary Model*, each in turn proposed alternative epistemic routes by which something could be brought to mind without that requiring its identification as such. Each failed. The first because, though it could explain falsehood where perception was involved, it did not respect the perplexing aspect of the puzzle, namely that it involves the act of *thinking* alone by itself. The *Aviary* picked up where the *Wax Tablet Model* left off and offered an exegetic illustration of the process of thinking involved when falsehood occurs. It too failed because focusing on the problem of *identification* it lost sight of the actual mental process involved when by an alternative epistemic route something is being thought. Each effort has been frustrated as a result of the stringent condition of thought and its incapacitatingly narrow comprehension of how something is thought, namely transparently only *as* the object of the thing in question. Part III of the *Theaetetus* will take up the topic of *knowledge* per se, and question the 'all or nothing' condition of thought. Knowledge will be distinguished from mere true belief, and the three proposed descriptions of *logos* will by implication demonstrate that what has thus far been called *knowledge* is nothing more than belief. Yet, thought, in fact, dialogue has proceeded uninhibited nonetheless.

Notes

[1] It is generally agreed that the early dialogues are the *Apology, Crito, Laches, Lysis, Charmides, Hippias Minor, Major, Euthyphro, Protagoras, Gorgias*, and *Ion*; the middle dialogues are the *Meno, Phaedo, Republic, Symposium, Phaedrus, Euthydemus, Menexenus*, and *Cratylus*; and the late dialogues are the *Parmenides, Theaetetus, Sophist, Politicus, Timaeus, Critias, Philebus* and the *Laws*.

[2] One of the features that characterises the early Socratic dialogues is their aporetic or non-constructivist nature; whereas, the later dialogues exhibit Plato's matured, and therefore complete, philosophical positions. However, this does not always find the late Platonic dialogues constructive; the *Theaetetus* is an example.

[3] See F.M. Cornford (1935) *Plato's Theory of Knowledge*.

[4] No historical attribution is being made regarding Plato's actual preoccupation with the Meno Paradox in the *Theaetetus*. Rather the objective is to show, whether acknowledged as such by Plato or not, that there is a compelling philosophical thread tying the two together. Furthermore, that the progress made in the *Theaetetus* is owed to identifying an earlier confusion which was responsible for the Meno Paradox, and which perhaps was in an embryonic stage of cognisance in the *Meno*.

[5] At 143a Euclid says he does not remember the conversation offhand, '...but I took notes of it as soon as I got home; these I filled up from memory, writing them out at leisure; and whenever I went to Athens, I asked Socrates about any point which I had forgotten, and on my return I made corrections...'.

[6] At 145 the appropriate names of various areas of expertise are given—astronomer, musician, calculator—and in the case of Theaetetus Socrates says, 'Then now it is time, my dear Theaetetus, for me to examine, and for you to exhibit, since although Theodorus has praised many a citizen and stranger in my hearing, never did I hear him praise any one as he has been praising you'.

[7] At 145a Socrates asks who the painter is that will decide if they are truly physically alike; is it Theodorus? The answer is established by essentially appealing to heresy; i.e. Theaetetus says, 'I have never heard that he was'. And later, after having agreed that Theodorus is an educated man, Socrates remarks that they should not take him at his word, but submit his words to scrutiny. This does suggest that he is also concerned with evaluating whether he who claims expertise is indeed an expert, and therefore knowledgeable. This is also reminiscent of the dialogue between Socrates and Hippocrates—recited by Socrates to a friend—in the Protagoras at 314a-c when Socrates warns Hippocrates that especially in the case of the 'commodities of the mind' one should first examine its quality before making a purchase. It is a rather difficult task to examine such commodities since

these cannot be carried away for consumption, rather one must submit one's ears to listening and accept the affects of listening. Essentially, Socrates accosted Hippocrates for being overly impressed with the reputation of Protagoras as wise, especially in the light of the fact that he is a sophist. So Socrates cautions him that because knowledge and the commodities of the mind are evaluable by the mind only, mere association with sophism is sufficient for infection.

[8] The prelude on learning argued that someone is wise/knowledgeable in the things he knows; and that learning is growing wiser about that which you learn; therefore, if Socrates knows nothing, he too is a student eager to learn, not the teacher (145d-146).

[9] Articles on the debate over Socrates' knowledge disclaimer include; G. Vlastos (1985) 'Socratic Disavowal of Knowledge', T.C. Brickhouse and D.S. Smith (1984) 'The Socratic Mission', *Phronesis*, M.M. Mackenzie (1988) 'Socratic Ignorance'.

[10] At 154c-155 Socrates opens a discussion of a number of assumption that together are responsible for contradiction in our minds: the first that nothing can be perceived a being greater when its corresponding sense object remains the same; the second that nothing can alter in magnitude without growing in size; and third, that nothing comes into existence that is not the result of a percipient experiencing something.

[11] See M.F. Burnyeat (1990) *The Theaetetus of Plato*. Burnyeat remarks that 'the entire elaboration of the three-in-one theory (he refers to the empiricism of Theaetetus, the Relativism of Protagoras and Heraklitus' Theory of Flux) takes for granted, as do later empiricists like Berkeley, that perceivers will simply "Read off" the correct description of their perceptual experience from the experience itself'. p. 50.

[12] There is disagreement about the duration of time that Plato supported the Theory of Forms. For instance, I will not present arguments to support Plato's adherence to it in the *Sophist*, though many have. However, there is more agreement that in the earlier dialogues the Theory of Forms is being defended; for instance, in the *Phaedo*, and the *Republic*.

[13] Frege's concern to distinguish psychologism from logic is viewed as a concern to make clear that a Thought—*Gedanken*—can be entertained without that obliging one to admit its truth since otherwise no sense could be made of intersubjective disagreements and intrasubjective inconsistencies in judgement. Moreover, the problem of psychologism also undermines the distinction between subjective and objective. See J. Hamilton (1991) *History of Philosophy*, 'Gottleb Frege', p. 374.

[14] H.H. Benson (1992) 'Why is There a Discussion of False Belief in the *Theaetetus*', *Phronesis*. See p. 173 where Benson also argues that Socrates has

already argued against the impossibility of false belief in his refutation of Protagoras.

[15] ibid. p. 171.

[16] It has become a fairly popular view that the sandwich scheme is meant to tie the discussion on false belief with Theaetetus' second definition of knowledge; and to thereby expose the model of knowledge (the acquaintance model) which supports Theaetetus' definition as involving the false assumption which has rendered the impossibility of false belief. See G. Fine (1979) 'False Beliefs in the *Theaetetus*', *Phronesis*; H.H. Benson (1992) 'Why is There a Discussion of False Belief in the *Theaetetus*?', *The Journal of the History of Philosophy*, 30:2.

[17] Socrates must be speaking of propositional beliefs because after asserting that there is false judgement in all cases, he adds, 'one of us *thinks* what is false' (187e6-7).

[18] Lewis and Benson have argued in favour of a weaker condition for knowledge. Their joint mistake, I believe, is trying to determine how much knowledge is needed to generate true beliefs regarding some object, x. That is, if for any propositional belief about x, S must know x; all beliefs involving x must also be true. So that, the following condition is just that if S knows x, then if S believes any proposition involving x, that proposition is true. But that is just the consequent of knowing; how can it also be the condition of knowing which has as a consequence the impossibility of falsehood? The mistake of Lewis and Benson, if I understand them correctly, is that they have been trying to answer the question; what must S be believing when S has knowledge of x? When the question that needs answering is, what must knowing involve, if believing is otherwise impossible. See F.A Lewis, 'Two Paradoxes in the *Theaetetus*', in *Patterns in Plato's Thought* (1973) ed. J.M.E. Moravcsik; and H.H. Benson (1992) 'Why is There a Discussion of False Belief?' in *Journal of the History of Philosophy*, 30:2, for his interpretation of this passage, as well as, Lewis'.

[19] Fine also develops this view. She argues that 'for any x such that one has a belief about x, one knows x'. Moreover, the knowledge of x is taken in its strictest sense to involve a hit or miss, all or nothing, affair compared to Russell. She argues, for any x such that one has a belief about x, one either knows *everything* about x or is totally ignorant of x. See G. Fine (1979) 'False Belief in the *Theaetetus*' in *Phronesis*, pp. 71 and 72.

[20] Though Socrates casts the condition of existence in terms of falsehood, or what is not, there is a parallel with the arguments found in Parmenides' poem on naming. Parmenides arrived at *esti* because on the assumption that all objects of thought, properties of objects and objects alike, contradiction would always result; i.e. something would always be itself and something other than itself at the same time.

Indeed, the third puzzle in the *Sophist* demonstrates the impending problem of contradiction.
21 Close to the end of the *Wax Tablet Model* Socrates says that their inquiry should now consider the possibility of thinking five and seven, but he says 'I don't mean five *men* and seven *men* or anything of that sort, but just five and seven *themselves* which we describe as records in that waxen block of ours'. This model is expected to take up the possibility of thinking and identifying two distinct things without this necessarily requiring that both things, then mismatched, are known. Perception coupled with memory are shown as two distinct epistemic routes for bringing an object to mind for thinking, and this is provided as the locale for falsehood. However, this analogy is unable to show how *thinking* of two things when perception is not involved could occur, which was, after all, the puzzle with which we began. When therefore, having acknowledged the apropos identification of the problem, numbers, like concepts, are explicitly distinguished from the objects or instances of these, it suggests that these may be expected to have a non-referential function. Therefore, Socrates must be suggesting that universals, unlike particulars, are meaningful even when these do not refer to, denote or stand in for an/the object they are of. For the moment, in the *Allodoxia Model*, this is not being argued for.
22 Again the scope of this dialogue must be distinguished from the *Sophist*. In this latter dialogue Plato will indeed be concerned to develop a semantic theory that will be able to explain 'what false thinking is'; and there, the Stranger will exploit the ability to think something without that actually requiring its so-called identification. However, for the time being, Plato is still dealing with problem of knowledge. Specifically, this case calls for some explanation of how the knowledge of universals is derived, if not from its instances. But if from instances, how are these ever recognised as actual examples, if there isn't already some preceding knowledge of what these concepts or universals mean.
23 See G. Ryle (1990) 'Logical Atomism in Plato's *Theaetetus*', *Phronesis 35*, pp. 21-46. Ryle also seems to agree that the internal complexity of thought, whether true or false, is exploited in the *Sophist*, and only hinted at in the *Theaetetus*. 'A truth or falsehood always has a certain internal complexity. At the very least it usually mentions one thing or person or happening etc. and ascribes something else to it or denies something else of it. It need not mislead us too much if we say that in even the simplest true or false statement there must be, at the least, a subject and a predicate....Furthermore, though this point, which is brought out clearly in the *Sophist*, is only hinted at in the *Theaetetus*, at least two of the pieces in a truth or falsehood are (a) out of different baskets from one another and (b) coupled or glued together in a certain definite way.' pp. 24-5.

[24] Angene also describes the case in this way, 'An easy way of making a false judgement would be to take a true judgement and replace its subject with some other subject of which the judgement's predicate was not true. This, if it were possible for the mind in firming judgements to get the wrong subject we would seem to have a way of thinking what is false. In such a case we would be thinking what is false about something which exists. Our judgement is false, not because we are thinking about what is not but because we are thinking what is *but* we are thinking it about the wrong thing'. See L.E. Angene (1978) 'False Judgement in the *Theaetetus*' in *Philosophical Studies 33*, pp. 351-365; esp. p. 357-8.

[25] W.V.O. Quine (1961) 'Reference and Modality' in his *Logical Point of View*, pp. 17-34; also 'Quantifiers and Propositional Attitudes', pp. 101-111.

[26] This becomes especially clear in the case of numbers supplanted into mathematical problems. Looking forward to Part III of the *Theaetetus* it will be argued that, for instance, '2+3=**5**' such that '2+3' (and for that matter, '12-7', '-5+10', etc.) stands for the number/object? '5'. Yet, were reference all there ever is to names, all these coextensional names should actual always render the same truth-value for any statement; and moreover, each should *mean* the same thing to the thinking subject or user. Yet, as Part III will show, it is possible to know the number '5', and yet not know or *understand* that '-5+10' also stands for the number '5'.

[27] M. Burnyeat (1990) *The Theaetetus*, p. 12. Burnyeat also argues that this initial stamping operation (learning, coming to know) remains shrouded in brilliant metaphor.

[28] L. E. Angene (1978) 'False Judgement in the *Theaetetus*', *Philosophical Studies 33*, pp. 351-365, esp. 252.

[29] However, Socrates does say 'when we are babies we must suppose this receptacle to be empty, and take the birds to stand for pieces of knowledge. Whenever a person acquires any piece of knowledge and shuts it up in his enclosure, we must say that he has learned or discovered the thing of which this is the knowledge, and it is what 'knowing' means' (197e8-198). This seems to imply a Lockean empiricism, though he does not argue for this.

[30] See M. Burnyeat (1990) *The Theaetetus of Plato*, p. 114

[31] Learning as something evolving out of repeatedly responding to various questions about the same thing brings the Slave Boy example to mind from the *Meno*. The elenchus produces knowledge in its interlocutors by posing questions that the interlocutor will be forced to assimilate in his head in such a way that it renders logically valid conclusions from already existing beliefs. The point is that the interlocutor may have a number of yet *unrelated* beliefs which may be *transformed* into knowledge when the *relations* between these has been understood

so that a more generalised belief regarding the relatedness of such beliefs would constitute a further truth belief, and so on for subsequently related beliefs. Remember Socrates places much emphasis on being able to draw the conclusions. In the *Meno* it is argued that Meno does not yet have knowledge because he is unable to work out the answers to related, though, yet unrehearsed, problems

[32] See D. Bostock (1990) *The Theaetetus*, p. 190; McDowell's belief that the Theory of Recollection in the *Meno* is here echoed, is reported and rejected by Bostock who argues that the two cases are far to dissimilar to support such a view.

[33] Already the similarities of the Aviary model and the TR in the *Meno* must be obvious. In both cases, a mathematical example is being used to show how it is possible to search for something already known in a way that is compatible with not-knowing. The important difference is that by the time the TR is developed the particular problem that Socrates is dealing with is the conversion of belief into knowledge. Already in possession of propositional beliefs, some of which may be true others false, contradiction sets in making the ability to distinguish between truth and falsehood pertinent. What is offered there is a TR which makes available this ability. However, in the *Theaetetus* what is at issue is how the mind can grab hold of something to think without that at the same time involving complete knowledge. The mathematical example is offered as a complex thought which is comprised of two known things. The suggestion being that it *should* be impossible to get the addition wrong *because* the complete knowledge of both identified numbers would guarantee truth. However, falsehood would seem to be possible as a result of a *misunderstanding* of what is claimed about the relatedness of the two numbers. *Thinking* is therefore here distinguished from the ability of the mind to grab hold of something for thought to get started, and consequently, it is how the mind thinks *about* its objects which is going to be blamed for falsehood.

[34] D. Bostock (1990) *The Theaetetus*. Socrates sets himself to investigate how large some number is, when, for instance, he asks himself what 7+5 is. This is something he knows in the sense that 7+5 *is* 12 which he knows, so it is tantamount to an investigation of how large 12 is. The same for counting external objects: when the number of matches in a box is 52, Socrates takes the question 'how many matches in the box?' to be the same as 'what is 52?'. Bostock remarks, however, that when the arithmetician is 'counting numbers themselves, he is doing a calculation; he is not just rehearsing the number series to himself', p. 187.

3 False Belief in the *Theaetetus*

Introduction

If Part III is going to be relevant to the present debate regarding the epistemological puzzle on falsehood, it must be shown to somehow respond to the stringent condition laid upon the act of thinking. Namely, this passage will have to be able to show how thought is possible when the so-called all-or-nothing condition, thus far referred to as exhaustive knowledge, is faulty. Moreover, the complete or not at all, hit or miss polemic regarding the ability to identify an object to think about must also be pertinent to how the three proposed illustrations of *logos* when attached to true belief alters this approach to thinking. Still more, the *logos* complement should also be able to say something about the Meno Paradox given that the *Theaetetus* from the outset linked the epistemological mishap regarding the ability to identify something for thought to both falsehood and inquiry. The *Jury Example* immediately dispels the faulty reasoning governing the thus-far problematic formula 'to know is to think something which is true' (i.e. to think something necessarily presupposes *knowing* that thing; hence identification guarantees that *what is thought is also true*) by demonstrating that even when *what is thought is true, that* it is being thought may only be the result of *persuasion*, and therefore not mark knowing it to be true.[1] Clearly this is intended to injure the professionalism of sophistry since eristic dialectics is designed to convince eager listeners to adopt a pre-established point of view *only*. Notoriously, youngsters depart intently satisfied that they have acquired *knowledge*; yet when asked to share this *knowledge*, they merely *repeat verbatim* the words of their *teacher*, impotent to provide complementary illustrations at any stage of their narration. The upshot is that the ability to identify some-thing to then go on and think about it casts doubt upon the stringent *knowledge* requirement upheld throughout. Hence, Socrates must be looking for some alternative condition to lay upon the act of identification; and hence an alternative understanding of the implications for the act of thinking thereby. The problem of falsehood is woven into the ongoing war between the eristic and elenctic dialectic methods of inquiry since its obstruction provides that 'any belief is as true as it is being believed'. Yet conviction is the kind of thing that can be induced such that conclusions are taken for true; whereas in the case of the elenchus, truth only follows once a false conceit or belief of knowledge has been shed. This was achieved by induced *aporia* but remained unreplaced because there seemed no available route for the dismantling of the imparted contradiction once aporia is reached. In effect, there was no way of distinguishing the true from the false without *knowledge*. This avenue then quickly gave way to the Meno Paradox, and it is here that we find inquiry lurking once again.

The appreciation of what stating, judging, asserting and so on entails only vaguely recognised previously is here indigenous to the *logos* constructions. Since as Socrates concedes, the problem of falsehood resides in entertaining *both* x and y simultaneously and then going on to substitute for a given assertion the one for the other, it makes sense that its resolution should turn on distinguishing 'thinking as stating' from 'thinking as naming'. The second is purely reportive or referential, whereas the first says something about it. Hence, albeit implicit, a distinction is drawn between 'what gets said by a statement' and 'what a statement is about'. The former is complex, whereas the latter is simple; the remainder of the dialogue will attempt to come to grips with this distinction regarding *how* each alternative, if in fact distinct, is knowable, again, if at all.[2] Hence, though there appears to be an underlying appreciation of this semantic point, the *Theaetetus* remains focused on the epistemological puzzle regarding the relationship between the condition for identification and thoughts *about* the identified object. The three successive *logos* constructs attempt to illustrate how knowledge differs from mere true belief. The first explicitly brings forth an important element of language, namely the medium by which ideas or Thoughts can be communicated; namely, the ability to *express* what one thinks. This is immediately cast aside because any competent speaker has this ability, and Socrates clearly rejects the possibility that *whatever* anyone has to express constitutes knowledge. Though commonplace, this is curious enough given that it flies in the face of the stringent condition laid upon thought, namely that it presupposes knowledge. Consequently, the latter two *logos* constructs should be expected to move some way away from this enigmatic formula towards a constructive advancement. The second, talks of the ability to enumerate the constituent parts or elements of which the object of thought, is comprised, but fails not just because it gets stuck in an infinite regress, but also because it appears that something can be said *about* so-called unanalysable simples or constituent elements that is indeed informative. Hence, the final *logos* construct exploits this insight and introduces the ability to discern the object in question from any other. This in turn will also fail because again the ability to apprehend the distinguishing or unique quality(ies) of any object would presuppose prior knowledge of the thing in question.

Getting Started on True Belief Plus Logos

Why does the interlude on false belief end with the Aviary? Why do Socrates and Theaetetus now revert back to their original question, 'what is knowledge'? Moreover, why does Theaetetus still persist that knowledge is true belief? Finally, how has the interlude affected Theaetetus' definition, if at all? Given the form of the elenctic method, even in the absence of conclusive answers (aporetic end), Socrates must suppose that learning has transpired. That is, the 'knowledge' acquired previously must be effectual and somehow alter the original understanding of Theaetetus' self-same definition of knowledge. Does the text support this?

In an attempt to remedy the contradiction that the Aviary Model involves, Theaetetus proposes that perhaps the mind is in possession both of pieces of knowledge and pieces of ignorance. That way, it could be argued that it is pieces of ignorance, rather than knowledge, that cause false belief. However, so long as pieces of ignorance are knowables, this would involve the contradiction of knowing and not knowing the same thing. Unless, of course, there were further layers of knowledge shutting second level knowledge away from conscious awareness: 'are you going to tell me that there are yet further pieces of knowledge about your pieces of knowledge and ignorance, and that their owner keeps these shut up in yet another of your ridiculous aviaries or waxen blocks, knowing them so long as he possesses them, although he may not have them at hand in his mind? (200c)'. Socrates is warning Theaetetus, therefore, that such a proposal would initiate an infinite regress. One might have expected the rebuttal to have endorsed the argument that pieces of ignorance could not be entertained by thought, yet Socrates argues that it renders contradiction instead. This is because Socrates assumes that these pieces would be known at another level of thought, though not immediately accessible. The

Aviary Model has already exposed the inadequacy of the levels of knowledge proposal; namely, that it is necessary but not sufficient to have identifiable objects for thinking in mind, since there must be some method by which these thoughts are delegated for understanding.

Theaetetus' proposal is true in an obvious way, however. It must be in virtue of *something* unknown that falsehood is possible. Though the Aviary failed, the manner in which it was set up was suggestive of some kind of proposal regarding the relationship between thoughts. The Aviary leaves this possibility wide open, but will collapse back into puzzle one (200b), unless it can first explain the manner and/or extent that these identifiable thoughts are known, such that the possibility of not knowing the relationship between all these so-called knowables (objects of thought) would not involve contradiction. If for all thought, there must be an identifiable object for thinking; and the ability to identify *x, y, etc.* for thinking requires knowing everything, then would it not also follow that the appropriately related beliefs (all those which are true for *x, y, etc.*) could be worked out with absolute precision? Moreover, grabbing hold of ignorance, *in* my ignorance, would surely render falsehood but that would occur without that person ever suspecting it. So that, on this account whether any claim was true or false would not be accessible, and therefore ineffectual. But if it is strictly inaccessible, it would follow as a consequence that all beliefs (and these require the knowledge of their objects) are (as good as) true for that person. This is perhaps why Socrates says previously, 'he will not *think* he is judging falsely', and further that, 'he will *think* he is judging truly, and his *attitude of mind* will be the same as if he knew the thing he is mistaken about' (200a-b). This attitude of mind does not expose an epistemological state as much as it does a psychological state. It may be true that falsehood is possible but so long as the knowledge which could expose it remains locked up somewhere out of reach, it is as good as impossible. Two ensuing difficulties arise from the Aviary which link it to the timely and recurring definition 'knowledge is true belief': 'how could a so-called *piece of ignorance* for something known be grabbed hold of *in* ignorance?' and 'how is the truth-value of any belief accessible when the *in* ignorance condition obtains?'.

Resuming the argument that 'knowledge is true belief' Socrates curtly exposes its failure in an example which embraces the sophistic profession. The counter-example introduces an indisputable and familiar case where someone has grabbed hold of true belief without knowledge.

Consequently, the mind need not be in an exhaustive state of knowledge to entertain thought. The condition of thought which the interlude laboriously tried to accommodate for the possibility of false belief no longer obstructs that possibility, therefore. Fine and others have argued that this refutation provides the philosophical bridge linking the interlude on falsehood with Part III of the dialogue. It is because the particular understanding of knowledge in play in the interlude renders false belief impossible, that this understanding must somehow be faulty since Plato believes false belief is possible. That much is obvious. However, why Socrates should have taken this terribly trying route to expose what the counter-example powerfully demonstrated is perplexing,[3] and overlooks the interesting dialectic which Socrates deliberately draws the readers' attention to. No emphasis whatsoever is given to the kind of knowledge, or the method for that matter,[4] involved in witnessing which Fine must place singular importance on.[5]

It is the interplay between the executors—the orators of sophistic profession—and the mediators—the jury members—of justice which is the outstanding feature of the example. Socrates instructs Theaetetus that orators and lawyers, 'men who use their skill to produce conviction', are employed by justice to persuade their hearers of *the true facts*, and thereby make them believe something for which they have no first-hand knowledge. And that this is achieved not by teaching since there is insufficient allotted time, but by persuasion alone. The dichotomy between teaching 'what is true' and persuading others 'that it is true' marks the difference between *demonstrative* and *sophistic* methods of inquiry. For each there was a corresponding epistemological bias: for Socrates the truth is objective but it can only be acquired by employing an existing belief-set; for the sophist there is only the truth of which the percipient is convinced. The dialectic manifests itself in these antagonistic methods of inquiry and the ensuing states of judgement which follow from either respectively. All along we have been working with the elenctic condition that true belief presupposes knowledge and tried to dispel the faulty assumption which gives rise to the implication that falsehood is impossible, and inquiry therefore meaningless. Now the method of sophistic inquiry shows how true belief need not necessarily presuppose knowledge. Anyone familiar with this method already recognises that the *state of mind* generated would not be dissimilar from the state of mind of someone who has got hold of a false belief in its stead. We have seen how the state of mind of elenctic interlocutors is the key to getting inquiry underway; and that the first stage of discourse always has the objective to devalue the so-called knowledge of its participants by entangling them in contradiction. Ameliorating this false conceit of knowledge, the interlocutors are in the appropriate mental state to embark on inquiry. So when the counter-example demonstrates that belief short of knowledge *can* be true, it falls short of success because it can not also provide the interlocutor with the insight to distinguish these alternative epistemic states. For even though the belief of which the jury is convinced is [may], indeed, [be] true, the jurors do *not know that belief to be true*, they merely *believe* it is. When justice is served the jurors convict the guilty and acquit the innocent; but unless the jury members were actually witnesses to the crime they can not know that their judgement is true. They do not, however, *know* for sure that they are not convicting an innocent man, or acquitting a guilty man.[6]

Socrates has provided Theaetetus with the motivation to seek out the truth unlike the participants of the judicial system outlined in the example; and he now remembers that he had on another occasion been introduced to a further epistemological distinction. That distinction acknowledges that any belief short of an account could not constitute knowledge, so that his revised definition now reads that 'true belief plus an account is knowledge'. This tallies with the need prescribed above for the ability to recognise and distinguish truth from falsehood within our own belief system, and therefore counters the fear that when engrossed by our own belief-set these are indiscriminately taken to be true, and are sometimes accidentally true, just because of their believability.

The seriousness of this judgement invites Theaetetus to defend a theory of knowledge which will both be able to tolerate the possibility of falsehood, and provide the means by which someone could be assured that his belief is indeed correct, though without demeaning the merit of inquiry at the same time. The theory must be weak enough to accommodate the possibility of falsehood, but strong enough to render beliefs viable, and the detection of falsehood accessible. Arguably the elenctic and sophistic methods are at opposite ends of this pole: the all-or-nothing condition of thought adopted by the elenchus entangled Socrates in the MP; while the relativism of sophistry in the impoverishment of truth and knowledge.

The Dream Theory

Numerous commentators have acknowledged the familiarity of the dream theory with something expressed earlier by the theory of recollection in the *Meno*.[7] We should be cautioned therefore that because the understanding that 'knowledge is true belief plus an account' given in the *Meno* at the same time involved them in a trial response to one of the most ruthless paradoxes—the *Meno Paradox*—that more is at stake here than 'what knowledge is'. Knowledge is intimately intertwined with truth; and the *Meno* especially highlights the problematic notion of coming to or acquiring knowledge of something prior to having grabbed hold of true beliefs regarding that thing, and knowing them to be true (*Meno* 75c8-d7). It will be insufficient a theory therefore, if it can not also demonstrate how knowledge is acquired without already assuming it somehow.

In the extremely dense passage from 201e-202d, Socrates sets up the argument to make the definition of *logos* or an account already perplexing. Briefly, it is argued that 'we and all things' are made up of composite parts and that anything that can be accounted for in terms of its parts can be known; whereas anything else can only be *named*. Consequently, given the running definition, 'knowledge is true belief plus *logos*', things for which there are composite parts are knowable; but all other things that can not be grasped thus are unknowable. We *can* think truly of all things irrespective of their composition (complex or simple); however, we can only know those things which can be accounted for. Looking back to the previous section, the possibility for true belief is not only short of knowledge, but its status is also precarious since there is nothing obvious about how these simples are grasped by the mind—in fact, Socrates says these are presented to the mind via perception—that makes their truth anything more than coincidental. So even if complexes are knowable in virtue of their parts, surely the precarious status of these simples or parts would be self-defeating when without knowing these their determinability amasked in complexities would be questionable, and at most accidental. So, already the understanding of what *logos* is logically prepared to add to true belief to acquisition knowledge is challenged. For if with the asymmetry of *logos* comes the asymmetry of knowledge, and it is impossible—as this reading implies—to know something (complex) in virtue of something else unknown (simples), then something has gone amiss. In what follows Socrates sets up three possible renderings of *logos*:

(i) to be able to express what one thinks, (ii) to be able to give an inventory or enumerate the parts of some (complex) thing, or (iii) to be able to tell what something is in relation and counter-distinction to all others things.

A great deal of ink has been spilt over the meaning of *logos*. The form of the arguments expounding the rendering of *logos* are fairly uncontroversial; however, how to supplant the intended meaning of *logos* for these arguments has been extensively addressed. The two main camps are divided between understanding *logos* as statement, as the interweaving or combination of names, and the other, in terms of analysis or explaining what the thing in question is.[8]

Either side has shown that both these renderings are sufficiently supported by the text; but the telling argument must also be able to show how the suggestion that knowledge is different from true belief by adding the extra condition of *logos* is intelligible. Plugged in for the first attributed meaning, knowledge must be expressible in a proposition. So that, since simples are unknowable, they can not be expressed as a proposition, though complexes can. For the alternative rendering, knowledge constitutes being able to analyse the thing in question such that it can explain what it is, perhaps, provide an exhaustive definition of it. Socrates expressly describes the dream theory as rendering simple elements unknown because

> We cannot attribute to it anything further or say that it exists or does not exist, for should we at once be attaching to it existence or non-existence, whereas we ought to add nothing if we are to express just it alone. We ought not even to add 'just' or 'it' or 'each' or 'alone', or any other of a host of such terms. These terms, running loose about the place, are attached to everything, and they are distinct from the things to which they are applied. If it were possible for an element to be expressed in any formula exclusively belonging to it, no other terms ought to enter into that expression (201e-202b).

Simple elements can not be accounted for because the *logos* of some such thing must not presuppose the knowledge of other things which could truthfully be predicated of them. Socrates seems to be saying that existence, and presumably other properties, could be used to describe simples truthfully; but that such a description could not render knowledge. Whereas, the converse does not hold, that is, complexes are accountable, therefore knowable, *because* they can be grasped in terms of their constituent parts or simples. But this does not imply, as advocates of *logos as statement* would have to, that simple elements are indescribable or that nothing can be said about them. The only available interpretation of Socrates' words entertains two thoughts: (a) because simples are unanalyzable—that is, can not be broken down into further parts—the properties which could be used to describe them would equally apply to other things (this, red, each, etc. could apply truthfully to a whole range of things); and (b) as the refutation at 203d-e makes clear, complexes indeed can be accounted for in virtue of other things; but this can not very well constitute knowledge until these other things in virtue of which these are described are also known. And that means, according to our working definition, accountable. The regress is in motion, and once again calls on the familiar epistemological paradox, namely that 'if knowledge is based on knowledge' how is it ever acquired; and if otherwise, then both falsehood and inquiry become meaningless.

Because (a) argues that an account must be able to describe something by bringing its unique and distinguishable qualities to bear, but that this is impossible, *logos as statement* is disqualified. For *logos* as statement only requires that some propositional claim can be rendered of something, not that that proposition involves any particular properties. But beliefs regarding simples are expressible propositionally, though this expression is short of providing an account that can satisfactorily differentiate true belief from knowledge. Moreover, any description of simples must not involve properties equally attributable to other things because this would make kindred simples indistinguishable. And (b) adds that even when unique expressions can be entertained for description, these too would have to be accounted for were knowledge to obtain for all subsequent beliefs; i.e. complex beliefs. And because these basic elements provide the foundation for all subsequent beliefs any defining properties of these must not presuppose the knowledge of other things.

(a) and (b) provide strong evidence for taking *logos* as definition or analysis. This reading adds to the first interpretation, the condition that the statements or expressed propositions involve uniquely attributable properties. This is compatible with the view that *logos* must be able to define or say 'what some thing is' which is after all supported by Socrates' application of primary 'what is X?' questions. On this account, the argument states that true beliefs could be expressed of simples, but that these would not amount to knowledge because it could not explain the essence or what that thing is.

The particular model enunciated by the dream theory leads to the asymmetry of *logos* between simples and complexes, which coupled with the definition 'knowledge is true belief plus *logos*' entails an asymmetry of knowledge. Simples are unknowable, and complexes are knowable. But the relationship between the two will prove even more disastrous. Because complexes are knowable in terms of simples, and knowledge is based on knowledge, it follows that complexes are also unknowable. The dream theory is therefore self-defeating, and this implies that either the particular model of *logos* is wrong, or else the conditions upon which the model is erected are somehow mistaken. Socrates already acknowledges the asymmetry of knowledge as a problematic feature at 200d10-e1; but in the example which follows as a sequel, emphasis is given to the contradiction rendered by this, and he suggests instead that they have misunderstood the meaning of *logos*. 'Is it true that an account can be given of syllables but not of letters? (203a4)', he asks. Syllables are complex things that can be broken down into further constituent parts; whereas letters, which make up these syllables, can not be reduced any further. So, when asked 'explain what 'SO' is?', Theaetetus naturally replies, 'S' and 'O'; its constituent letters. But when asked 'explain what 'S' is', Theaetetus objects that 'S' is simple and therefore can not be stated in terms of parts. Socrates endorses these beliefs, and concludes that syllables are known through their constituent letters, though letters lack such parts so that they can not be known. Yet, when on his own admission Theaetetus adds that 'S is a consonant, nothing but a noise...while B not only has no articulate sound but not even a noise (203b-c)' he inadvertently contradicts himself. For this statement is as obvious a case of accounting for the *peculiarity* of these letters as is the statement that 'SO' is 'S and O'. This contradiction compromises their understanding of *logos* because it suggests that the particular model of *logos* is questionable; and in fact, there seems to be an alternative way to account for simples after all. Identifying the absurdity in arguing that 'someone knowing and recognising SO as the first syllable of Socrates' name does not also know and recognise the individual letters 'S' and 'O'' (203a-e), Socrates suggests that syllables could alternatively be understood, and this naturally reflects an alternative use of *logos*.

Sums and Wholes

For the most part the 'sums-wholes argument' is not recognised as an independently viable argument. It merely redefines syllables in terms of simples, and the same regress ensues. But surely this is obvious. The infinite regress cast in the above argument would apply no matter where the rudimentary level of constituent things was established. Moreover, complexes just are not simples; and so to recast them in terms equally applicable to simples must involve a different understanding of *logos*. The real question then is, why does the same regress ensue for this argument?

Is any complex just the sum of all its parts, or are complexes themselves independent entities? Can these entities or wholes be understood independently of their sums? For if the foundationalism of the dream theory is not to be compromised the definition of knowledge as 'true belief plus *logos*' must dispel the asymmetry of *logos* because it fostered an impasse to knowledge acquisition. Any improvement on the dream theory will therefore, have to show either that (i) simples can be accounted for, or (ii) that no account need be produced of these, but that they are knowable nonetheless.[9] This would imply therefore, that there are different *kinds* of knowledge, and corresponding methods of acquiring knowledge. (i) must defend a theory of knowledge appropriately applicable to simples, and how knowledge of that kind suitably supports knowledge of the second kind. Socrates openly rejects the possibility of reducing elements to further constituent parts, but no where does he claim that the theory is not applicable to basic elements. Quite the contrary. The sequel is a onerous attempt to *redefine logos*. (ii) requires an alternative definition of *logos* that applies equally to both simples and complexes, but which at the same time demonstrates that the one does not necessarily entail the other.

The alternative suggestion is that complexes, like syllables, are themselves in one respect also *unitary* entities which are distinct from, but arising out of, letters (203e-204). It would not be objectionable to suppose that a body, to take another example, though made up of arms, legs, etc., is itself a singular entity identifiable as an object of thought. In fact, it is in just this way that true belief short of knowledge can be expressed about some thing. A body can be grasped and recognised as a body without actually knowing that it is made up of the spleen, etc. along with arms, legs, etc.. The question is, however, whether knowledge of a body is sufficiently accommodated by enumerating its parts, and whether indeed, there is an alternative way of knowing the body. Only with a keen eye on what this question entails can sense be made of this passage. For right after Socrates enunciates what this second alternative entails, he infers that wholes must be partless. Not only is this an invalid inference, but moments ago Socrates himself described them as 'arising out of letters' (203e4). His meaning can not have been, therefore, that as *objects* they are partless; rather, he must have understood the *method by which wholes are grasped for knowledge as not entailing their parts*. That is, both the method by which knowledge is acquired or wholes are learned, and the condition which constitutes knowing must bypass the knowledge of parts. Sums and wholes characterise different epistemic routes for learning and the example which follows is an attempt to show how they may differ.

Taken in sequence the sixth number designates the actual number six, 'two times three', 'three times two', 'four plus two', and 'three plus two plus one' each amounts to or designates the same number six. Is there any difference between the sum 'six' and the numbers which amount to six? With nothing to differentiate between 'the numbers amounting to six' and six, it would make little sense to talk of *logos* apart from the parts of which anything is comprised. Moreover, on the 'knowledge is based on knowledge' condition the knowledge of either would entail the knowledge of both. This, however does not follow. For, already in previous sections it was shown that someone could know that six is the sixth number in sequential order, and perhaps that 'two times three' is equal to six; but the knowledge of the designated number six does not entail knowing every possible way of attaining that number.

Does Socrates argue for this? Or is he going to defend the view that there is no method by which wholes can be grasped independently of parts? An acre, for instance, is compared to the number of square feet that make up an acre; the same for the number of feet in a mile. Presumably the point is that an acre just *is* 'x number of feet' and similarly for miles. Socrates then proceeds to argue that a sum is the same as all its parts (204b10-e6). Applied, this conclusion renders that 'the sum six' is the same as 'two times three' and any other possible variation that amounts to the number six. How does this affect wholes? At first glance, there seems nothing obvious about inferring that the distinction between sums and wholes must be false because the sum of all things *is* all of those things. But the argument has an interesting twist. Only after Theaetetus is shown that sums and wholes can be described in the same way does he let up and admit defeat. Still, even if Socrates is correct that sums and wholes can be accurately described as 'something from which nothing is missing', it does not follow that they are the same in virtue of all possible descriptions. In which case, the distinction may still be applicable. That is, so long as *is* is taken as description. This rendering is not supported by the text, for as the acre example makes clear, it is the *is* of identity which is in play, not description.

The secret to understanding this argument is to clearly establish the objective of the passage. We began with the need to revise the model of *logos* for the inclusion of simple elements in order to counter the impasse to knowledge acquisition. The particular model proposed a system of enumerating the parts of the object in question, but simples being partless could not thereby be accounted for. Hence, the revised version of the model had to bypass enumerating parts, and proposed instead, that complex things too can be ascertained in a different light, as wholes. In one respect unitary simples can be grasped as individual or aggregate wholes. On the understanding that *logos* must be able to substantiate true belief by some expression which successfully grasps 'what that thing is', both Socrates and Theaetetus had it in their head that any defining expression just *is* the thing in question. Socrates had argued that 'an expression must exclusively belong' (202b) to the object in question since otherwise the expression could not successfully identify the uniquely defining elements of the object in question. This argument had assumed that the object in question is partless, and consequently concealed the assumption being made about descriptive expressions. Not only must these be able to establish a uniquely defining expression which doesn't presuppose the knowledge of other things, but what is being said about them must belong to the object itself. As a result a definition would be a long hand expression of the same thing which the naming of the thing would be a short hand version of. Each could be substituted by the other for each expression is identical to the thing it is about. 'What some thing is' cannot be substantiated in virtue of wholes by bypassing sums because the 'expression must exclusively belong' (202b) to the object in question, so that any conclusive expression (something from which nothing is missing) just *is* that thing. Their confoundment is the result of conflating the objective to express 'what some thing *is*' with the indivisibility of something into constituent parts. So that, when complexes are described in terms equally applicable to simple elements—alternative (ii)—*all* things become equally unknowable anew.

The Present Standing of Logos

Two alternatives presented themselves to resolving the Dream Theory: either (i) a theory of knowledge appropriately accommodating unaccountable simples must be established which can at the same time prescribe a method by which knowledge obtains, or (ii) an alternative definition of *logos* equally applicable to both simple and complex elements must be founded where the knowledge of the one need not entail the knowledge of the other. Contrary to (i) Socrates has focused on revising the working model of *logos*, and in doing so, he suggests a similarly applicable method by which both are grasped by the mind for thinking. All objects of thought are grasped singularly, as individual, singular entities; though as objects some are partless, and others are not. Irrespective therefore, of the divisible composition of objects, the mind grabs hold of all objects singularly as individual entities. That the mind indeed does so raised the question whether the method by which objects are grasped as individual entities could be accounted for as individual entities without the knowledge of its composite parts. The effort was aborted because the uniquely defining expression was expected to describe the object in question in terms of properties which belong to the object corporeally or somehow physically, and this rendered the confusion of identity.

Both (i) and (ii) are equally tied by the condition which initiates the epistemological regress; the accountability of complex elements does not constitute knowledge unless the things in virtue of which it is known are equally knowable. The understanding of learning—that is from simples to ever more complex combinations of these (206a-b)—stated at the end of this passage lends itself to the view that the foundationalism of the dream theory must begin with simple elements because so long as these cannot be accounted for because of their simplicity all else stands outside of knowledge. The suggestion, however brief, is that irreducible elements are distinguished and grasped by the mind for thought via the senses, and 'from our own experience of elements and complexes, we should conclude that elements yield knowledge that is much clearer than knowledge of the complex and more effective for a complete grasp of anything we seek to know' (206b-c). The physicalism of grasping something for thought again begs acknowledgement. The reason which purports a clarity of knowledge for simple elements by sensory perception is the physical way in which some thing is presented to the mind without 'the confusion of the arrangement of them in spoken or written words' (206a5-6). The succinct exposition of simples and how these are grasped with a clarity of mind which words seem impotent to accomplish does not seem to endorse a competing account for these;[10] rather, the suggestion seems to be that an account must imbue an image of an object for thought with the clarity which any true expression about it could not.

Logos: Three Possible Versions

There are only three possible interpretations of *logos*, and none of these successfully disassociate knowledge from true belief: the first (i) proposes that any account must be overtly expressible in language; the second (ii) that any account must be able to enumerate the parts that come together to make the thing in question 'what it is'; and (iii) argues that (ii) is insufficient since complex elements made up of the same properties could thereby be confused, and to this Socrates adds that the constituent parts must be placed in order or particularly arranged.

Indeed (i) is swiftly dismissed because anyone can readily express their thoughts in speech, with the exception of those born deaf or dumb. It would be hasty however, to assume that (i) is also insignificant. For (i) dislodges the commitment to the condition that *logos* must be a uniquely defining expression incorporating *only* those things of which the object in question is comprised, or in Fine's words, 'an account must be proprietary (*oikeios*) to what it is of (202a7)'.[11] An account is specifically described as an 'overt expression to one's thoughts by means of vocal sounds with names and verbs, casting an image of one's notion on the stream that flows through the lips, like a reflection in a mirror or water' (206d1-4). Still there seems to be a strong correspondence theme in play here—what is expressed of the object must designate it for thought—but just as the image reflected in water does not belong to the object, neither does the combination of names and verbs in proper syntactic order belong to the given object. Rather than having bits of speech corresponding to bits of the given object, the defining expression as a whole must designate that object. Consequently, both simple and complex elements may be knowable in terms of truths about them, rather than parts of them.

Still, this is not the conclusion adopted by Socrates. Instead, Socrates returns to the dream theorist's model of *logos* as the enumeration of parts. Same model, different criticism. Socrates' counter-argument neither involves the unaccountability of simples, or the infinite epistemological regress that it initiates. Leaving this debate aside, Socrates maintains that even after having enumerated all the elementary parts of some thing, still knowledge may not obtain. The problem should have already been obvious. Even when something can be accounted for in virtue of its parts, it is possible that the very same parts equally apply to some other object. So, someone could enumerate the letter of the words 'dog' and 'god' and still get them confused (207d2-8). The obvious parallel is the arithmetic problem employed to refute the Aviary Model such that someone could know the numbers '11' and '12' and yet still not recognise that the sums [or parts] '5+7', '2+10' all amount to or stand in for the same thing, '12'. Evidently, the question 'what is X?' means more than 'what is it made of ?', and its corollary 'what description stands for the thing itself?'. Before terminating this dispute, Socrates reiterates the argument with an interesting addition. He says, 'whenever in writing 'Theaetetus' he puts down all the letters *in order*, then he is in possession of the complete catalogue of elements together with the correct belief' (208a10-13) but that this still falls short of knowledge (208b4-8). The arrangement or order by which the enumeration was to follow was not previously included in the description of *logos*, however. An accommodating expression would, as (i) already implied, have to appeal to the principles of arrangement, for composition and the like which no longer provide accounts mentioning *only* the thing and/or its proprietary parts, for 'principles for concatenating letters into words govern the production of all words and are proprietary to none'. [12] Someone that is well trained with what is called technical knowledge and can always get the word 'Theaetetus' spelled right, may not also be able to recognise when the same letters appropriately combine to make up other words. The ability to get things right does not count as knowing the word 'Theaetetus' for he does not *understand* what is going on when he evidently spells it out into its elements.

In fact, this is fitting with the third and final rendering of *logos*. Socrates' concluding effort encompasses what most people understand *logos* to mean, that is, 'being able to name some mark by which the thing one is asked about differs from everything else' (208c8-10). An example is given as being able to say of the sun that it is the brightest of the heavenly bodies that go around the earth (208d1-3). The dream theorist's model and this one are commonly described as being able to account for some-thing without fixing upon something common to other things (208d9-10); i.e. the condition of propriety. That the knowledge of some thing involves the ability to distinguish that thing from all other things is obviously meant to sound familiar. It was the preliminary condition which got this Socratic debate underway. Hence Socrates says that *logos* understood in this way presupposes knowledge, and we have been working on the assumption that true belief is possible without knowledge. Yet, if *logos* is the ability to identify the distinguishing character of some thing, then as the condition of thought supposes, anyone already thinking of that thing must already possess the appropriate knowledge. How else should anyone ever be sure that he was talking about the intended person when making references to him? This addition inadvertently adds nothing extra to true belief at all; in fact, we have come full circle (209e-210a). Again, were knowledge rather then true belief expected to render the distinguishing feature of that thing, we would be involved in vicious circularity.

Conclusion-The Present Standing on False Thinking

Despite authoritative arguments which maintain that the semantically significant distinction between *naming* and *stating* is recognised by Plato, it has been argued that because the *Theaetetus* is through and through epistemological, whatever inkling there is of such an interest it is left unexploited. There are indeed many instances when semantic considerations are intrinsic to the points being drawn out, but no definitive argument is developed to suggest that Socrates is interested in this taking root for the explanation of any of the ongoing puzzles of the *Theaetetus*.[13] Part III of the *Theaetetus* is expressly concerned to undermined eristic dialectics, and simultaneously replenish elenctic inquiry. Left with the stringent condition of identification, Socrates resumed the dialectic question 'what is knowledge' with an eye to how this, albeit destructivist, pursuit could shed light on the problematic assumption that thought presupposes knowledge. In other words, Socrates had by now identified the problem of falsehood as a problem of identification because he could not make sense of how it is possible to think *of* something in hand without the certainty that *it* is, in fact, the thing for which the *name x* has been supplanted for thought or speech. Nonetheless, Socrates was not unaware that thought need not entail knowledge, and that inquiry or the pursuit of knowledge is a noble objective. He would have to show how people could be made to *think* certain things, despite at least initial ignorance, without at the same time making a mockery of the ability to successfully communicate thoughts or ideas to others effectively. Of course, this is only part of the problem which Socrates is concerned to explore. For tied up with the ability to entertain thoughts without knowledge, is how to obstruct the radical relativism of sophistry without being able to at the same time explain how, after getting something in mind to think, the truth or falsehood of that thought becomes discernible or can be judged by the very person having that thought. In other words, if Socrates is to resist the consequences of sophistry in defence of the elenchus, he must able to show how thought does not presuppose knowledge—which is commonplace we have said, despite its evasiveness—*and* how it is possible to think *about* the things concatenated in mind or judge such things as true or false without compromising this ability. Were Socrates to argue that the mind is furnished with things to think via *experience* (to bypass the question as to how something is concatenated in the mind), there will be no easy way for him to explain falsehoods and their discernibility. Remember the intention, first of the Wax Tablet Model and then the Aviary Model was to illustrate how when perception and memory are involved, or differing epistemic routes respectively, that some-thing can be wrongly *identified* so that properties which truthfully apply to the intended object render falsehoods when attached to the wrong object. Each attempt was, therefore, an attempt to resolve this epistemological puzzle by appealing to how something can be mistakenly identified. Neither illustration was prepared to accept that wrong or false predicates could be attached to the right object were it successfully identified, however.

By Part III Socrates directs inquiry away from the process of identification to 'what constitutes knowledge' and its fairly straightforward bearing on that process. That is, if it is the case that knowledge, in fact truth and falsehood, is not meaningful, as Ryle and others endorse, unless something gets stated, so that names of objects can not be known as such, then a solution to this problem will have to recognise the implied semantic distinction between *naming* and *stating*. Still, this was no more than intimated thus far. From the three *logos* constructs we get (a) the informative acknowledgement that knowledge does indeed involve making a claim, (b) that somehow what ever is going to get said about something [else] must somehow belong to or be a part of 'what that thing is', and finally (c) coming to grips with 'what something is' need not necessarily entail properties indigenous to it, but the context in which these are found and recognised as somehow distinctive from other surrounding things. Each in turn is shown to be lacking, and even the last, (c), is shown to rely on the presupposition of the knowledge condition which Socrates was trying to repudiate. Still, there is something to be gained from this destructivist dialogue. To begin, even though the hidden semantic significance of (a) is not exploited, it is all along assumed, namely that knowing something involves being able to state a thought about it. So the problem which (b) and (c) subsequently take up regards 'what gets said' or the predicate part of any statement. Each in turn considers, first (b) the physical properties which actually make up or out of which the given object is composed, and second (c) moves away from the object [the sentential subject] completely and talks about its *difference*. Again this is an epistemological exercise, so we must keep in mind that Socrates is presently concerned only with what knowledge must look like, and *how* it can be *acquired*. Hence (b) is no surprise. It has been fairly obvious throughout that Socrates understands—in fact since the *Meno*—that knowledge or the ability to answer the 'what is *x*?'[14] questions requires knowing all the necessary and sufficient properties *of x*. This is why it is then problematic to say, 'Socrates is ugly' and for that to be false. For knowing Socrates guarantees knowing 'ugliness' because part of 'what Socrates is' is ugliness.[15] In turn, of course, for the statement 'Socrates is ugly' to be meaningful, both 'Socrates' and 'ugliness' must be identifiable and meaningful things or concepts. Hence the impossibility of falsehood and inquiry are at once before us. The next step (c) takes Socrates some way away from this proprietary approach to ascertaining something. The full magnitude of the contextual approach was doomed to fail because Socrates at this time was still frustrated by the problem of identification without knowledge. In other words, though the ability to identify 'what something is' with reference to what other things are not, has the potential to capitalise on the ability to think of something in terms of 'what it is not', once again the cost of identification gets the better of him. Instead of looking for some quality which sets the thing in question apart from all other things—for instance to describe the letter 'h' as a hissing sound—Socrates again reduces this search to the quest for the unique quality(ies) of the thing in question which would once again require knowing that thing. For how else could anyone set out to define all the unique qualities of some thing unless knowledge of that thing had been previously acquired. It would be rather like saying to the child to whom you promised a pet dog what distinguishing qualities it had before you had ever decided on what dog you would get.

Finally, how anyone could ever get it into his head to think *of* something and then go on to think about it 'what is not' remains a mystery because Socrates could not get past the proprietary approach to knowing 'what some-thing is'. To know some-thing it is mandatory that all those qualities that make it what it is and not something other are acknowledged. For, the viciously circular argument goes, unless these qualities were acknowledged, the thing in question could be easily confused or mis-taken for another similar thing. This is why, even when for (c) or the third *logos* construct the proprietary condition was laxed, Socrates still could not explain how anything could be said *about* the thing in question apart from its composite parts that would add to true belief, unless that thing had been previously known. The identification problem is not resumed again following the dialogue on *logos*, but we can guess that the failure to define knowledge constitutes a failure to accommodate this problem also. The threads of argumentation have evolved from the enigma of thought; namely that it is impossible for the mind to get some-thing in mind to think by the name of x such that S is thinking *of* x, unless previously S knew x. The paradox of falsehood and inquiry followed as ensuing puzzles from this. The ability to identify an object of thought was not the direction that Socrates sought to resolve this enigma, rather he exploited first the epistemic routes through which an object comes to mind, placing responsibility for falsehood not on the process of thinking as such, but the alternative states, perception and memory. With the Aviary again the identification condition was not compromised, instead Socrates explored the possibility of looking for particular object amongst a stock of other things—again this beautifully brings out Socrates' commitment to the view that knowledge of the thing in question is required in order to look for and finally find it—and mistakenly retrieving another object in its stead. The arithmetic example employed to illustrate this argument seemed to imply a hidden agenda regarding the ability to think *of* the same thing under one name, and not under another. That is, '12', '5+7', etc. all denote or refer to the same object, yet when looking for '5+7' instead of '12' the number '11' is retrieved in its stead. The implied semantic point regarding a difference in reference, transparent versus opaque, is not capitalised on. Instead the locale of falsehood would appear to lie with how some object is thought *about*, or to refrain from conspicuously semantic lingo, that some-thing can be known, and the number '12' successfully retrieved for thought, so long as the process required for identification does not also require a further ability, namely reflection which does not involve the actual object '12' denoted by the sum '5+7'. So what does knowledge entail?

That which is at the centre of confusion is the proprietary assumption regarding how some-thing must be for thought if the nominata are going to be *of* the objects named. It is the correspondence theory of truth which would seem to feed into such an assumption since a statement obtains truth when it corresponds somehow to the object or state of affairs in the world that is being judged. In fact, this is an intuitively sound belief. We naturally believe that a statement is true when it accurately describes the world it is about, and false when it is inaccurate. The reason that Socrates is stumped is because in the process of trying to develop a theory of knowledge he bungles the function and meaningfulness of language. That is, he suppose that all words in a sentence are names *of* things that must be identifiable and therefore known completely to have found their way into thought to get named. At every turn Socrates' efforts to explain the possibility of knowledge *acquisition* have been obstructed because he could not figure out how words could be used otherwise. This is why in the *Sophist* the topic of falsehood will take a slightly divergent route and instead of trying to determine what knowledge would look like and how anybody could *think* some-thing that is false/what is not, he *reformulates* the puzzles in order to determine what false belief *is*.

Notes

[1] G. Ryle (1990) 'Logical Atomism in Plato's *Theaetetus*', *Phronesis*. Ryle succinctly puts it, 'So their thinking falls short of his knowing, even when what they think is the same as what he knows', p. 28.

[2] Following a brief exegesis of the relevant modern debate, Ryle says 'In other words, the view that sentences are *either* mere congeries of ingredient names *or* themselves composite names of higher order complex objects [statements rendered complex wholes will now be about higher order objects; i.e. the statement 'Caesar killed Brutus' is rendered the higher order object named 'the-killing-of-Brutus-by-Caesar'] results in just the trouble that Socrates sketches in his criticism of his dream. What I know (savoir) or think must be something stateable; and a statement cannot then be construed in reverse as the name of something which I could at most have knowledge (connaitre). What a sentence *says* cannot be reduced to what its words name *or* to something extra of which it is itself a name [i.e. higher order objects]. What is said or told in a sentence is not just *another* subject of predication. *Saying or telling is one thing, naming is another* [my italics].' ibid., p. 34.

[3] G. Fine (1979) 'False Belief in the *Theaetetus*', *Phronesis*, p. 78; H.H. Benson (1990) 'Why is There a Discussion of False Belief in the *Theaetetus*?', *Phronesis*, p. 172; Also M. Burnyeat (1990) *The Theaetetus*, p. 119. Burnyeat also questions the need for the interlude when its objective is cast in terms of indirectly refuting what the counter-example directly refutes with such ease. Though this objection is watered down somewhat with his talk of modern vs. ancient philosophical expectations, Burnyeat ultimately believes that there is more at stake in the interlude than a simple distinction. pp. 120-21.

[4] Witnessing seems to suggest perception as the means by which knowledge, at least if empirical data, may be acquired; yet, as Part I argued, knowledge is not perception.

[5] Fine argues that the Acquaintance Model of knowledge follows directly from the argument that states that the jurors could only have knowledge, as opposed to true belief, if they had been witnesses to the crime or derived from first-hand experience. Certainly there is a discrepancy here; is knowledge just the experience, or is it merely derived from there and followed by something else?

[6] One has to wonder whether there is any intended innuendo regarding the indictment brought against Socrates, and his eventual conviction. The jury had been convinced that indeed Socrates was guilty of the named crimes; i.e. introducing new gods and corrupting the youth of Athens. See *Apol.* 18b-c where Socrates denies the charges levied against him, and where he specifically says, 'a great many people talked the youth of Athens into believing that Socrates can make the weaker argument defeat the stronger', where he is obviously referring to the sophists.

[7] See G. Fine (1979) 'Knowledge and *logos* in the *Theaetetus*', *Philosophical Review* *88*, p. 366; D. Bostock (1988) *Plato's Theaetetus*, p. 203, though he believes that the 'dream' aspect is attributed to the idea that this theory genuinely quotes someone else, but because the source dates later than the dramatic time of the dialogue, Socrates and Theaetetus could not admit to knowing its proper author and therefore had to call it a 'dream' rather than something that actually occurred.

[8] See D. Bostock (1988) *Plato's Theaetetus*, p. 203; G. Fine (1979) 'Knowledge and *Logos* in the *Theaetetus*', *Phronesis*, pp. 371-78; G Ryle (1990) 'Logical Atomism in Plato's *Theaetetus*', *Phronesis*, pp. 38-44.

[9] See G. Fine, ibid., esp. pp. 375-378. Fine presents the respective modern debate appealing to both Russell and Descartes. Fine argues that it is the Russellian viewpoint that Ryle's interpretation of the argument adopts.

[10] It has been argued by Ryle and others that Socrates opts for our alternative (i), and that he is arguing that the epistemological foundationalism is accommodated with the understanding that simples are grasped not by description but by sense perception, and that this is comparable to the distinction Russell makes between knowledge of description and knowledge of acquaintance. Correspondingly, the *logos* of simples is disanalogous to the *logos* of complexes. In fact, this interpretation lends support to Ryle's propositional rendering of *logos*, since simples on this view would be known by some intuitive apprehension, or special acquaintance of and therefore unpropositionally. For an excellent refutation of this view, and the similarities between the foundationalism of Russell, Descartes and the Dream Theory, see G. Fine, ibid., esp. pp. 376-78.

[11] G. Fine, ibid., p. 383.

[12] ibid.

[13] Regarding Ryle's eminent article 'Logical Atomism and Plato's *Theaetetus*', esp. pp. 35-36, he seems to suggest that the unknowability of simples, which can only be named, expresses Socrates' understanding that there is a significant semantic difference between *naming* and *stating*. The first can not be known, whereas the latter can. For regarding the first nothing gets said, whereas in the second something does. However, this overstates or makes too much of what it is the intention of the Dream Theory to illustrate. The Dream Theory is an epistemological exercise that wants to worry the reader about the possibility of justification or *logos* of some-thing (that the ability to know requires expressly claiming something to be such and such is only acknowledged with the first account of *logos*, and that fleetingly) when that thing is not comprised of any further parts, such that there are, as it were, no further things or properties that belong or are a part of it, and can thereby be used to describe it. This sets us up to query the proprietary approach to *logos*. That, this coincides with the modern debate regarding the meaning and function of name, and the meaning and function of a statement is useful, but it is not until the *Sophist* that it is acknowledged by Plato.

[14] It is well known that these questions are expected to be able to identify the quality(ies) that runs through all the things or instances of the x in question, and further that this is tied up with the idea that two [different] things can only be called by the same name because they share a common property or nature; Socrates and Theaetetus are both men. Again this lends itself to the view being defended

here regarding the ability to think something and know it, without at the same time knowing all those names standing in for *things* which impart what that thing is.

[15] For a full account of Socratic elenctic definition and Platonic definitions see G. Nakhnikian's paper 'Elenctic Definitions' as well as R. Robinson's paper ' Socratic Definition' in G. Vlastos (ed.) (1971) *The Philosophy of Socrates: A Collection of Critical Essays*, pp. 125-158.

4 False Belief in the *Sophist*

Introduction

The *Sophist* is a dialogue that may be addressed as a sequel to the *Theaetetus*. It also finds Socrates suspended of his capacity as director of inquiry, and replaced by an Eleatic Stranger. The topic of discussion is baptised by Socrates but then handed over to the Stranger. He is assigned the deceptively simple task of setting things right on the proper application of the names sophist, statesman and philosopher. The difficulty of the task is located in the form of refutative argumentation adopted by each, and therefore involves the evaluation of the justifying epistemological systems supporting each. Read together, the *Introduction* and the *Meno* chapter demonstrate that the elenctic and sophistic methods of argumentation have definite similarities. By implication there are legitimate grounds for confusing the one for the other, and falsely applying the title philosopher to the sophist and the converse. This is a matter of some importance given that many, most prominently Plato, maintain that Socrates' alleged 'criminal activity' was the result of his purported familiarity with the sophistic circle. The application of the Socratic method always ended in the same way; with the contradictory of the interlocutor's originally proposed knowledge-claim, and his confoundment as well as humiliation. Not much distinguished Socrates' method from the sophist's apart from his proposed objective, namely truth. If anything however, the only truth that a life-time of destructive elenchi seemed to attain was the verification of its inaccessibility. With that, the philosophic stage-setting prepared the way for the *Theaetetus*. Though the definition of knowledge was at the forefront of conversation, falsehood lurks in the background, until following the rebuttal of empirical relativism, it is expressly addressed. When truth is not relative or subjective, false belief must be reckoned with; but what sense can be made of 'believing what is false?'. Stumped by the ontological status of the occupied objects of any falsely claimed belief, the *Sophist* naturally takes up the question, 'what is falsehood?'. Its solution will involve debates on overlapping projects already discussed in the

Theaetetus, but this time round beliefs will be taken as complex propositional claims which will take us some ways into semantics.

Stage Setting

The stage setting of the *Sophist* is even more involved than the three phased report of the dialogue in the *Theaetetus*. To begin, the cross referenced remarks ending the *Theaetetus* and beginning the *Sophist*, not only state the obvious; that the aporetic end of the former was only temporary, and that the *Sophist* has the job to pick up where it left off.[1] For it follows unquestionably, that Plato must have either written the *Sophist* looking back to the *Theaetetus* or the *Theaetetus* looking forward to the *Sophist*; so that, consequently, the philosophical expedition of the latter is tacitly committed to resuming the paradox set forth in the former. More significant, however, is why the *Theaetetus* is cut off mid-swing. Socrates adjourns he says, because he has a previous engagement, namely he must report to the portico of the King Archon to meet the indictment brought against him by Meletus (*Theaet.* 210d). Consequently, the *Sophist* is dramatically set at some point before Socrates' trial.[2] Needless to say, Socrates had been, at least informally, if we can trust Plato's word,[3] indicted on charges of

> criminal meddling, in that he inquires into things that
> are below the earth and in the sky, and *makes the*
> *weaker argument defeat the stronger*, and teaches others
> to follow his example' (*Apol.* 19b-c).

Socrates, in his defence, denies the charges flat out, concurrently establishing what he obviously took the charges to involve, namely his misrepresentation and association with the sophists. For he says, 'there is nothing in these charges and if you have ever heard anyone say that I try to educate people and charge a fee, there is no truth in that either' (*Apol.* 19d8-e). And earlier, at *Apol.* 18b-c Socrates obtrusively places the blame for his present quandary with his precursory adversaries. Saying,

...I have already been accused in your hearing by a great many people for a great many years, though without a word of truth, and I am more afraid of those people than I am of Anytus and his colleagues, although they are formidable enough. *But the others are still more formidable. I mean the people who took hold of so many of you when you were children and tried to fill your minds with untrue accusations against me*, saying, there is a wise man called Socrates who has theories about the heavens and has investigated everything below the earth, and *can make the weaker argument defeat the stronger* (my italics).

The framework of his defence seems to stand or fall depending on the viability of his arguments to disassociate himself from those men, namely the sophists, who at one time or another had their hands on the would-be politicians or statesmen, who now charge Socrates for embracing *antilogic* as a foul method that always placed Socrates at an *unfair* advantage. Notice that Socrates fears *most*, not the statesmen who are responsible for prematurely ending his life; but 'those men in whom they—the statesmen—place the fate of their soul unreservedly'. The echoes of the *Protagoras* highlight the importance of 'getting straight on the distinguishable qualities of one's would-be "teacher" *prior* to resigning oneself to its unavoidable effects'.[4] Seen in this dramatic light, the *Sophist* must at least have the intention to exonerate Socrates, and draw from those arguments which at his trial were ineffective, by presumably providing the means to distinguish between the elenctic method, which Socrates attested to by the will of the god of Delphi for the expropriation of ill-founded claims to knowledge, and the eristic method espoused by those alleged teachers of wisdom. The *Protagoras* reminds us both how arduous a task it is to successfully affect the minds of those already polluted by sophistic argument; and simultaneously, why the pedagogic objective need to be satisfied *prior* to inquiry.

This is beautifully staged by Plato's reference to two Homeric passages from the *Odyssey*; the first is taken from Odysseus' speech to the Cyclops Polyphemus and the second, is borrowed from the memorable scene concocted by the conspirators, Telemachus (Odysseus' son) and Odysseus, who swore revenge on Antinous and Penelope's other iniquitous suitors.[5] Theodorus' companion, conspicuously unnamed, from Elea and comrade of the circle of Parmenides and Zeno, is the butt of Plato's innuendoes, not only because he is an intruder, but because he is soon to take on the protagonist role normally assigned to Socrates. It is well-known that Socrates' role had always been to *judge* the existing beliefs of his interlocutors, and inevitably escort them to the 'good life' (*Apol.* 36c-d; 38a4-5); so that his substitution by this Stranger raises two related questions: Why is Socrates being suspended? What or whom has this Stranger in Parmenides' name come in judgement of? Looking forward, is the Stranger then identifiable with a god, like Zeus, who comes disguised to survey the law-abidingness and behaviour of human beings, or is he an anonymous god come in human form? Moreover, if the stranger is a god, and Theodorus is responsible for his introduction, is he not equally culpable for the political crimes of which Socrates has been accused, and which are inseparable from his pedagogico-philosophical offence according to which the youths are corrupted by their exposure to the so-called unknown maieutic god. Much is riding, it would seem, on the ability to identify who the Stranger is, or more accurately, what the Stranger is. For the challenge which is just beginning to unfold does not involve putting a name to the Stranger's face, but instead involves putting a title to his claim. That is, the question 'who is the Stranger?' does not ask for the Stranger's historical identity; it asks for a justification for Theodorus' claim that he is a philosopher (2164), and divine at that (216b11).[6] Of course, did we know what it means to be a philosopher it would be an easy task, undeserving of such an elaborate discussion, to figure out the validity of such an assertion. As it is, the point being made is that gods, like sophists, take on many appearances; and this makes the controversy concerning the forthcoming tripartite relationship between sophist, statesman, and philosopher pertinent. Not least because the suggestion that gods assume impenetrable disguises introduces an old Platonic concern intimately tied up with the relativism of empiricism which is the key to the sophist's protective niche. Unless, once again, the essential criteria determining the nature of these personified methods can be shown to somehow belong to them, the measure of all things will be accessible only with regard to their exoteric appearance or image. Notice, when at 216c-217 Socrates says that the Stranger would not be easier to discern were he a philosopher rather than a god who comes in disguised form, the difficulty is owed to:

the ignorance of everyone for whom philosophers show up in all sorts of apparitions and haunt cities, looking down from on high on the life of those below. Giving the appearance to some of genuine worth, to others, no worth whatsoever, sometimes taking on the apparition of statesman, other times of sophist, and still others, they give the appearance of being altogether crazy.

The suggestion fostered by Socrates is that philosophers are variously and conflictingly talked about because man in his ignorance incompetently applies the name to all sorts that *appear to be the same*. Wherefore, statesman, philosopher, and sophist can, while being the one, at least give the appearance of the other; and by implication any attempt at disassociation becomes self-defeating, something which Plato successfully recalls in the mind of his readers by dramatically drawing on the historical events leading to Socrates' execution.

The tripartite relations set against each other by the dialectic participants (Socrates/Stranger/Theodorus) and the personified subjects of their discussion (God/Philosopher/Sophist; Philosopher/Sophist/Statesman) are also preserved in both Homeric passages. The Cyclops Polythemus, and Antinous are the figures of ill-repute; Zeus, the god of strangers, comes disguised to judge men of such dubious character and invisibly accompanies respectful strangers; and Odysseus *disguised* and an *anonymous* suitor speak the words of admonition sealing the fate of these disreputable men. Since Theodorus has brought this Stranger to the Socratic circle as an unnamed guest, and Socrates subsequently reacts by first questioning the credentials of his newest member asking, 'is he a stranger or a god in disguise?', it follows that the Stranger is being identified with Zeus. The confusion of this identification is hidden behind Theodorus' conjecture that his Stranger is godlike in the same way that all philosophers are; and the extant role of Zeus in the cited passages.

The ordinary and commonplace reading superficially suggests that philosophers are like gods among mortal men; but Zeus for Odysseus was first (Bk. IX) patron-god accompanying him on his journeys and therefore owing him respectful passage,[7] and later, taken to be god in human form intent on retributive justice. Zeus was named by Odysseus to Polythemus as the guarantor of his safety, in whose name Odysseus and his men indeed managed to escape; Zeus is custodian of Odysseus' word (emphasised by

Polythemus' disregard of these words on the grounds that he is an atheist) but has no physical presence. Following Antinous' maltreatment of Odysseus in the second citation, the anonymous suitor castigates him with the words 'gods looking like strangers from afar become all things and wander about the cities viewing human hubris and righteousness'. Contrary to the manifest mortal form of Odysseus beforehand, his appearance, said to camouflage his historical identity, may be concealing his god-like form, and ulterior motive; i.e. to *judge* and consequently *punish* mortal man. For the Cyclops the stranger is Zeus; for Antinous the stranger is Odysseus mistaken for a punishing god. The apparent incongruity of these Homeric passages, in fact, reinforces the question at the forefront of the discussion, namely 'what is the Stranger, friend or god?'. For as god he is a friend to his suppliants (the Cyclops was not), but as avenging justice he is foe to all mortal sinners. The pending question awaiting disclosure is, therefore, 'in what manner has the Eleatic Stranger come in judgement, as co-patron or retributive assailant?'.

Confirming the taxonomic interest in the tripartite figures as personified subjects of methods of speech, thereby linking avenging justice to refutation in speech specifically (216b3-6), the intended reading of Socrates' and Theodorus' initial dialogue is facilitated. At 216a8-b6 Socrates speaks these words,

> He (Homer) asserts that not only do different gods accompany all those human being who share in a just shame, but that also, in particular, the god of strangers proves not least to be their companion and looks down on the acts of outrage and of law-abidingness of human being? So perhaps your stranger who attends you might also be one of the Mightier, come to look us over and refute us who are poor in speeches, and is a kind of refutative god?

Theodorus in response says,

> No, Socrates this is not the stranger's way. He's more measured than those whose zeal is devoted to contentiousness. And the man, in my opinion, is in no

way a god; he is however, divine, for I address all the
philosophers as of this sort.

To which Socrates subsequently argues that the indiscernibility of such a
god-like man is proved difficult by the arbitrary use of the words sophist,
philosopher and statesman. Theordorus' qualifying reply implies an
important modification of the Homeric passages; whereas, gods *punish* the
sins of mortals, the divinity of philosophers does not reside in his capacity
for refutation either in speech or manner, but is disposed to some other
end.[8] Expectedly, this strikes a nerve in Socrates since the elenctic method,
though claiming to be *dialectic*, has been purely destructive with an
admonishing spirit. To a degree this is not unjustified, for after all, Socrates
does claim at *Apology* 21b-d that the elenctic method was the outbirth of
his mission to establish the truth of the words of the Delphic oracle, 'that
no one is wiser than himself'. That which his experience in engaging, first,
the most renowned figures of wisdom, politicians, and then the layman in
conversation indeed relayed to him was the understanding that his so-called
superior wisdom lay in the acknowledgement of his own disavowal of
knowledge. By implication, anyone of professed knowledge, in a manner of
speaking, is chastised by refutative argument accomplished by disclosing
the contradictoriness of his doxastic beliefs. The blow to the ego of elenctic
participants can not, of course, confirm that the Socratic elenchus is *really*
indistinguishable from sophistic argumentation, which is after all sold for
hire in case of public defence against offences often really *punishable* by
law. In other words, refutative argument may have numerous suitors and
correspondingly various forms, some of which may be philosophical,
others not.

    In his response, Socrates is cautious and warning Theodorus of the
indiscernibility of the philosopher two issues are raised: (1) the appearance
of the philosopher must be genuinely mistakable for the appearance of the
sophist or statesman, even madmen; (2) the philosopher is genuinely
distinguishable from these others; (3) ignorance of the truly defining
features of each is responsible for gripping on to faulty appearances, and
some alternative method must be made accessible to us for their
discernability. In other words, some method of apprehension suited to the
task of making the fine distinction between images, phantasms, or
appearance and actuality. Already obvious even at this early stage of
development is that the empirical relativism of the sophists would in no

way be suited to the task. But we must see whether any other alternative is being recommended either by Socrates' or the Eleatic Stranger's presence. Anyway, 1-3 confirms that the status of Socrates, the Eleatic Stranger, and the sophists are simultaneously afflicted by the same difficulty and consequently have all fallen under suspicion.

Some headway has now been made to answer the opening question: Why has Socrates given up his protagonist role to the Stranger, and what has this Eleatic newcomer come in judgement of? Without, for the moment, attending to the Stranger's immersion in Eleatic philosophic inquiry, from the aforementioned setting Socrates sets up the topic for discussion with his expressed reservations about the Stranger's credentials which subsequently engages them in a dialogue concerning the need to justify the contention that philosopher, sophist and statesman assume definitive adverse forms of refutative argument. The same kind of distinction that Socrates himself understood his acquittal to be depending on; for this reason Socrates could not be expected to employ the same misunderstood method to persuade or teach his audience the cause of their confusion without at the same time making himself out to look like a sophist; something which his hearing historically verifies. Moreover, (3) requires some third party to demonstrate how the refutative methods of argumentation differ, such that the method of delivery is not previously assuming the appropriateness of the one over the other. It must be able to attend the minds of its participants to reason unafflicted by appearances and preconceptions or prejudices. Given (1) any attempt to teach others that (2), requires that some other method of argumentation substitute for the usual elenctic method. For, the elenchus could not be trusted to deliver the truth, unless from the outset its dialectic character was not under dispute. The merit of the Socratic elenctic method can consequently only be judged by a dispassionate outsider. For an answer to the subject of judgement we must turn to the Eleatic and his professed philosophical liaison, Parmenides.

The Stranger as Eleatic Spokesperson

The philosophical persuasion of the Stranger deserves special attention, especially given that he has been assigned the role to designate the criteria of philosophical inquiry by way of establishing the true relations between the tripartite subjects of inquiry.

The arguments provided in the *Introduction* were presented to show that the philosophic persuasion of the Stranger is not accidental. These arguments aimed to show that Parmenides' poem presented a particular challenge regarding the nature of truth and naming, and further, that Plato in the *Sophist*, proposed that an answer to Parmenides would simultaneously satisfy the present task. Further, that the *Sophist* like the *Theaetetus*, was haggling over the terms of *expressible falsehood* because without its discernibility the project of inquiry would be meaningless, and the distinction between dialectics and antilogic would be undermined. Consequently, the names sophist and philosopher would be variants of the same method or synonymous terms. The credibility of the sophist rests on the relativity of truth and therefore the indiscriminate application of truths for the perceiving subject. It would follow therefore, that falsehood is impossible; and so long as truth remains unattainable for Socrates, he would have to temper the elenchus to strive only to *change* the *content* of the existing beliefs of his interlocutors, rather than *judge* the *status* of those beliefs.

As Eleatic spokesperson, the Stranger's presence makes the initial problem about naming the sophist, the statesman, and the philosopher pertinent to the general difficulty about falsehood because naming for Parmenides also involved the mixture of being and not-being. The problem regarding naming has to do with the ability to logically attribute distinguishing properties to anything whatsoever when occupied with any search calling for qualification. For the nature of distinguishing properties gets stuck in expressions of the sort found in Parmenides' fr. 8. In order to express the difference between at least any two *things*—e.g. the sophist and philosopher—in effect, requires saying what something is-not. Namely, that it, say x, is different and not the same as this other thing, say y, in terms of some properties, say a, b, c; such that x is different from y ($x \neq y$) because x is not-a, not-b, and not-c. The problem Parmenides had with attributing (and by extension naming) is the same problem that Plato is having with falsehood; for each involves the logically impermissible expression, 'what is-not'. For both Plato and Parmenides, the impossibility of this expression lies in its being unidentifiable for thought and speech.

Concluding, the Stranger facing up to the challenge presented by Parmenides guarantees to reconcile the problem of method for Socrates because he will be expected to resolve the challenge on the terms laid down by Parmenides. This requires starting a priori, with leaving the world of phenomena behind, in a fashion comparable to Socrates (abstract deductive reasoning) and coming clean on the thus-far elusive expression 'what is-not'. By adopting the method of abstract deductive reasoning the resolution to the challenge will justify the end, namely truth, of such an exercise, without having to succumb to the opinion of mortals; though, at the same time, making such an exercise applicable to their world.

Having arrived at the phantasmal nature of the sophist, and laying claim to his distinguishability thus, the Stranger lays the relatedness of falsehood and Parmenides bare: the application of such terms as '"appearing", "seeming" without really "being"; and the "saying of something which is not yet true"' (236e-237a) repeats the problem found in the *Theaetetus*, 'how may one say or think that falsehoods have real existence, without being caught in contradiction by the mere utterance of such words?' Explicitly billing the possibility of 'appearing' with the possibility of 'falsehood' when taken to imply 'what is not actually' the case or 'not-being', the arguments *against* sophistic relativism are identified with the arguments in *favour* of the possibility of falsehood. Still more conclusive is the Stranger's explicit attribution of the 'contradictoriness of uttering the words not-being' to Parmenides by name. He says,

> the audacity of the statement lies in its implication that
> 'what is not' has being, for in no other way could a
> falsehood come to have being. But, my friend, when we
> were of your age the great Parmenides from beginning
> to end testified against this constantly telling us what he
> also says in his poem, 'Never shall this be proved—that
> things that are not are, but do thou, in thy inquiry hold
> back thy thought from this way'. (237a1-12)

So that finally, it stands to reason that indeed Socrates, the Sophist, and Parmenides are equally suspicious characters; and the place of judgement seems to match the puzzle evolving from the so-called intention and application of the respective methods of inquiry. It would follow that, if we are right about the motive of Parmenides' poem, and he sought to express a challenge that would otherwise be inexpressible, the Eleatic Stranger might have come to judge whether Socrates has lived up to his method both in *word* and in *deed*. Taking the *Theaetetus*, Socrates himself remarked that he and Theaetetus would engage in dialogue in search for knowledge, and all the while apply the term as if they knew what its meaning was; and still more, they would speak of images, so on and so forth, not knowing what ontological status could be attributed to it. Still more interesting, Socrates would claim no knowledge, and yet engage others in argument, in the end assuming the face of a retributive god, and evoke shame and humility in all.

Parmenidean Puzzles on Not Being 236e-243c

The dialogue continues in the same light by reinstating the problematic implications that followed from Parmenides' challenge. The first argument (237b7-e7) demonstrated the unmentionability of *what is not* on the grounds that nothing gets named and consequently nothing gets thought. Obviously the job of a name is to put the thinking subject in touch with its object and it is for this reason that naming *what is not* is nonsensical, it just does not put the thinking subject in contact with anything at all. Already this assumes that there is an external world so that, it has already been argued, Parmenides can not intend his monist conclusion to be taken literally. Again this is important because it suggests that Parmenides understands that it is possible to *express what is not*, but that we are wrong to think that the ability to do so in any way reflects the *truth* about things. This would place the present company of purported philosophers on par with the men of *doxa*, thus reinforcing our suspicions regarding their true intentions. The following argument (238a5-c10) will consider the possibility of talking about *what is not* instead of naming it straight out, much in the same way that Parmenides considers an unnamed subject of inquiry in his poem. Still this proves unfruitful because the truth of an assertion about a nonexistent subject could not be inclusive of the set of things named by its predicate term. This follows because *all* names irrespective of their contribution to a statement were treated in precisely the same way by Parmenides, so that a statement would be true when the subject and predicate terms were extensionally equivelant. Of course, this argument moves away from Parmenides in an important way. Parmenides' argument against the possibility of predication had been that it involves contradiction because talking about something was as good as talking or saying what it is not. This argument, however, seems to take on board a new understanding of the relation between subject and predicate terms. Even though the argument fails, there is the implicit acknowledgement that predicates refer to a quality that the subject is expected to have, hence description. Together these two arguments make a mockery of the status of the present company which a third argument (238d-239b) propounds. If after all, *what is not* can neither be named nor described successfully, the reader should be wary of what these acclaimed wise men (Socrates, Parmenides' suitor and the subjects of the debate, the sophists) have been all the while talking about. From these arguments a number of important points get inserted: (a) *what is not* is not really inexpressible, it is just nonsensical because it can not be meaningfully accounted for, and consequently we do not know what we are talking about which makes any supposed teacher look ridiculous. (2) Reinforced is the objective to show how it is possible for truths about the external world to obtain which both the *Way of Truth* and the *Way of Mortals* failed to accomplish. (3) It is clear that the job of language or naming specifically is to bring the thinking subject in contact with the external world but that a straight word-world understanding of that relationship can not make sense of this. (4) *what is not* would seem to plague all thought and speech at least implicitly. Remember Parmenides' peculiar argument which claimed that attribution of any kind is impossible as it always involves contradiction because a predicate term implies what the subject term is not. And finally (5), that language which is the medium in which meaningful thought occurs does more than just pictorially represent reality to the mind. The point about description would be that the mind contemplates the world rather than merely representing it. Points (1)-(4) all point to the obvious, namely that we are comfortably using the terms we presumably have no understanding of in a successful and meaningful way. In fact, we are presently reflecting upon precisely these inaccessible terms much in the same way that Socrates and company indeed talked about things which they presumably were not entitled to on the grounds that they lacked the requisite knowledge of such things. It would seem that in order to get to the heart of things, we must first acknowledge the meaningfulness of having such thoughts, otherwise we are stumped before we begin, and must therefore leave the epistemological questions aside until we have first understood how language makes it possible that thinking is meaningful prior to knowledge.

This is reinforced by the following two puzzles, first on the impossibility of images and then on the impossibility of falsehood, which in the process brings the Parmenidean Challenge to the forefront of the discussion of the sophistic challenge. At 239c, the Eleatic Stranger says that 'until we meet with someone who can perform this feat [describe what is not] let us say that the sophist has found an impenetrable lurking place'. We are told that this comfortable niche follows from the sophists empirical relativism (239d-240) because if *what is not* is inaccessible to both thought and speech, then we have no other recourse but to refer the sophist to examples of images in order to get to the meaning of the term. Still, the sophist would have to be able to explain the ability to acknowledge an example as an instance of what it is being claimed to be an example of without prior knowledge of what such a thing would be like. This should recall in the readers' mind the typical Socratic problem regarding the Priority of Definition. Despite these problems, the Eleatic Stranger confines the debate to discourse (240a-b) which thus counters the sophist's obvious refuge in statements of the sort 'what you refer to *appears* otherwise to me or not at all' in his effort to resist the possibility of invoking images in his mind by example. In fact, the Stranger's project would seem to provide the sophist with a superior place of refuge since the Parmenidean Challenge involves the ability to meaningfully talk about *what is not*. We must be able to proceed, therefore, to inquiry about that which for the time being remains inaccessible to language. Our job would be descriptive in kind since the objective will be to determine what can truthfully be said about something unknown. Being unknown, the subject of our inquiry will also have no extension. The strict word-world understanding of naming must consequently be in dispute. The argument on images is a fruitful one because it introduces the peculiar status of that thing which is not parasitic on a real object, but nor is it nothing. Images are copies of real things, so they are something, likenesses (240a-c). Since we are told that this is the queer way that *being and not being* combine, it can not be that images are the contradictory of *what is*. If *what is not* is not necessarily the contradictory of *what is*, then the *existential* use of these terms which is responsible for such a reading must be dropped or at least should not be universally adopted for all naming expressions. *What is not* is of something, perhaps in the same way that images are of something which do not actually exist. This would suggest, of course, that in not existing, such names do not strictly belong or correspond to the external world.

Falsehood presumably means unintentionally thinking of something contrary to how it actually is. This sounds too commonsensical to have required so much fuss. Most people would probably intuitively say that when someone believes something falsely, the given belief involves talking about something in an untruthful way, or in a way that does not correspond to how things actually are. The trouble with this intuition is that it overlooks important epistemological and ontological questions. A discussion of the impasse to falsehood with respect to the ontological status of the objects of thought had been considered in the *Theaetetus*. There the specified task was to expose the enigma of falsehood as arising out of the epistemological assumption that 'to identify something requires knowing it'. So to think would be to know, so that there seemed no way to think something that did not actually correspond to how things actually are in the world. The discussion of *being and not being* in the *Theaetetus* wanted to explain the movement from object to thought, but this question has been reinstated as a more complex relation between object, word and thought. So what appears an easy question, in fact, involves a number of complex questions about how the mind and the world interact, and how language meaningfully makes that possible without at the same time getting stuck in the impasse to falsehood and inquiry.

Falsehood is reconsidered here to acknowledge the non existential rendering of *being* and *not being*. Falsehood has now been described as a case where 'something which is in no way at all is thought of as being in some way'; or conversely, the case where 'something which certainly is, is thought of as not being in any way at all'. Or in short, it is thinking of something in some way *contrary* or somehow *opposed* to how it really, or in fact, is. Again it has already been argued that this is a rather ordinary belief but which is expected to solve a rather complex and perplexing enigma. And, of course, this distinction goes some way in clarifying things. It basically says that when in language we give expression to our beliefs and make judgements these judgements involve non contradictory notions. Rather, probably in the case of both truth and falsehood, while beliefs require something to take the subject position (or something *to* which the belief pertains), a judgement is a necessarily complex assertion which involves saying something *about* the given subject. The understanding that falsehood involves speaking of something in a way *contrary* to how it really, or in fact, *is*, suggests that perhaps this *contrariety* involves not the referent object exactly, but how we have come to *understand* its meaning, if you will. The point is that contrariety need not imply that there is something new, with ontological independence, which is being attributed to something else; rather because contrariety recognises that two things are somehow related, each must be *describable* in terms of some common properties, and in a way share or are part of the same reality. The problem which this proposal will involve is how language can apprehend the truth unless it is of some object to which it refers? For if this reality is to be derived from the self-same object of reference this looks suspiciously like what Parmenides warned us not to do, namely to think of something, in fact, a name denoting that thing, as something other than what it is, in fact. Evidence in the text supporting this reading is found at 241b-c, and the closing remarks which end this section:

> He [the sophist] will say that we are contradicting what
> was said just now, when we have the face to say that
> falsehood *exists* in thoughts and in statements, for we
> are constantly being obliged to attribute what has *being*
> to what is not, after agreeing just now that this was
> altogether impossible.

The solution to this is described as patricide in virtue of what must be said in the sophist's defence, namely that 'what is not, in some respect has being, and conversely what is, in a way is not' (241d2-7). Not necessarily committed to the idea that the objects for thought and speech must actually exist (this is, of course, what they are trying to come to grips with in the case of no referring expressions or names), there is still the problem of Parmenides regarding how names relate to the things named. Not only does this imply that something is being named, but also that the name tells us *what* that thing is, and this implies meaning. The problem, we have encountered more than once so far, is that when a name is expected to refer to something, and that something (even in the event that it does not exist in the world as such) is what the name means, then attributing other names to it would be like saying it is not what its name implies that it is. That, of course, gets us stuck in the familiar Parmenidean paradox about naming: that because a name is expected to pick out the thing named, such that it is that thing (this is where the meaning of thing named is implied) and how we understand that thing to be, no name can tolerate the attachment of other names because that would imply that the named thing is not equal to itself and this had got us stuck in contradiction. Theaetetus and the Eleatic Stranger have taken a giant leap forward when they identified the problem as common to both being and not-being, and that somehow Parmenides had gone seriously wrong when he took it that naming works in the manner outlined above.

The Parity Assumption 242c-243c

Having just admitted that the solution to the enduring paradox may involve patricide, the Eleatic Stranger now reprimands all PreSocratic philosophers[9] who indulged in the application of terms regarding being (given that the project of most PreSocratics, especially the earliest, was to develop cosmological ideas) without previously explaining their use. Specifically his complaint is lodged in their inconsideration for the ignoble commoner for whom everything goes amiss; though, of course, he says, he counted himself party to the expressions involving the unreal. It turns out that if any theory about the world is going to make sense, we must first be sure of what we are saying; for not knowing what our utterances commit us to, we are also in the dark as to what makes them true, and therefore, when, if at all, we are talking of the thing we intend to, or if everyone understands these things in the same way. We should not forget the implications of the combined Heraclitean-Protagorean theory of knowledge found in the *Theaetetus*. I don't want to make too much of this very brief interlude except to add that the Stranger's interest in the layman must imply that he views language as something common to everyone, and this more than likely means that names must mean the same thing(s) for everyone alike.

We must not leave any assumption unturned, and it would seem that in the same way that previously the Stranger had thought himself party to the understanding of the name *unreal*, but is no longer; perhaps the same may be the fate of the name *real* or *being*. His words are:

> Possibly then, our minds are in the same state of confusion about reality. We profess to be quite at our ease about the real and to understand the word when it

is spoken, though we may not understand the unreal,
when perhaps we are equally in the dark about both.
(243c2-6)

His point is not just inductive; namely that because he has by
inquiry discovered reason to doubt his previous understanding of the
unreal, it may turn out that for all previously assumed understanding of
names inquiry will show these also to be faulty. A bolder semantic claim is
being made about how names, whether of being or not-being, must be
understood to relate thought to its object or sentential subject to an
assertion involving it. Again, this will be wrapped up in an epistemological
project regarding truth. For, once more, the Stranger et al want to be able to
demonstrate not only that falsehood is a logical possibility, but that sense
can be made of the epistemic status of the objects for thought when
something is falsely believed of it. What's more, again putting the
Theaetetus to work, one of the arguments which had been raised against the
Heraclitean-Protagorean theory of knowledge was that people end up
talking about something different from what they either intend or
understand themselves to be talking about. The insistence that the object of
thought pins down the measurement for truth led Socrates to endorse a
strict correspondence theory of truth. The ability to talk of anything
whatsoever that is accessible to everyone such that language becomes a
successful medium for communication requires that everyone understands
the same thing when employing any kind of naming expression (whether in
the subject or predicate place of a sentence). And in this way, they had got
stuck in the self-same problem which is now under discussion; that the
objects which are for thought must in the same way be for language,
namely mind independent (the word-world point of view).

The very astute observation being made is that it doesn't really
matter whether when we formulate our beliefs they involve being or not-
being. What is important is how, for thought and language, we relate and
therefore come to acquire the use of naming expressions. Once this is
established we will also be in a position to comprehend what makes these
thoughts and assertions true and meaningful. The conclusion therefore, is
that the abstract logical deductions, like in the case of Parmenides, are
useful only when we first understand what makes the premises we employ
true, and if, there is a method of evaluation readily accessible for anyone's
use. In what follows, the Eleatic Stranger sets out to try to ascertain the

meaning of naming expressions involving being for the various cosmological and generally metaphysical theories of his predecessors.

Given that the project of discussion is set up in this manner, the sequel to this argument should address both being and not-being *simultaneously* which is significantly resumed immediately following the anticipated failure to establish the nature of *being* (251a).[10] Both these referring expressions must concern the remainder of the dialogue, and the anticipated non-aporetic end of the dialogue must satisfy an answer to both.

Parmenidean Puzzles On Being 243c-249d

Both Theaetetus and the Eleatic Stranger are agreed that being and not-being are equally puzzling terms; but Theaetetus seems to have understood the objective of the present dialogue in a slightly different way. For, when Theaetetus says 'we must find out what those who use the word [being] think it *stands for*' (243d4-5), the Stranger says we must find out 'what this expression *conveys*' (243e). Clearly, the first asks for a denoting expression, and the latter for a connoting expression. Theaetetus would have missed the point of the previous section if what he confesses is the need to find the object to which this expression refers. For any expression involving not-being is obviously empty; and consequently meaningless. Yet, the Parity Assumption which has just been admitted requires that being and not-being are meaningful; and that both are meaningful in the same way. Perhaps, the point that the Stranger is making is only that throughout the ages all these theories have been meaningfully understood; each in turn trying to discredit and surpass his predecessor. That comes to admitting that all these conflicting theories, each employing or making use of the word 'being' in a different way, are equally meaningful, yet not all these are also true. This implies that meaning and truth are two related, yet separable notions. This shift in emphasis, from truth to meaning, is accompanied by the notion that something thought or uttered is not meaningful in virtue of the truth of that thing thought or uttered. In light of the first paradoxes on not-being this is certainly a significant admission; for these had reduced any expression involving the form as meaningless *because* nothing corresponded to it, and therefore no truth could be mustered up for it. In other words, its meaninglessness followed from an inherent theory of truth as correspondence. Assuming the meaningfulness of these pluralistic cosmological theories then, the Stranger proceeds to the task of figuring out how being was understood (or what meaning was assigned to it) for each with an eye to some alternative understanding of what *something* so-called thought or uttered is after all.

In the brief lines preceding the Stranger's anticipated act of patricide, pluralist cosmological theories in general[11] are discredited when being is taken in a transparently referential way because, as we might have guessed, it renders language impossible. The familiar point being, that if what-is is a name for which nothing can be predicated, in line with Parmenides, then language could only meaningfully entertain the word '*esti*'; and that, of course, is hardly meaningful since it doesn't *assert* anything. Thus we are quickly led into a discussion of *Parmenidean Monism*.

An Inheritance of Mistakes on Being and Not-Being

Monism and the One

This section can conveniently be divided into two corresponding to the two basic and interwoven principles of Eleatic philosophy; 'being is one' and 'being is whole'. Again the problem concerns naming and the pluralising effect naming has on the world following from the familiar ontological commitment of Parmenides' theory. That is old news. There is also new news. The 'wholeness' of being is a rather interesting addition at this point, since it brings the *complexity or simplicity* of the object of thought to the forefront of discussion.

Actually even old news is sometimes innovating. As we know monism followed as the result of the intolerability of attribution, and that was due to the pluralising effect that naming has on the world. This is admitted and more. Indeed, it is asserted that 'the one is real'; and surely, this is as conspicuous a case of attribution as any. Fault is found with this assertion because it is inconsistent with numerical monism. That is, at the end of fr. 8 Parmenides concludes that there is only one thing in the world[12] which exists; and yet, since a name must be of something, when it is said that 'the one is real', 'the real' in turn must too have a corresponding object which it stands-in for in thought and speech. Hence, there are at least two things in the world; 'the real' and 'the one'.

Rather than get us involved in the contradictoriness of such assertions, we are reminded of the anticipated conclusion of fr. 8 given at fr. 8.1-4.

> There still remains just one account of a way [*alitheia*], that *it is*. On this way there are very many signs, that being uncreated and imperishable it is whole and of a single kind and unshaken and perfect.[13]

Many commentators admit that this fragment is inconsistent with monism[14] and have tried to explain it away by employing the ladder analogy.[15] This solution is misplaced when fr. 8 is read as a challenge, however. In fact, I have argued that Parmenides implores us to find out *why* such assertions are meaningful; and of course, this was expected to also be able to meet the standards set forth in the Way of Truth. Truth corresponds to how things actually are; yet, thought and speech seem to be nonetheless meaningful when the objects of thought, or names of these, don't correspond. Yet, early on in the *Introduction* Parmenides argued that thought is full, or in other words it always involves *something*. This *something* doesn't always correspond to how things actually are—and so it just does not correspond at all—and so when we think or talk of it, what is it that the thought or speech is about exactly? The form of the argument is important because while the first part of the argument involves the pluralising effect of naming; the second, argues that even if the names—'the one' and 'being'—do not correspond to things that exist in the world, names cannot themselves be *something because they would then be inexplicable because they would be unnameable*. The argument is given as follows:

> ...it is equally absurd to allow anyone to assert that a name can have any being, when that would be inexplicable....If, on the one hand, he assumes that the name is the same as the thing, either he will have to say it is not the name of anything, or if he says it is the name of something, it will follow that *the name is merely a name of a name and of nothing else whatsoever*. (244d-e)

Hence inexplicable. The form of the argument is thus: if for any name there is a corresponding object in the world which it is of, then naming pluralises. Yet, this is inconsistent with its monistic end. Moreover, because monism can not tolerate attribution of any kind it is also self-defeating since it can not even be formulated in language The only thing that can be uttered is the word *esti* (note that the English translation would involve two words 'it is'), but that, as we have already noted, does not say anything—*ouden legein*—in fact, it is meaningless. To resist this counter-argument, either the monist will have to admit that a name does not require a corresponding object in the world which it is of, in which case it is not of anything [at all]. Or, names do indeed name *something*, but that a name does not stand-in for some object which it is of; rather, a name is *the name of a name* and nothing else whatsoever. The argument is presented as an exhaustive choice between understanding naming to be of nothing or something. The first argument did involve existence; and, of course, this is how from monism pluralism was contradictorily derived. However, in this second argument *being* is not understood in this way; for it is argued that if the thing named and the name itself are one (to avoid pluralism), then either there is nothing in a name; or it is a name of a name. In this way, the name is of *something*, namely a name. But the Stranger says, this would be inexplicable. No other reason for this presents itself to account for this, since the Stranger doesn't straightforwardly tell us, except what can be surmised from our foregoing knowledge of Parmenides: following from the Parmenidean understanding that for every thing thought or spoken there is an object which it is of, if the name *is* that thing itself, then it can not in turn be named. The point being that were we to go on and name it, pluralism would follow all over again.

This last argument is intriguing mostly because for the first time there is talk of a naming expression serving some function other than just bringing the thinking subject in touch with the objects which they are of. It would be stretching things a little bit to argue that the Stranger at this point understands naming expressions in such a complex way, such that their function is more than one. However, that the Stranger has entertained the possibility that thought may be full or it may attend upon something which it is the job of a naming expression to fulfil and that this may involve naming a name suggests its conceivability. Though no headway has yet been made, this encompasses a movement away from the ontological status of the things names are understood to represent for thought and speech to an isolated interest in how names are for language specifically. It is important to remember that Parmenides gets stuck in monism because of his understanding of the idea that names furnish thought and speech with *something* because names are of existent objects in the world. This led to a theory of truth as correspondence which was in the end shown to be self-defeating since he deduced the world away.

Monism and the Whole

The relation of part to whole, and sum to whole is certainly not a new theme in Platonic dialogue;[16] most apropos is its elaboration in the *Theaetetus* (204a-206) immediately preceding the three proposed schematic forms that *logos* when added to true belief may take to engender knowledge. The course of conversation which prepared the way to the appropriateness of this topic of discussion concerned the problem of foundationalism. In an effort to distinguish knowledge from mere truth the discussants' progress was impeded because still interested in the *objects* of thought or knowledge, the suggestion that the enumeration of elements could justify true belief could not also explain how the elements, themselves partless or simple, could in turn be accounted for. Foundationalism fosters a problem because the enumeration of parts is expected to justify belief; and yet, if the very parts upon which justification depends are themselves not accountable, then it would invalidly follow that some object is known in virtue of unknowables. The relationship of sum to whole exposed the possibility of thinking of complex and simple objects of thought in an alternative way. Sums are different from wholes because even when they refer to the same object, the one treats the object as an aggregate sum of physical properties or parts, whereas in the case of wholes the point is made that even complex objects are individualised objects (i.e. a car is a single object but it is made up of a large number of parts). The mathematical examples served to show the difference between sums and wholes: 2+4; 10-4; 2x3 etc. are different expressions; yet, each refers to the same numeric object, six. There are different routes or ways of arriving at the same referent object, and what is more, there are different contexts by which some object can come to be understood or known (see *Section II Sums and Wholes, Chapter Four True Belief Plus an Account*).

The relation of sum to whole takes a slightly different course in the *Sophist*. Making explicit reference to a segment from fr. 8 of Parmenides' poem, specifically fr. 8.32-45 and perhaps also fr. 8.22-5, which read:

> Nor is it divided, since it all exists alike; nor is it more here and less there, which would prevent it from holding together, but it is all full of being. So it is all continuous; for what is draws near to what is. (22-5)

> But since there is a fullest limit, it is perfected, like the bulk of a ball well-rounded on every side, equally balanced in every direction from the centre. For it needs not be somewhat more or somewhat less here or there. 17 (32-45)

The Eleatic Stranger invalidly argues from the premise that the real is 'a well-rounded sphere...' that it must have a middle and extremities; and thus is determinable in terms of parts. Of course, given that fr. 8.22-25 endorses material monism outright in order to resist the possibility of qualitative variance or heterogeneity, it is doubtful that even Parmenides expected the 'sphere analogy' to be taken literally. Nonetheless, were it thus, the inference that a homogeneous sphere extended in space must admit of parts is invalid, take the case of the smallest atomic particle. However, it does not also follow that a sphere could not validly be *described* as having a middle and extremities. This faulty inference would seem to be riding on a neglected distinction between the physical properties or parts which belong to and in a restricted sense say what something is, and a purely conceptual undertaking concerning what can truthfully be said about something such that it is not inconsistent with what it is. This is the assumption which caused the similar debate in the *Theaetetus* to fail. With an eye on how something comes to be known, the discussants took wholes as being long hand expressions of the same thing which the naming of the thing would be a short hand expression of. So when the numeric object 'six' is described sometimes as 2+4 or 10-4, these expressions denote what 'six is' in the same way that physical properties (limbs, heart, brain, etc.) are said to denote what something (a man) is, such that they are expected to literally belong to it.

Getting himself involved in definitional knowledge and seemingly conflating the words 'sum' and 'whole', the Stranger says that in admitting divisibility, being can also be described as 'unity' in virtue of the aggregate sum of its parts; or as 'being a sum or whole'. That the discussion on 'sums' and 'wholes' was epistemologically dressed in the *Theaetetus*, of course, overlaps with the more general purpose of the present dialogue; but the specified task of the current debate is foremost about establishing *what is*. This is still ambiguous, and many have thought of what is as a quantitative exercise regarding how many things exist in the world. This unfortunately is both divorced from the scope of the debate, and is inappropriate to Parmenides. That Parmenides was a rationalist epistemologist and not at all a cosmologist is an often neglected fact. That monism is the first thing that comes to mind when thinking of Parmenides should not imply that his objective was to establish *what there is*. Monism was the consequent of his rationalist a priori deductive project; and specifically, being was relevant to that project *only* as contained by the world of a thinking subject. In other words, being or *what is* is for thought.[18] The relevance of the present debate is therefore, not about *what there is for the world*, but rather *what being is for thought*. Again *being* was introduced to the current debate as something deserving of equal attention as not-being *because* as in the case of not-being, it is unclear what it means to think of or formulate thoughts involving *being* either silently talking to oneself (for thought) or aloud (for *speech*).

Henceforth a double scenario, with relative inherent paradoxes attached, is expounded for being:

(a) *What is* has unity, and in terms of its aggregate parts it is also whole.

(b) *What is* is not whole at all.

Without laying this somewhat jagged argument out in full, the gist of it can be made clear in the following way: the one real thing [for thought] is [the] whole; yet, following invalidly from the description of the well-rounded sphere as determinable in parts [middle and extremities], option (a) proposes that for complex objects, these are in a sense 'one' [as an aggregate sum], but they are not unity; hence unity and oneness are two distinct names and plurality follows as a consequent. Alternatively, if (b) the real thing [for thought] is not whole, it might be, on the one hand, (b$_1$)

something from which a piece is missing following from the definition of wholeness as a unified aggregate sum.[19] Alternatively, (b2) were the whole not to be, then it would be impossible to attend upon being for thought, as too would the notion of coming to be, and quantity would also be deceiving.[20] This brings to mind the utility of the well-rounded sphere in fr. 8, and the likelihood that Parmenides' objective was to suggest that the ability to think of something, whether simple or complex, visually requires some kind of borders of determinability for identification. Keeping in mind that the paradox of monism was the consequent of the deductive a priori project traversed on the *Way of Truth*, the pertinence of this passage concerns the enigma involving what thought grabs hold of when thinking of something, such that, thinking also attends upon truth. Truth, which any correspondence theory of truth would require, obtains when thinking involves thinking *of x as x*. So that the difficulty laid bear forthwith challenged the ability to entertain the thought *x* where *x* is a complex object *with parts* without at the same time thinking of *x* in terms of those parts which strictly speaking are themselves—because divisible into unique parts/objects—other than *x* or *not-x*. Contradiction by definition implies falsehood, and the scenario is therefore rejected. Consequently, the thought *x* is either *whole* or *complete*; hence it is equal to itself or *one*, and this implies simplicity, or, it is not *whole or complete* and it cannot be entertained nor indicated by thought. (fr. 2 is a reminder of this).

The Stranger concludes with a string of logical implications following from the argument on wholeness which repeat those found in the concluding fragments—fr. 8-5-49—of his spiritual father regarding the impossibility of birth, number, etc.. In effect, having arrived at this conclusion the Stranger has reached the *Parmenidean Challenge*, and is now properly perplexed about *being*. Concerned therefore, that he has not accurately understood the nature of being, he turns the eye of the debate to alternative philosophers who took up the issue of *being* from a different, perhaps logically prior, angle. *Monism* took up trying to answer what the *ultimate* reality, which the everyday world of diversity is the appearance of, is made-up of;[21] whereas, *materialism* and *idealism* may or may not agree that the *ultimate* or *underlying* reality is one or more than one, but disagree as to the *nature* of this *underlying* reality. So, true to the Socratic method, the Stranger turns away from analyses concerned with what *being* refers to, and towards the conceptual understanding of what *being* means or what amounts to a definition or *logos* of *being*. The job which the Stranger sets for himself is curiously described as a *battle between the gods and the so-called giants*; where the first refers to the *idealists* and the latter to the *materialists*.

The two philosophical traditions that the *materialists* and *idealists* suggest that the Stranger sees the puzzle for falsehood and language to depend upon what it is that thought *thinks* and whence these thoughts come. This had been previously broached with the *Allodoxia Model* in the *Theaetetus* when the extension of a name was implied to be insufficient to account for how language works; names do not always stand in for the object they are of. The battle of the Gods and Giants will address this head-on and it will consequently take us into waters where epistemology and metaphysics meet.

The Battle of the Gods and the Giants

Eluding first to the argumentative character of the materialists (Giants), the ES reiterates dialogic conditions familiar to us from Socrates. Constructive discourse can only unfold when able participants are jointly interested in the truth. This would not be typical of someone who aimed *only* to defend his view against objections. Both our hard-line materialist and idealist are appropriately tamed to meet this condition.

The redeemed materialist is made to accept that body is animated by soul and that soul, though intangible is something real. In turn, soul is variously described; but not without making the point that these descriptive terms do not lie alongside soul as if some kind of independent physical body. Such a view would usher in the pluralising affect of naming which Parmenides faced. Pressed further, he is also described as admitting what both the tangible and intangible have in common such that both share in being; it is their *capacity to affect or be affected* (AA). Of course, the earlier concession—that body in animated by soul—already pre-empted an interest not in objects per se, but in the capacity of objects to *act*.

The hard-line idealist, like Parmenides at the end of the Way of Truth, is robbed of the world of existing things. The Stranger's idealist however, adopts the view that there are two levels of reality with two corresponding means of accessibility: *being* is described as immutable with no physical extension and is received by way of reflection (soul); and *becoming* is variable   and ascertained by the senses. Plato's *realism* evolved from his claim that the tangible world of things could not confer truth because descriptive names become relative to their application, and thereby baffled by the question of how relative names are meaningful, he posited a world of immutable *forms* where these remain unaffected by this relativising context. That the *idealism* propounded by the Eleatic Stranger here should echo the Platonic Theory of Forms when the inherent catalyst so narrowly converge, and that the inevitable enigma of interactivity is found once again before us, prompts speculation regarding the objective as well as historical orientation of the present puzzle. Again the Stranger's intent on revision rests on his ambition to secure the truth; so the kindred metaphysical perspectives must be expected to bare some relation to the truth; yet, given the purpose to expose the confoundment on *being*, they must ultimately be intolerable. Strictly speaking, *idealism*, unlike *realism*, maintains that the *mind* is ultimate reality such that everything entertained by thought *is* only *something* for mind. *Realism* actually assigns *existence* to the *ideas* occupied by thought *independently and external* to the mind entertaining such ideas. This two world view of the reformed idealist can not, of course, postulate a *world* of immutable forms without therefore collapsing into *realism*. When the Stranger argues for the *idealist*, therefore, that there is a pertinent distinction to be drawn for the realm of *thought* and the variable corporeal to which thoughts apply, he does not adopt the view that these *thoughts* (exactly the ideas or objects entertained by thought) *exist* somehow aloof from their application. Neither, can they be just those things to which thought is applied, for then *idealism* would collapse into *materialism*. The character of the subsequent argument must therefore be able to bypass the threat of both *materialism* and *realism*, without at the same time rejecting either (a) that the objects of thought are somehow aloof from the world of variability and corporeality; and (b) that thought must also truthfully apply to this corporeal world. The echo of the *Parmenidean Challenge* is definite. As a result of a misplaced understanding of 'what is not' Parmenides logically deduced the inapplicability of 'what is'. So, his challenge involved reinstating the applicability of truth, and what comes to, complex thinking. (a) and (b) together are expected to demonstrate that thought must somehow interact with the world, but that the objects of thought do not also literally belong to that world.

How can the mind ascertain truths of the world of existing things or what method can describe this intercourse in a truth preserving manner?

The ES puts AA to work again. The acceptance of AA hinged on maintaining that souls have various qualities which are not themselves assigned to the corporeal world of change. Hence, AA does not have to elicit change in the *nature* of the *affecting* or *affected thing*; i.e. justice does not cease to be justice when affixed to soul, Socrates, Mother Teresa and so on. A physical interplay between universal and particular is therefore not being recommended. Rather, particular objects can be apprehended by way of deploying features defining the *context* of its *affection*. The proposition which AA seems to involve concerns not just the obvious point regarding *predication*, but it also suggests that the running requirement that *thinking* requires an identifi*able* object, which in turn implies *knowledge* of the given object, is somehow mistaken. Specifically, AA conjectures that the mind can entertain *thoughts* about something (some object or state of affairs) without at the same time *thinking* of an *object*. This seems to be what is involved when the mind entertains *thoughts of affection*. When *thinking* occurs in terms of AA, we mean that something is *thought about* in terms of how it relates to something else without actually *thinking* of that thing in particular or the *context of affection* as something literally part of it. Nor, of course, is this *context* an object itself; it is more easily understood as an *idea*. This, is nothing more than a peculiar kind of *idealism* somewhere between *materialism* and *realism* as promised. The Stranger wants to hold on to two apparently contradictory notions, as his derogatory hint about our 'childishness' confirms, regarding the ontological complexity of predicates. Complex thoughts involve the kind of sentential complexity which the isolated usage of simple naming expressions (proper names) can not endure, and for this reason, for the first time, we are being introduced to an alternative ontological claim—which will obviously revise the running theory of truth as correspondence—to accommodate precisely this confusion.

The Methodological Discussion

Disappointed that neither arguments for or against the variability of *being* propose viable means of *thinking* or *(coming to) knowing* it, the Stranger compares our fate to that of a child begging for both, 'we must declare that *being* or the *sum of things* is both at once all that is unchangeable and all that is in change' (249d4-5). Given the obvious contradictoriness of this conclusion, the Stranger recommends a different strategy and sets down the *rules* according to which the sequel will carry on. By way of example—two contradictory terms, movement and rest *are being*—the Stranger demonstrates to Theaetetus that they are equally in the dark with respect to *being* as *not-being*. The reason for this, as the example successfully established, is that *all* naming expressions irrespective of how these are *related* to each other for *thought* are treated as referring expressions (referentially transparent); hence with the job to pick out and denote these things for *thinking*. This treatment, of course, plagues *all* sententially complex thoughts and any *non-referential* (referentially opaque) expression to utter confusion as Parmenides confirmed. Acknowledging this, the Stranger concludes that the difficulties which they have confronted thus far regarding both *not-being*—including *falsehood* and *non-existential* expressions—and *being* involve a *singular* problem about *how* names are related to the world, to each other and *how* names are learned in a way that also facilitates the communication of their *meaning*. The so-called problem of *not-being* is not as much an ontological puzzle as it is, therefore, a semantic puzzle about how language works. The so-called *rules* will reflect this realisation; these are given below as the *Parity Assumption*, the *Late Learners, Communion of Kinds*, the *Alphabet Analogy* and *Dialectics*.

First, the *Parity Assumption:* We are told that the problem that plagues not-being is the selfsame problem that plagues being. We must therefore explain both these terms in the same way. Owen was the first to give this assumption proper attention;[22] however, his argument relies on exposing the ambiguity of the verb 'to be', whereas I argue that these terms must be explained in terms of how any name, whether sharing in being or not-being, is thought of as itself, and not something other than itself. The Stranger lays the blame on the shoulders of the PreSocratics who unbeknownst predisposed their disciples to confuse questions regarding *what there is* with questions about *what can be thought or known* and *what can be uttered.* The *Parity Assumption* states outright that the *Parmenidean Challenge* is the fault of a strong inheritance of cosmological prejudices regarding the nature of being as something that exists. Not-being was, by implication rendered non-existent and the contradictory of being. Not only must being and not-being be explained in the same way, but the explanation must be able to respond to the *Parmenidean Challenge*. This requires being able to explain not just the isolated problem of predication, but generally how *the thing named* is related to *what we want to say about that thing*, without at the same time causing the subject to think of the intended thing as something that it is not. Second, the *Late Learners:* The Stranger tacitly endorses the rule that whatever is going to be our conclusion regarding *being* and *not-being* we must be prepared to take its implications seriously; and this would involve from the very outset, the need to reinstate the possibility of language since this is an ongoing assumption without which all thought and the exchange of beliefs would have to be suspended. Our problem has all along been how anything gets thought as the thing that it is (by itself). This is why predication of whatever kind (involving being and not-being) becomes intolerable. It is not possible to think or speak that 'man is good', because man is not what *is* good. The late learners would defend the commonplace idea that language is possible, and at the same time prohibit us from thinking or talking of something as something else. This is a reminder of the problem of multiplication or the problem that 'naming pluralises' which was first encountered in Parmenides, and previously in our discussion of monism. Third, the *Communion of Kinds*. Applying the rule, Theaetetus and the Stranger examine the views on being by determining their consequences (251e5) based on the acceptance or rejection of combination. Where it is possible, the immutable world of the idealist (at rest) and the variable world of the materialist (in motion) are rendered impossible because neither rest nor motion partake in being. This translates as a problem for language such that no talk whatsoever is possible where rest and motion are only paradigmatic of the problem of being. Where combination is possible, contradiction plagues all assertions for in saying both rest and motion partake in being each would supervene upon the other, bringing therefore motion to a standstill and vice versa. Hence, any theory on being must first be able to explain the possibility of combination before it is to be taken seriously. Otherwise, things (e.g. man) can only be called by their own names (e.g. man) which the rule following from the late learners rejects. They conclude that perhaps not everything can partake or combine with everything else or not at all; but that only some things are capable of combination, which the alphabet analogy attempts to clarify.

Fourth, the *Alphabet Analogy*. It addresses the ability to formulate complex thoughts or statements which the problem of predication is an isolated occurrence of. Having already introduced semantics to the debate and established that the problem of *being* and *not-being* is really a problem about how language works, the rules regarding combination are compared to the case of the letters of the alphabet (253a). We are told that not all letters combine with all other letters; special weaving letters, known as vowels, have the job to unite other letters. The difficulty is obviously in determining which letters properly combine with which other letters. We are told that the expertise here required belongs to the grammarian, just like in the case of combining sounds, the musician would be the proper expert to consult. When adopting the analogy to thought, it is clear that first and foremost we must acquire an understanding of how words are put together (combined) such that something gets thought or said in a meaningful and accessible manner. The matter of its truth will reintroduce the significance of ascertaining its metaphysical status but it will be axiomatic on how language works.[23] In other words, the assessment of truth has everything to do with *what is getting said*, so that consequently, how and by what rules words are related in a sentence to facilitate thought and speech will also establish the method for measuring truth.

And fifth, *Dialectics*: the cataloguing of universals, implying the rules of their application to particulars. This requires a fuller consideration of the text. The Stranger does not straightforwardly define the method or rules of dialectics; rather, the dialectician is characterised by his ability to discern (253d-e):

> (1) (i) *one* form everywhere *extended throughout* (ii) *many*, where each one lies apart, (2) and many forms, different from one another, embraced from without by *one form*, and again (3) *one* form connected in a *unity* through many *wholes*, and (4) *many* forms, entirely marked off apart. That means *knowing* how to distinguish, kind by kind, in what ways the several kinds can or cannot combine (my numbers and italics).

What suggests itself as a precondition must meet the terms of competency provided as 253b-c:

> Well, now that we have agreed that the kinds stand toward one another in the same way as regards blending (e.g. as with letters), is not some science needed as a guide on the voyage of discourse, if one is to succeed in

pointing out (1) which kinds are consonants, and (2) which are incompatible with one another—also, (3) whether there are certain kinds that pervade them all and connect them so that they can blend, and again, (4) where there are divisions [separations], whether there are certain others that traverse wholes and are responsible for division?

The greatest controversy regarding the first passage is whether (1) is talking about the *extension* of some *idea* or *concept* (i), so that we are talking specifically about how so-called *universals* relate to *particulars* (ii) which are described in virtue of *participating* in it. Or rather, is the alluringly Parmenidean use of words here no more than accidental; such that, *oneness* (i) and then *manyness* (ii), indeed extended, in both instances refer to *ideas or concepts themselves*. This latter interpretation can not, however, account for (2), since seen in this light (1) and (2) say exactly the same thing but in the reverse. Namely, at (1) there is *one form* which subsumes a number of other *forms*; whereas at (2) there are many *forms* which are subsumed by *one form*.[24] In fact, (1) seems to be interested in the relatedness of universals with particulars; (2) with the relatedness of distinctive *concepts* or *universals*; whereas (3) and (4) are concerned with *how* (1) and (2) occur. That is, (3), corresponding to (1), argues for the discernment of a *universal* when attached to a [complex] particular by way of other intermingling *universals*. Someone skilled in dialectics should be able to ascertain—namely to acquire knowledge of—something [new] about some particular, *x*, regarding its participation in *some universal descriptions*. That is, when *x* participates in the *universal a*; because *a* intermingles or is subsumed by *b*, *x* can also be understood in terms of *b*. (4) then is about the discernment of *universals* independent of their *relatedness to other universals*. Of course, this task precedes all others; and is presupposed for (3). That is, unless there is some method by which the *meanings* of *universals* can be objectively determined, arguments at (3) will tend towards circularity. Were we to name those *universals* which do not intermingle or are not subsumed by any other *universal* as *Great Kinds,* and *b* is a *Great Kind,* we must be able to justify *a* by demonstrating its consistency with *b*, which in turn requires defining *b* without reverting back to *a* and so on, for all other intermingling *wholes*. It is significant that (3) refers to a *unity* in virtue of which *one form* comes together, and *wholes* in terms of which that *form* is ascertained. The last time *unity* and *wholes* were discussed, the Stranger was involved in dispelling the ambiguity of *being* (p. 51-4). It was argued that something is a *unity* in terms of being an aggregate sum of parts,[25] whereas a *whole*—following from the Parmenidean Challenge—is *for thought identical to, and therefore, determined with respect to, itself.* Compared, this recommends the reading provided because firstly, it consistently makes sense of (3) and the summarised conclusion, that *all this* (1)-(4) comes to *knowing how to distinguish kind by kind.* Secondly, it has the advantage of being relevant to the problem of language under discussion in a way that its alternative is not. For, the argument which maintains that reference is made *exclusively* and *specifically to kinds* or *universals* cannot show the relevancy to *predication* which has incited the problem of language.[26]

Regarding the correspondence of the passage outlining the ensuing skills of a true dialectician, and the set agenda of his science, clearly the summarised conclusion of the one meets the individual tasks pieced together in the other. For though the agenda fragment does not, of course, mention *particulars*, it does reflect or spell out what is involved in *knowing how to distinguish kind by kind, and in what ways the several kinds can or cannot combine provided* at the end of the first. Apart from the application of dialectics, what is important is that for the first time names are treated as complete [or whole] and yet complex. For names, such as those used to describe *particulars*, can be accounted for in terms of how they relate to other *forms*, such that they are said to be subsumed or that their meaning is entailed by the meaning of some other name [i.e. standing for a *form*]. There must, therefore, be an underlying logical structure of language to explain how *one* thing can be grasped, and in effect entailed by, *another thing* without either *becoming* that thing, or *other than itself*—hence contradiction. The goal of the remainder of the dialogue is to impart this knowledge, and thereby solve the problem of *being* and *not-being* and consequently, falsehood.

Conclusion

The historical baggage of PreSocratic thought has been made responsible for the misplaced understanding of *being* and *not-being*, and consequent epistemological and semantic philosophies had been exposed are insufficient as a result of this. All attempts to construct a metaphysics: materialism, idealism, realism, monism, pluralism, failed miserably because each in turn set restrictions that could not possibly conform to the meaningful communication of thought, most notably their own philosophical thought. Thought does not become meaningful in virtue of some existent object all by itself. According to AA thought can attend upon things with respect to their capacities; these capacities are not, in turn, expected to suggest facts or states of affairs to which thoughts as a whole would be expected to correspond all over again. Rather, it must somehow be possible to think of things with respect to their capacities, hence with respect to *how* these are, without thereby getting stuck in the relativism of their behaviour. Nonetheless, thought must apply to the world. The next chapter is being set up as identifying the problem for false belief as a problem that involves the way in which words relate to the world, each other and in what way these words are meaningfully relayed to others. The sequel should be expected to develop a theory of meaning which will at the same time develop a corresponding metaphysics to settle the problem regarding the strict word-object premise.

Notes

[1] Compare *Theaetetus* 210d2, 'but tomorrow morning, Theodorus, let us meet here again ', and the *Sophist* 216a, 'here, we (Theaetetus and Theodorus) are, Socrates, faithful to our appointment of yesterday'.

[2] Nearly a month elapsed between Socrates' condemnation and execution because a day before the trial a sacred galley had been sent on a mission, and according to custom, no one could be put to death prior to its return. The delay of the galley's return kept Socrates alive, but awaiting his death in jail.

[3] Of course, the formal charges levied against Socrates were for the introduction of new gods, and for corrupting the youth.

[4] 'But when it comes to something which you value more highly than your body, namely your soul—something on whose beneficial or harmful treatment your whole welfare depends—you must not consult either your father, your brother or any one of us who are your friends on the question whether or not to entrust your soul to this stranger (Protagoras) who has arrived among us.' 'Instead upon hearing the arrival of Protagoras without question Hippocrates is ready to submit himself to his teachings'. And to this Socrates says, 'some of these men (that go from city to city speaking on various subjects of knowledge for a fee) are also ignorant of the beneficial or harmful effects on the soul of what they have for sale, and so too are those who buy from them, unless one of them happens to be a physician of the soul'. Moreover, 'the risk you run in purchasing knowledge is much greater than that in buying provisions', for 'when you have paid for 'services to the soul' you receive it straightway and are affected by it accordingly' (*Prot.* 313a-314c).

[5] The first Homeric passage from the *Odyssey* is taken from Book IX. 269-71; and the second from Book XVII. 485-87. The first is spoken by Odysseus to the Cyclops Polyphemus: 'May your excellency fear the wrath of heaven, for we are your suppliants, and Zeus takes all respectable travellers under his protection, for he is the avenger of all suppliants and foreigners in distress'. Whereas the second is spoken by an anonymous suitor to Antinous: 'Antinous you did ill in striking that poor wretch of a tramp. It will be worse for you if he should turn out to be some god. And we know the gods go about

disguised in all sorts of ways as people from foreign countries, and travel about the world to see who do amiss and who righteously'. See Samuel Butler, trans. (1944) *The Odyssey of Homer*, pp. 109 and 220.

[6] See S. Rosen (1983), *Plato's Sophist; the Drama of the Original and Image*, p. 62.

[7] For the passage cited from Bk. IX. 269, Odysseus appeals to Zeus as the avenger of suppliants and foreigners in distress in the hopes of assuring their good treatment by the horrendous Cyclops. It turns out that Polythemus is a disbeliever, and goes about devouring Odysseus' men. Later when Odysseus gores Polythemus eye, the neighbours hearing Polythemus' cries, remark 'if no man is attacking you, you must be ill; when Zeus makes people ill, there is no help for it, and you had better pray to your father Poseidon'. Zeus is a punishing and unforgiving god; faltering from the path of righteousness the fate of man is already sealed. In the second passage, Odysseus has returned home disguised as a beggar. He has been struck and abused by Antinous, who is in turn reprimanded by an anonymous suitor, saying 'gods looking like strangers from afar become all things and wander about the cities, viewing human hubris and righteousness'. Taking no heed of the warning Antinous continues until it is the death of him. Hence, there is the suggestion that Odysseus (whose likeness was restored to him in Bk. XVII) is Zeus in disguise.

[8] In Rosen's commentary on this passage, he says 'Philosophers, like gods, are hard to distinguish, but one can make this suggestion about them: whereas righteous gods punish the sins of mortals, one philosopher appropriately punishes another by refuting his defective arguments. Socrates thus makes an important correction in the passage from Homer. According to the proud young man, disguised gods view human hubris and righteousness. According to Socrates, gods also refute, or in other words, punish, and thus distinguish between better and worse....In sum, if the Stranger is a god, he will both distinguish mortals by their looks or natures and administer punishment or judge their merits' (p. 63-4). And later that gods are said to refute, but philosophers not (p. 65). Rosen argues further that the stranger's subsequent identification of refutation with the art of sophistry, reminiscent of Socrates, suggests that in this passage Socrates is defending himself in advance against his identification with sophistry. See S. Rosen (1983) *Plato's Sophist: The Drama of the Original and Image*, pp. 63-4. Rosen says that this later ammendation to the Homeric passages is curious due to Socrates' reputation, but conjectures that the implication is that Socrates' form of refutation is likely being distinguished from that of nonphilosophers. This is, of course, not at all curious. Nowhere is Socrates defended against the accusation that the elenchus is friendly; Socrates is however, defended against the accusation that the sophistic form of argumentation (antilogic) is identical to the elenctic form (dialectic).

[9] At 242c10-243a4 the some remarks are made. 'In our part of the world the Eleatic set, who hark back to Xenophanes or even earlier, unfolds their tale on the assumption that what we call 'all things' are only one thing' obviously refers to Parmenides. 'Later, certain muses in Ionia and Sicily perceived safety lay rather in combining both accounts and saying that the real is both many and one and is held together by enmity and friendship; "In parting asunder it is always being drawn together say the stricter of these muses"'. The first

must refer to Heraclitus and the Pythagoreans. 'The milder relax the rule that this should always be so and tells us of alternate states, in which the universe is now one and at peace through the power of love, and now many at war with itself owing to some sort of strife' refers to Empedocles.

[10] See G.E.L. Owen (1970) 'Plato On Not-Being' in G. Vlastos (ed.) *Plato: A Collection of Critical Essays, Vol. I, Metaphysics and Epistemology*, pp. 223-67.

[11] Where the doctrine of Anaximander is the model of dispute, the Eleatic Stranger first argues that 'hot and cold' are three, and then one real thing rather than the two ordinarily understood by the assertion 'hot and cold or some such pair *really are* all things'. It repeats what has been the Parmenidean problem with naming.

[12] This passage only entails *numerical* monism; but it has been argued in the *Introduction* that at the end of fr. 8 Parmenides gets stuck in *radical* monism. That is material, numerical, and predicative monism.

[13] G.S. Kirk, J.E. Raven, J.E.M. Schofield (1983) *The PreSocratic Philosophers*, Second edition, p. 248, 295.

[14] Again in the *Introduction*, it has been argued that this fragment is not at all an embarrassment. In fact, it more than reinforces what has been argued to involve the Parmenidean Challenge. For it requires that language is not diminished to the nonsensical utterance—*esti*—which doesn't assert anything, and shows of necessity that precisely because Parmenides supposes someone to be reading his poem (hence numerical monism is out of the question) that he would have to employ terms which he can not yet make sense of. Not that they do not make sense, or the world does not exist.

[15] It is basically the idea that we employ words that our theory could not recommend only to make the point that those words can not rightfully be employed. The paradox which the ladder analogy tries to solve involves saying something like: 'it is senseless to say that *x* is *a*'. But in order to say that you must necessarily employ the very utterance or words that you are saying are senseless, namely that '*x* is *a*'. Of course, were it strictly senseless, then it would not accomplish anything to say it. So, the ladder analogy argues that in the same way that a ladder is used to give us a boost to reach higher places, so too could a so-called linguistic ladder be used to facilitate communication; and once used it could be discarded in a non-committal fashion.

[16] It has been discussed at length in the *Parmenides*, in the *Theaetetus* and the *Sophist*.

[17] G.S. Kirk, J.E. Raven, M. Schofield (1983) *The PreSocratic Philosophers*, Second edition, pgs. 251 and 252-3, nos. 297 and 299.

[18] Comparison of the Parmenidean and Cartesian project has already been made. However, I would like to add that the challenge of foundationalism that both these a priori deductive methods erected their project on proceeded on the basis of inferences drawn from *thought*. For Parmenides withdrawing from the world of *Doxa* left him with thought. Specifically with thought contemplating thought, and from there he derived that thought must be full, or of something (NB it was only as a consequent of his correspondence theory of truth that this led him to deduce simultaneous conclusions for the world external to the thinking subject). Hence, Parmenides' starting point or building block began with the *objects* of

thought and thereby moved into territory regarding what could be logically thought of it. However, for Descartes, the Cogito being his building block, began with an inference regarding the subject of thought. That is, left also with thought contemplating thought he moved to deduce the certainty of his own existence (as a mind).

[19] I do not want to get involved in this immensely hoary argument except to remark that it is unclear whether its rebuke follows because *being* would share in *not-being*; or whether specifically anything would not be equal to itself. The point being that it is different to refer to a table as a *table* [a complex object made up of an aggregate sum of auxiliary parts] and the parts which comprise it.

[20] Fr. 2 first introduces the idea that the object of thought must be individualisable; but in fr. 8.48-9 spells it out 'for being equal to itself (any object occupying thought) on every side, it lies uniformly within its limits'. In other words, either some object is equal to itself such that it *complete* or *whole*, or else it is *incomplete* and consequently, it is not equal to itself. This would be tantamount to the mind attending upon x as *not-x*.

[21] If we are to accept that Thales is the father of philosophy, we would argue that metaphysics began with his *material monism* which evolved from his interest in cosmological questions regarding the origin of all things which he understood to involve a single material, namely water.

[22] For G.E.L. Owen's 'Plato on Not-Being', see *Logic, Science and Dialectic* (Collected Papers), ed. M.C. Nussbaum (1986), pp. 104-37.

[23] In Everson's (1994) *Companion to Ancient Thought 3: Language,* he remarks '..one does not have to accept any particular thesis about the relation between language and thought to recognise that linguistic confusion breeds bad philosophy' p. 5. Claims from language, it is argued, have since the time of antiquity—Parmenides is cited as an example—led to strong metaphysical conclusions. Throughout this exact proposition has been acknowledged; and this passage transposes this realisation to Plato himself, who now understands that all misunderstands regarding *being* and *not-being* have arisen from semantic blunders. Further, that the analysis of language which shall proceed will require a particular theory of the world which will allow the subject to acquire the ability to skilfully and meaningfully employ language.

[24] R. Chadwick remarks in his (1984) *For Images: An Interpretation of Plato's* Sophist, that 'the first ability, which is also the first mentioned in the *Phaedrus* account (265d) and is referred to in the *Philebus* as the business of dialectic (14-15), is that of finding one Form extended throughout many, each one lying apart. The many things lying apart are widely held to be individuals because of the genitive absolute construction for 'each one lying apart' .... On the other hand, the fact that dialectic in the *Republic* and in the *Phaedrus* (265-6) studies only the Forms should raise doubts. Moreover, just four lines above (253d1-3) the business of dialectic has been described as dividing by *Kinds* (my italics), not taking the same *eidos* for a different one nor a different one for the same; and the very same speech (253d-e) that lists these capacities ends with the summary: 'and that means, knowing in what ways each can and cannot combine and how to divide according to Kinds', p. 55.

[25] This also overlaps with the a passage in the *Theaetetus* (204a-205) when in an attempt to determine what *logos* is, a distinction is made between sums and wholes; such that, sums are the parts of which something is made up, and wholes—in not just being the same as the sum—singularly refer to some complex thing in virtue of its *meaning*. This was given at 205 as the ability to ascertain *what it is* in the context of other things (e.g. letters assume certain sounds).

[26] Even the Theory of Forms got stuck in the problem of participation—which, in effect, comes to predication—because after having postulated some accessible (?) means of ascertaining *forms*, it was unclear how these could then, without losing their *wholeness* be applied.

5   Resolving Falsehood

Introduction

In what follows Plato will show that *not-being* is not metaphysically problematic and that it makes sense to talk in terms of *what is not*. Settling this difficulty Plato then shows how it is meaningful to assert of one thing that it is something else without that involving either contradiction or a non-thought. Truth will be separated from meaning; and in turn, the capacity or function of a naming expression will be made clear. Forms are both denotative and connotative; but nothing is meaningful in isolation; words acquire meaning for application. Still names name; and verbs say things about their actions. The threat of relativism is resisted and the promise of a middle ground between *materialism* and *idealism* is developed.

The Great Kinds and the Thought Experiment

Abruptly the methodological passage ends, and shaking off the impervious philosophical link to dialectics, the Stranger recasts the interest in the present voyage in terms of catching the sophist. In fact, we are recommended to take our leave of the philosopher, and to cast some light on the darkened niche of the sophist which will *at the same time bring us closer to the philosopher* if only because in apprehending the sophist, we determine what the philosopher is not.

Making something of the idea, lingering since the discussion of *logos* in the *Theaetetus*, of context, the AA condition is exploited to assist in the explication of *combination* or predication. Context is almost unsuspectingly assumed from the outset of the present discourse when the Stranger proposes a thought experiment where, he says, only a select number of *universals* need be considered (254c4). The paired opposites, motion and rest, sameness and difference plus *being*, are selected, and thereafter the twofold objective of the thought experiment is given as, first *saying what each is like,* and the second, *to show how these have the power of combining with each other* (2545-7). Selection already assumes context since by definition a choice of preference in relation to others is made; hence the decision to take *these* kinds is based on their reference to the rest. Again it is implicit that these *kinds* are neither idealist forms, nor physical entities since the earlier contradictory consequences regarding the combination of rest and motion in *being* do not follow. Hence, already AA and the promise of some metaphysical theory which somehow compromises the *idealist* and *materialist* positions are in play. Preceding then the actual task of determining the compatibility of the combination of *kinds*, is the establishment of the *nature* or definition of these kinds which inadvertently involves attribution. Put differently, the determinability of combination depends on *what we know can already be said about some kind*, and this will not involve listing aggregate parts, but rather taking on board the eye-opening discovery that names are at the same time *whole and complex*. The Stranger goes on to lay bare how the logical relatedness of motion and rest helps to unpack their complexity, and thereby their meaning, remembering at the same time that the solution that this expects to provide for *combination* must be equally applicable to all statements including false statements; i.e. *all* statements must be meaningful in the same way. How one sees the background strategy is going to directly affect how one is going to read the ensuing, and very controversial, solution to the problem of falsehood. For this reason it is essential that what follows is seen in light of the *Parmenidean Challenge* regarding thought; that all the *rules* established in the methodological interlude are not neglected, and finally, that the answer really does [try to] solve the problem of falsehood *with reference to the status of not-being*.[1] The debate over how the solution proposed by the *Great Kinds* is to be interpreted is exceedingly thick; yet, one might say that two main thrusts of argumentation make the fundamental disagreements clear: the first involves the manner by which the solution is elaborated, and specifically whether two distinct phases are introduced for two distinct and separable problems; whereas the second concerns the solution to the problem of *not-being* per se, namely does Plato seek to accomplish this by dispelling a confusion between the *is of identity* and the *is of predication*,[2] or alternatively, on a different sense of 'not', distinguishing thus that which is *different/other* from that which is in *opposition*; or again, could it involve a difference in *naming* as such?

The arguments which have been defended thus far all involve the presence of Parmenides and his trouble with *not-being*. However, *not-being* is not, as Jordan has argued,[3] primarily important to Plato regarding what Jordan calls the 'compresence of being with notbeing'—which I take to mean what Plato calls *combination* and hence the focused concern on predication. Predication is an isolated problem which involves the relatedness of *being* and *not-being*, but Plato takes this problem to be a problem for *language* and therefore involves, as his clearly semantic focus confirms, a greater difficulty regarding *complex* thought and the meaningfulness, accessibility and truth of overt expressions. This concern is not at all divorced from the project of Parmenides. Frs. 2 and 6 in Parmenides' poem specify that what is puzzling is how *something is for thought and speech;* while the *no way track* and the *backward-turning thoughts* of mortals shows the relevance of *not-being*. When an expression becomes meaningful in terms of the numerical object it represents or stands for in thought, two implications follow: firstly, the naming expression must correspond to something that exists—an ontological claim; and secondly, thought is meaningful only as an entity; i.e. *all* naming expressions have the function to denote or refer the thinking subject to its object of thought. Words name things—a semantic claim. In turn, nominata are understood as simple because the semantics of Parmenides made it impossible to name something complex because that would involve naming some-thing *other* than its corresponding nominata—semantic atomism. That Plato picks this up as the problem he wishes to resolve is confirmed by the Parity Assumption—*being* and *not-being* as independent naming expressions are puzzling *for the same reason and in the same way*—,[4] the clearly semantic[5] concern regarding the function of naming expressions *for thought*—which is perfectly consistent with what Plato was trying to do in the *Theaetetus*—and finally, the explicit puzzles on Parmenidean concepts, especially regarding *wholes* and *unities* which, of clearly referential import, are concerned with how the mind can grab hold of some object for thought with some naming expression, and meaningfully be thinking of that thing *as itself* when the thought involves the form 'x is F' [or 'F is G' for that matter]. [6] That is, this discussion had hinged upon the relatedness, yet, distinctiveness of *unities* and *wholes*; the first, involved ontological import such that something was an aggregate sum of *physical* parts, whereas *wholes* were complex objects *because* these involved *varying conceptual attachments*. The problem therefore, which this proposed was how to, in effect, think of a so-called complex object *in virtue of varying conceptual attachments or attributes* without thinking of it as *something else* [the pluralising effect was the result, of course, of treating these *attachments* as entities]. Thinking of the letter 'h' as a *hissing sound* in the *Theaetetus* comes to mind as a possible example of what is involved in this puzzle; namely, the ability to think of something [what better to make the point than a simple object] in terms of something that does not strictly belong to it [the condition of propriety]. At this point it is essential not to lose sight of what exactly is going on, and how the string of arguments are woven together. The problem raised regarding falsehood was raised as a problem for *not-being*, which in turn, was revealed to plague utterances involving *being* in precisely the same way. The problem is one regarding language, specifically it lies in the *referential capacity* of a naming expression, and its determinant meaning thereby. From Parmenides, thought is meaningful only when *what is thought* corresponds to what that thought is *about*, such that it is about *some-thing*. Sentences were treated as bits of naming expressions, as it were, and each with the role to denote its object. Where there is no object as such, the utterance by implication is saying nothing (is about nothing) and is thus unintelligible. Plato is now willing to take on board the *rules* and therefore semantic complexity of thought in speech. Most have been led to thereby hold that Plato makes an important discovery regarding what a statement involves; namely in its most economical form, a subject and predicate, such that the function of the first is to name something which, in turn, it is the job of the latter, to say something about. Such a view lends itself to the interpretation that the solution to the problem of *not-being* involves drawing out the distinction between the 'is' of *identity* and the 'is' of *predication.* That the complexity of language, and in fact *rules* of language are going to be somehow important to how Plato sees the resolution to this puzzle is absolutely consistent with the view being defended herewith. However, this can not be isolated from the serious metaphysical dispute which has raised corresponding puzzles for epistemology in the *Theaetetus*, and semantics in the *Sophist*. Even though the logical function of a naming expression involves two different uses of the verb 'to be', that which constitutes the solution must say something about how a naming expression can ever get something said without at the same time referring thought to the thing it names, and how, when the plausibility of predication is demonstrated via combination, a so-called predicate-name acquires this different function for thought and is at the same time related to its subject-name without introducing a relativising context.

The body of the first number of passages is positively odd. There is something queer about either identifying or predicating things like *sameness* and/or *difference* of other things. What exactly is the meaning of the statement, 'motion is not sameness' and so on for the various combinations of the selected forms? The peculiarity, is, of course, that *sameness* and *difference* are not strictly predicates, but terms specifying a logical relation.[7] This is especially strange given that the combining of forms is meant to make it possible for a form to have the *name* of something different from itself. Sameness and difference are not ordinary naming expressions since these do not refer or denote an object. One might object that perhaps this introduces a new kind of naming where the function of a name is not to stand in for an object in thought. Yet sameness and difference are not even predicate names, they are names of logical relations. That which is presumably accomplished in this passage is to show how all these kinds are equally compatible with *being* such that, and here again is the peculiarity, *being can be called by such names.* There is also the asymmetry of the selected forms. Motion and rest are contraries, and therefore obviously exclude each other; yet, these epithets seem patently different in kind from *being*, difference and sameness. The latter, it has already been noted, have logical force, whereas the former have not, and in what follows all the work will be done with reference to the latter. In fact, no argument, or background scenario, makes an appearance to suggest that the choice of these two contrary kinds, motion and rest, are anything but accidental; that is, any contraries could have been utilised.[8] It must therefore be that the essence of the passage lies in the relations of difference, sameness and *being*, and determining their effectiveness in an argument concerned with showing the possibility to *think* that *what is not, in fact, is,* whether truthfully or falsely.[9]

The function of a *name* under issue in the discussion of the pluralists demonstrated that naming pluralises, and later in the discussion of the monist, it was suggested for the first time that a *name* must somehow be different from the object it denotes (wholes versus unities). In turn this was picked up when the discussion on *being* shifted from an interest in its *number* to its *nature*. This movement away from an exclusive concern with designata to an extended interest in its *nature*, of course, suggests that the 'names' linked together to explicate *how being* is must acquire a different status—i.e. other than that of denotation. We should now be prepared to take on board both the means of accessibility and meaningfulness of an ulterior function for a *name*. Read in this context, it would seem that Plato is offering us two alternative routes for coming by a name *for thought*; i.e. a name is not only accessible in terms of identifying the object it denotes; such that it acquires meaning for thought when the name-object is thought of *as* itself. In other words, under this transparently referential function of a name, the name-*x* is meaningful only when *x* is really being thought of. This is the reason why falsehood on the face of it seemed unintelligible; for it involves naming *x* when, for instance, thinking of *y* (*allodoxia*) or not-*x*.

Having cast the philosophical puzzle in the proper context, let us resume the argument as such. The process of actually counting out, and thereby separating out the Great Kinds is accomplished by deriving implications for the paired contraries, motion and rest, when called by the alternative names, *being*, *sameness* and *difference*. The *nature* of these forms or concepts, motion and rest, is logically contrary, and therefore, nothing which is said of the one can jointly be said of the other (255a6-7). From 254d-e the gist of the overall argument is provided: motion and rest are incompatible due to the contrariety of their *natures*,[10] yet *being* must be compatible with both because both motion and rest *are*. Conclusion, *being* cannot be subsumed by either forms and must therefore be a uniquely meaningful concept or form. So, now there are three. In fact, in the same manner that *being* is a unique form in virtue of which these others are *what they are*, each of these three forms is in turn understood *as being the same as itself*, and *yet different from each of the other two*. Enter two further *forms*; *sameness* and *difference*.[11] The point seems to be the following: even in the case of forms these cannot be meaningfully thought of unless, as the contextual setting implies, somehow logically concatenated in the mind. It would in a way be comparable to blurting out to someone just the word 'man' in isolation. It does not mean anything to the listener until you say something of it. This would be the original semantic problem that plagued the Theory of Forms as a result of thinking of these as somehow logically prior to and independent of the contents they figure in.[12] I find the identity-predication interpretation unsatisfactory because it is unable to say anything about why *these* particular forms, which are not after all strictly predicates, are employed. In fact, the counting out of forms is accomplished by a preceding knowledge of the *natures* of the *forms* motion and rest, which determines the *logical* behaviour of a term, hence their recognised contrariety. The ensuing *forms* are then counted out in like manner: the only argument provided is that in being contrary, both must *be* [what they are] in themselves or otherwise [it is implied] be what they are in virtue of something else [constitutes being subsumed by some other form which is in turn what it is in virtue of itself]. Understanding this argument requires a prior understanding of the concepts of *being, sameness* and *difference*. Of course, it is also true that the argument requires this preceding understanding of these concepts *because* these alternative concepts say something *about* motion and rest which is not actually part of what it means to either *be* motion or rest. Hence, in not being *identical* to these, or any of each other, yet accessible in terms of each alternative, predication is something that begins to make sense. For it is important that for any assertion of predication the predicate-term is not subsumed by the subject-name [whether a proper name or concept] so that it is actually cognitively informative. That just means that in knowing the meaning of the subject-name, this did not already imply the knowledge of the predicate-name. There are therefore at least two things going on simultaneously: Plato is dealing with a *cognitive* problem which has to do with the process of thinking itself, as well as the specific *semantic* problem regarding predication. The required cognitive apparatus reveals that the act of thinking is always logically complex—hence the relevance of the forms *being, sameness* and *difference*—whilst the actual argument employed to separate out the five Great Kinds hinged on drawing a distinction between statements of *identity* and statements of *predication*. The distinction is derived as a consequence of the former: that is, the complex process of thought demonstrates that when thinking '*xxx*' it need not involve the simple thought '*x*', nor yet that '*x* [or *G*] is *F*' only makes sense in terms of *F* being the same as *x*. The name *F* may be something distinct from *x* [or *G*] without that entailing the contradictory belief or thought that '*x* is not-*x*'.

Applying the same chain of argumentation, the latter forms, *sameness* and *difference*, are separated out as distinctive and all-pervasive concepts. That is, the forms *being, sameness* and *difference* each (255e) can at the same time blend with all other forms. Yet, sometimes a form is *spoken* of [thought of] as 'what it is' *in itself* and sometimes it is spoken of as 'what it is' *with reference to something else* (255c16-18). When speaking [thinking] of a *form* as itself *it is what it is in virtue of its nature*; whereas in case of speaking [thinking] of a *form* with reference to something else *it is what it is in virtue of its difference*. These alternative ways in which a form can be thought of would imply therefore, two ulterior ways for a concept to figure in speech, and that recommends an antecedent sentential analysis of how the subsentential expressions contribute to the meaning of the thought as a whole. For it is *how* a name figures in speech that will determine its contribution to the given thought; i.e. in virtue of its *nature* or in virtue of its *difference*. Of course, that which has remained at the periphery of the present debate is the exact status of the all-pervasiveness of *being*. Again the line of argument adopted will not support the view that these all-pervasive forms are *attributed,* not *identified*, with motion and rest. Rather, once more the point must be relevant to how the mind can meaningfully grab hold of something for thinking; in which case, is Plato arguing that even a *concept* must refer to a set of existent objects in the same way that a proper name or *particular* would denote an individual object? For names only pluralised because each bit of a sentence was treated as a proper name; that is each name denoted its own individual referent object. Yet, so long as the predicative relation of a sentence is intact, it could be argued that a predicate name denotes a class of things which the subject name is expected to be a member of. Hence in case that it is, the statement is true, and in case that it is not, the statement is false. The only help Plato provides in this matter so far is (a) that in motion participating in *being* because it *is*, motion is nonetheless not 'the same' as *being* [repeated for *being* and *sameness* at 255bc2]; and the inference (b) if *being* and *sameness* have no difference in *meaning*, when we say that motion and rest both *are*, we shall thereby be *speaking* of them as being 'the same'. (b) states that two names with a shared meaning must necessarily be about or refer to the same *object* (so if good and virtue have the same meaning, if *x* is good, it must also be virtuous). (a) however is specifically concerned with the application of names. Namely, when some object named *x* is said to participate in *F*, it does not follow that *x* and *F* are the same thing. It only means for the statement 'Socrates is good' that the man Socrates can be ascertained in terms of 'goodness'. Were both these names purely referential, we would expect Socrates *to be* one of those things subsumed under the class of things called by 'goodness'. Instead, it is clear that these two names can not be understood merely as co-referential since then, it would have to follow, according to (a), that whenever 'goodness' is named it could thereby be substituted by the name 'Socrates' without affecting the meaning of the statement, which is not, of course, the case.[13] The implication which follows is that *forms*, as well as being denotative—it is clear that Plato maintains that words acquire meaning because there are existent objects in the world that behave in a particular way—are also connotative. No argument suggests itself to attribute to Plato the recognition that some names *only* denote, and therefore can only stand in for their nominata; but it would nonetheless seem to be implicit. The debate is turning on the use and meaningfulness of *universals*; particulars (e.g. including for Plato things like *the* table and Socrates), which presumably would involve *things* as instances of universals, have proper names which do correspond to—in fact they come directly from—the world. Therefore, a word or name need not denote an object to meaningfully contribute to the meaning of the sentence entailing it, for a name, specifically *forms*, have meaning independently from the things that acquire, whether truthfully or not, the given name. The meaning of a name, of course, is a question for its *nature* to define.

The Solution Applied to Statements

When applied to its usage or function in assertions, how is the meaning of a name when understood to be what it is in virtue of its own nature going to differ from the meaningfulness of a name in virtue of its difference from everything else? In what follows, it looks as though the so-called meaningfulness of a name—by participating in sameness or difference—will depend upon how it is fed into a statement, or in fact, what the thought contained by its assertion intends to convey in putting these various words together. In what follows both true affirmative statements are formulated, as well as true negative statements, hence with the objective to demonstrate the blending capacity of a name when plugged into a declarative sentence. This suggests something that has already sneaked into the debate as seemingly trivial, namely that words or names having ulterior functions *for* thought overtly expressed in statements *acquire* a different meaning. That is, the meaning of a word is no longer going to be an isolated affair whether standing alone or part of a sentence, rather it is primarily the contribution of words in a sentence that will decide the meaning[fulness] of the particular word in question [use of expression at 256b].[14]

The ensuing passage is extremely dense and we must be sure to notice all of the distinctions being drawn in each application of a name for a statement.[15]

(i) 'Motion is not rest in any sense'—in being altogether different
from rest

yet (ii) 'motion is' [by participating in *being*]; i.e. in virtue of
referring to something.

That is, the thought or statement involving the not-being of motion; i.e.
'motion is not-rest', involves its not-being something else. It does not, in
other words, require the thought of something which is not at all [-motion].
For indeed, motion does partake in *being*. Presumably the worry is that the
assertion 'motion is not-rest' means that 'motion is identical to not-rest'
and therefore involves the thought of something 'that is not'. But it is
impossible to think nothing, and so on and so forth.

and (iii) 'Motion is *different* from *the same*'; hence motion is not
the same.

Without appealing to the alternative usages of the verb 'to be', it is argued
that in the same way that 'motion is different from the same' and hence
'motion is not-the same', so too is 'motion not-rest'.

but (iv) 'Motion *is the same as itself*' [by participating in
sameness]; i.e. refers to its *nature*.

Yet, motion is the same with respect to its own nature. In other words, the
assertion 'motion is the same' and the assertion 'motion is not the same'
are both meaningful [and true], yet apparently contradictory. However,
sameness obviously does not assume the same function for both assertions
as the explanatory notes clarify. In the first case, 'motion is not the same'
because the *form* motion is different from the *form* sameness [i.e. motion
and sameness are two distinct *forms* not one]; yet, in the second case,
'motion is the same' because it can be understood to partake in *sameness*.

Hence, (v) 'Motion is *the same* [as itself] and *not the same*' [by
participating in *difference*].

The apparently contradictory statement 'motion is both the same
and not the same' is clarified by appealing to the alternative usages of the

name *same*, which it is forthwith argued for *difference* and all other forms. Hence the explanation can not be derived from the ambiguity of the use of the name *the same*, but from the ambiguity of *how* some name is used.[16] Namely, given that the forms, *being, sameness* and *difference* are all-pervading, all names are something which can be understood in two different, and yet reliable ways. The ambiguity is therefore with *how* the name retains its meaningfulness for a particular statement. For that which divulged the ulterior usages were the statements in which the name 'motion' appeared (compare (ii) with (v)). Implication,

> (vi) if Motion participates in Rest it would not be outrageous *to speak* of it as *stationary*; though, *in fact*, Motion does not participate in Rest *at least so long as the argument on nature is accepted as true* [(i) again the nature of forms determines its logical behaviour].

and (vii) the same in turn for how motion stands in relation to *difference*. Concluding,

> therefore (viii) it must be possible for that which 'is not—different from existence—to be for all forms, since all of these are by partaking in difference, *not being*. So that for every form there is much that it *is* and an indefinite number of things which it *is not*'.

The chain of argumentation begins with admitting the contradictoriness of motion and rest, and yet concludes by saying that even though nothing truthfully can be said of the one that can be said of the other, it makes *sense* to *speak or think* of motion as stationary. It is just false. The true is now distinguished from the meaningful. All these statements make sense to the reader; yet they do not all say the same thing, hence nor are they all true for the same reason. The upshot is that the understanding that 'something is not-something else' does not involve thinking of not-being as such, but rather, it involves thinking of something which is-not or is-other than something else. Notice, however that the example used to illustrate the point was an affirmative predicative statement, but that this was employed to explain the meaningfulness of a thought expressed by some phrase prefixed by 'not'. Compare the examples 'Motion is Rest' and 'Motion is the same and not the same'. The second suggests an apparent contradiction which is explained to be the result of thinking of the expression 'the same' in the same way in both instances. Two things are going on simultaneously here: Plato demonstrates that all forms are both *what they are in virtue of their own nature* as well as *different from an indefinite number of other forms*. Moreover, an important semantic contradiction is being eliminated via the explication of the alternative ways that something can be thought of as *being*. The generalised point is that for any affirmative expression it is meaningful in virtue of its own *nature*, whereas negative expressions are meaningful only with reference to everything else. In coming clean on what has been accomplished here the Stranger says 'when we speak of 'what is-not', it seems that we do not mean something contrary to what *is* but only something that is different' (257b).

What have we learned from the mixing of these Great Kinds? We have learned that it is possible to talk about some one thing without jeopardising *what that thing is*, when we take on board the way that things in the world *relate* to each other either in virtue of their difference. The point is that, difference is not actually *part* of the thing in question. Rather it is a feature of its context (*relative* to other things). We would not, therefore, expect what the thing is in itself to be inhibited. This is what comes from the distinction drawn between the nature of something in itself and difference. The first concerns *what* the thing is, the latter *how* it is (in relation to other things). There is no ontological commitment in the case of the latter, and it is for this reason that *what* the thing named is (and consequently, how it is thought) is uninhibited.

Exegesis of the Solution

The solution to the puzzle on not-being has been explained by the introduction of three distinct all-pervasive forms (motion and rest are employed only to apply the Great Kinds). Each of these forms—*being, sameness* or *difference*—do not, as it were, actually denote or have any object in the world to which they apply in the same way that a proper name has. All three are, in fact, applicable and consequently meaningful, as a logically prevalent semantic imposition on a *name* as such. That which is not, is therefore, only different; so that the meaning of 'not-tall' would be 'what is equal', 'what is short'. By extension, for statements prefixed by the word 'not' the meaning would be 'something different from the words that follow, or rather from the things designated by the words pronounced after the negative (257b-c3).'

Knowledge finds its way to the foreground once again, and the Stranger argues that in the same way that knowledge is parcelled out over many distinct areas of specialisation, so too is *Difference*. In turn each area marked off from the other is assigned a different *name*. So in the case of the *Beautiful* the nature of *difference* is here parcelled off into the *Not-Beautiful* where the meaning is *the different from the nature of the beautiful*. Inserting the previously provided function of a name in the case of *difference* versus *sameness*; it is the nature of *difference* [like *being* and *sameness*] that it becomes meaningful when applied. When something becomes meaningful in terms of partaking in *difference* it is 'what it is' *with reference to something else*. The *Not-Beautiful* is meaningful with reference to the *Beautiful*. The *Not-Beautiful* is, therefore, any indefinite number of things that is different from the *nature* of the *Beautiful*. The *Not-Beautiful* is 'what it is' in virtue of being set up against 'something' that *is* in virtue of being itself [or the set of definite things compatible with its *nature*], and in turn *also is something* [by partaking in *being*] *just* because it *is not-the-thing in question*. The not-beautiful, the not-just, the not-tall and so on *are equally something* as the beautiful, the just, and the tall. Two obvious implications follow: firstly, the thinking of 'what is not' does not involve thinking of no-thing whatsoever, hence nothing, an empty, or non-thought. Secondly, the truth of a statement [or name] prefixed by 'not' is determined by all the indefinite number or instances of things [or concepts] which are *different* from the nature of the name or series of words affixed to the 'not'. For example, 'Socrates is not-tall' is true so long as 'not-tall' can be substituted by one of the range of names which are *different* from 'not-tall', like 'short', such that Socrates is a member of things so-called (258a-d). Still this leaves both the complexity of the thinking process involved, as well as the corresponding semantic unity and the meaningfulness of a name in the context of its sentential contribution to the sentence as a whole, out of the picture. This would be taken up from 259d regarding the impossibility of discourse—language—without the weaving of forms. That is, this argument would seem to satisfactorily explain the ontological status of a name prefixed by 'not' so as to avoid the problem of not-being and the semantic emptiness of such expressions. However, the argument which is in the process of development supports the view that names are not meaningful in isolation; that the sentential contribution of a name determines its meaning, and that the function of a name may not, depending upon its meaningful contribution to the overall meaning of the sentence entailing it, be purely referential. Names have been uncovered to be semantically complex, and therefore legitimately cognitively assessable in terms of varying senses, so to speak. Finally, the logical behaviour of a name, whether thought of in virtue of itself or difference, will determine the actual meaningful contribution and function of a name for the sentence entailing it. When a naming expression is prefixed by 'not', the logical function of the name and therefore meaning is determined with reference to *difference*; otherwise the logical function of a naming expression and meaning is defined in terms of its own *nature*. In turn, the logical function of a name will also provide a determinate set of truth conditions for the sentence as a whole entailing it. This will become clearer following the discussion of the specific role of *onomata* and *rhemata* for a statement.

Catching the Sophist

Catching the sophist is again paralleled with the overthrow of the Parmenidean Challenge. The Stranger has demonstrated that 'what is not' does not involve the contrary of 'what is', but something that equally is in virtue of being different from what the name to which it is prefixed is in virtue of its own nature. We have therefore trespassed far beyond the prohibitions of Parmenides who warned that 'never shall it be proved that the things that are not are' (258d). This is not however achieved by succumbing to the tactics of sophistry which are in the finale no different from the beliefs acclaimed by the common man who, backward turning, also presumes that 'what is not also is'. For the Stranger argues, in the splendour we have been accustomed to hear Socrates speak, that whoever wishes to challenge the results of the present debate should do so not by reducing the arguments to a tug of war, presumably by concocting out of these a contradiction. The theatrics of sophistry no longer pose a threat to the truth-inciting discourse of dialectics for we are no longer forced to fold under the duress of those arguments that spoke of things and their contraries as equally viable.

The ill-fated lovers of phantasms are now obliged to speak with the kind of precision that makes language possible: both the exact *sense* and *respect* in which a name or term is used must be clarified. The fallacy of equivocation was, of course, rampantly put to work by sophistic rhetors and the case of *being* was no exception. The argumentative method of speech adopted by the sophist would therefore appear to have been slightly restrained, for he is now obliged to account for his application of names in speech. Just as the relativism of sophistry may be the offspring of 'a too recent contact with reality' (259d6),[17] the Stranger also speaks out against those who, now on a semantic level, would separate everything off from everything else, thus undermining the possibility of language.

That which makes discourse possible is the weaving of forms, but that which remains unexplained is how thinking can actually entertain what is not in terms of falsehood. For though more generally the Parmenidean challenge regarding *not-being* applies also to the case of falsehood, it is still unclear how exactly referring to the same thing by alternative names in the case of predication applies to thinking of one thing as something else which is not actually being thought of. Nonetheless it is clear that the Stranger considers that significant headway has been made, and that faced with compromising argument confirming the existence of *not-being*, the sophist would have to give way to the possibility of deception, images and phantasms (260c-d). Though, diverting the focus of the debate away from the ontological status of the objects of thought and returning its focus to the propositional expression of thought entailing these, the Stranger argues that the sophist notwithstanding may maintain that still *not-being* cannot be entertained by thought or speech (260d-261). The insistence on the weaving of forms is the result of the previous stretch of arguments on the Great Kinds, and as specified in the passage outlining its agenda, meaningful propositional expressions may be general or particular, but they must always include at least one form or common term that would *connect* the content of speech. For again, where this is impossible Parmenidean monism remains the only alternative, and speech without predication can admit only that 'it is'[18] which would reduce language to a game of indexical discourse, so to speak. This observation underscores exactly the point of the subsidiary reply to the Great Kinds, namely that irrespective of whether, in fact, it can be proved that 'what is not' *is*, the present debate is after its accessibility to thought and speech. The separation of the ontological from the semantic not only reminds us that 'what is not' may be meaningful in terms of *difference* and that because it partakes in something else which has referential capacity; but it also calls attention to the complexity of thought and speech. That is, a propositional claim which entails both a singular terms and always at least one form, suggests that there is a significant *logical relation* in virtue of which any such claim becomes meaningful. In other words it is how each subsentential part of a statement contributes to the complex assertion that makes it meaningful. Is there any account of *not-being* therefore, which carries obvious non-existential import, that can explain how its subsentential contribution can meaningfully claim anything about anything else? And does this necessarily commit Plato to a through and through referential appreciation of language as Stough argues[19] or is he offering an alternative way in which a name may contribute to the meaning of a statement without referring?

The actual formulation of false thinking in terms of *difference* is absent until 264d, but since predication and falsehood are afflicted by the selfsame problem regarding the ability to think 'what is-not', we should expect false thinking to be similarly described as predication—the ability to apply more than just one name to a singular thing. This, it has already been shown, depends on the recognition of at least one form entailed by any propositional claim. We should be looking for arguments in the sequel that will be able to explain how the contribution of forms to the meaning of a statement as a whole can solve the problem of falsehood in thought and speech.

Onomata and Rhemata: A Pertinent Syntactical Distinction

Embarking on the final inquiry on the ability to think or speak 'what is not', the Stranger recommends that they proceed as they had earlier with the Great Kinds asking about the manner in which words blend for statements. The opening thesis statement clearly suggests that the matter of blending in the case of a statement is a question of how words stand together when spoken in succession. Presumably the point is that 'Socrates beautiful' are two words spoken in succession but this doesn't mean anything because nothing is being *said*. Yet, 'Socrates is beautiful' is a statement where 'Socrates' is the subject-name about which the statement is saying something, and 'is beautiful' is the predicate-name which says something about it. Clarifying for a slightly confused Theaetetus, the Stranger specifically says that the two kinds of signs in speech to signify *being* have distinct functions: *onomata* are names which are given to the things that *perform actions* (262b11), whereas *rhemata* are terms *signifying the action performed* (262b7). In the examples provided the role of *onomata* would be to refer or stand in for the subject of a statement, whereas the role of the *rhemata* would be to actually *state something* (262d-e) rather than simply *naming* something as it were. Something gets said in terms of providing information about facts or events in the present, past or future (262d1-4). However neither do *onomata* or proper names nor *rhemata* independently signify either the nature of something that exists or does not exist or action performed or not performed respectively (262c1-4). For any *use* of a name to be meaningful it must contribute to the stating of something, so that it is in saying something that it becomes meaningful, and not necessarily in referring to something. For after all, proper names do independently refer to or denote the objects which they name, yet the stranger denies this. Apart from the explicit and recurring reference to the complexity of thought and speech which argues that a statement, in fact, thought (263e4-6) requires both a proper name and predicate name, it is clear that Plato is breaking away from more than just the word-object correspondence theory of Parmenides, but his argument on *forms* has introduced a more sophisticated theory of meaning.

Two conditions are propounded: (1) every statement *as a whole* is either true or false, and (2) one subsentential element of a complex statement must be about some-thing to which the expressed thought corresponds. At least one element would function as a proper name to stand in for the object which the statement is about. A false statement is not going to be about a non-existent thing therefore, since (2) applies to (1) which is inclusive of both true and false statements. In the examples provided 'Theaetetus' is the name employed to denote Theaetetus the man in both the true statement 'Theaetetus sits', and the false statement 'Theaetetus flies'. If for the name 'Theaetetus', and for any subject name of a complex statement, there is a man to which this name corresponds it would follow that the truth of the statement will be expected to comply to what names can actually be used to describe Theaetetus. But what exactly will make this statement meaningful irrespective of its truth-value? We should at this point be careful not to disregard that the debate is hinging not on truth but on the meaningfulness of thinking as such. We should be concerned therefore with whether the meaningful contribution of a predicate name to the statement as a whole requires that there is something to which it corresponds that the speaker recognises?

The above would seem to imply that a truth consists in the correspondence of the statement with the 'things that are' or 'facts'. This would lend itself to the popular view here under attack, that 'Theaetetus sits' is about the corresponding object Theaetetus, and that the fact 'sits' is being asserted of him, such that the statement 'Theaetetus sits' would reflect the existing fact, Theaetetus sitting as a complex object of perception. Such a view is riding on the assumption that each word *stands for* one element in the complex fact, so that the statement as a whole is complex and its structure corresponds to the structure of the fact. The failure of this line of argument simultaneously dismisses the 'hit and miss' approach: i.e. substituting 'stands' for 'sits' in our example, it could not be argued that 'stands' is not a non-existent fact, but only 'different from the existing fact' yet nonetheless existent. This too fails, as the 'Theaetetus is flying' successfully spells out, because Theaetetus could never fly. In other words, the meaningfulness of *this* statement would nonetheless have nothing to refer or correspond to. Hence, a false statement is not going to be a true statement about a 'different fact'. This can not successfully explain falsehood to the sophist since there will never be an existing complex fact in the world to which a false statement can correspond, and the puzzles on the nothingness or emptiness of false assertions resume.[20]

The Stranger provides us with a hint as to how he plans to resolve the problem of thinking 'what is not' in the case that what is being thought is false without that involving the impossible thought of a non-existent thing, event, fact or state of affairs. The very brief interlude sandwiched (263d5-264c) between the discussion of truth and falsehood explicates that the mechanism involved when thinking such that something gets *said* is *judgement*. Thinking has on very many occasions, and in dialogues other than this one, been described as 'silently talking to oneself' such as to resemble discourse but of covert kind. Just as statements are the outward expression of propositional claims, so too are judgements the conclusions of an inward expression of propositional claims (*Tht* 189e8-190a5). This seems important because the conclusion is summarised to show that even were it assumed that the mind is furnished with *things* to think about by sense perception, judgement involves asserting or denying the content of that thought as its conclusion or statement. As the syntactical arrangement of words in mere succession already intimated earlier, that which makes a statement meaningful is not the name which denotes the subject of thought, nor yet the verb which states something about it, rather it is the content of the claim being made which ties or weaves these two together.[21] Plato is not willing to suspend the referential function of the proper name,[22] and so he must, if this argument is true, have something to say about the function and contribution of the predicate name to the statement as a whole which would not compromise the obvious non-referential capacity of a false assertion. It is important that the Stranger has successfully managed to distinguish, albeit implicitly, that a statement is defined independently from its actual truth-value, namely in virtue of fulfilling (1) and (2). Hence a statement becomes meaningful only with respect to successfully specifying a subject, and saying something about it, and this is different from then saying something about that statement, namely whether it is true or false. Determining the actual truth-value of a statement, we have already noted, will depend not on specifying the subject, but rather on what gets said about it, i.e. the predicate name.

Resuming the problem of false thinking or judging proper, the Stranger must recall the argument on the weaving of forms, which, it has been argued on another occasion, is that upon which discourse depends (259e). At least one form enters into the meaning of any statement or judgement. Forms, it has been argued above, have two alternative ways of functioning. Forms can either specify a member or members of a particular class of things much like a proper name; or they can speak about something in virtue of its difference with respect to something else. The statement 'Theaetetus sits' like the other 'Theaetetus flies' both take Theaetetus the man as the specified subject, but differ with respect to what each is stating *about* Theaetetus. We can say about what the statement says—as opposed to what gets said by the statement—that the first is true and the second is false—this is what the Stranger refers to as the *character* of a statement. The first is true because it says of 'Theaetetus sitting' *that* he is sitting; whereas the second is false because it says of 'Theaetetus sitting' *that* he flies, or something different (263a-c). We can further say that the second, like the first, does state or say something and in this case, it is meaningful because the form or general term attached to the naming subject 'flies' *exists* even though it is different from the things that exist in the case of Theaetetus (263b15-17). Conditions (1) and (2) make it clear that each subsentential expression or name must itself be meaningful, though incomplete, if it is going to meaningfully contribute to the statement entailed by it. Further, an *onoma* functions in a statement to specify the subject of thought, and is therefore referentially meaningful, whereas the *rhema* functions for the overall meaning of a statement by saying *something* about it, and is therefore non-referentially meaningful for the sentence as a whole. The point is that a form can denote objects that can truthfully be called by its name and it is in virtue of having such objects that it also is *something*, recall 'false statements state about you *things different* from the things that are [hence things that are not as being] but things that exist [nonetheless], [only] different from things that exist in your case' (263b10-c).

The secret to understanding this argument is to recall that all statements must be meaningful in the same way, so we should find only one theory developed to explain predication irrespective of whether the naming expressions involved are affirmative or negative. Again recall that *onomata* function like proper names in that they refer the mind to the object of thought [i.e. *what* the thought is about]; whereas *rhemata* say something *about* the object without themselves *being what* that object *is*. In the section The Solution Applied to Statements, which was on the function of *forms*, demonstrated that universal naming expressions, usually the kind plugged into the predicate place of a statement, are meaningful in virtue of their own *nature*. Naming expressions, however, acquire meaning within the *context* of their use. This is the view that the meaning of a name can not be determined in isolation. The brief interlude on judgement made the point that, in fact, judgement [or more accurately the judgeable content of a statement] precedes the analysis of concepts, and consequently, to ascertain the *actual content of any assertion—that which gets said*—first the *logical*, not ontological as such, contribution of each subsentential expression must be laid bare. In other words, the use or function of a naming expression will depend upon its logical behaviour for that particular thought or statement. The logical behaviour of a name was, once more, defined with respect to how it was related to the *onoma* or proper name of the statement entailing it, where the function of a proper name is to specify the sentential subject. In the case that the predicate name was prefixed by 'not' the logical contribution of the predicate name would be defined in terms of *difference* or otherwise in terms of *sameness*. So for the affirmative, yet false, assertion 'Theaetetus flies', this is meaningful because independent of *what the statement actually says*—this determines only its truth-value—each of the subsentential elements successfully contribute to the sentence as a whole so that *something in fact gets said*.

Falsehood has already been set down as involving the logical form 'what is-not', and all that has been said thus far has been directed toward explaining precisely the possibility of entertaining something intermingled with *not-being*. *Not-being* has been shown to be meaningful for thought and speech—i.e. a statement is only the overt expression of silently thinking to oneself—with reference to *difference*. False thinking is therefore described as a combination of *onoma* and *rhema* stating about its subject 'what is different *as* the same or what is not *as* what is'. This is a straightforward cross reference to the *Theaetetus* and the *Allodoxia* or Model of Misjudgement. There the model breaks down because Socrates could not explain how something, *x*, could be taken for something else, or thought of *as* something else without that compromising the confidence of the thinking subject that he really was thinking of *x* (see *Chapter Three: Theaetetus On False Belief*, p. 55); nor yet how it is possible to truthfully think of *x* as *y* or *F* when *x* and *y* or *F* are not the same, or when *x* just is not *y* or *F* (see *Chapter Three: Theaetetus and False Belief*, p. 57). The argument of *Allodoxia* here becomes complete: false thinking involves making a judgement 'Theaetetus flies' which does not square with the facts because Theaetetus is neither flying now, nor at any other time did he fly. This thought therefore entails thinking about Theaetetus in terms of things different from the things that are. The predicate name, here a *form*, is meaningful therefore with reference to being different from the *form* 'sits' or not what it means for something to sit. The predicate name, though it does not correspond to the facts, would not be an empty name, and therefore we are no longer faced with the sophistic objection that this is a non-statement because it does not *state anything*. The *form* 'flies' is now meaningful, and consequently it can also meaningfully contribute to the meaning of the sentence in which it appears as a whole irrespective of the truth-value its determinate conditions for the statement render. The name 'flies' is, like any affirmative expression, used in virtue of its own *nature* and it would thereby have meaning for the thinking subject who was acquainted with numerical objects called by that name.

The Sophist Caught

Going all the way back to the division of kinds or the art of angling, the stranger asks us to recall that the essential ingredient of sophistry was *image-making* which was in turn broken down into two, *making likenesses* and *making semblances*. The problem which halted further elaboration was the *not-being* of appearances and false statements. Now equipped with the above arguments on *not-being* and falsehood specifically, the *image-making* of the sophists should by the same token be explainable. That part of sophistry which denies the possibility of falsehood has already been explained; yet the Stranger labours extensively over trying to account for the metaphysical status of the appearances 'without really being' rendered by him. Appearances are the kinds of images which the sophist creates in the minds of his listeners much in the same way that a sculptor might deliberately contort the shape of his [original] subject to inspire a particular mood or image in his beholders. Thinking back to the *Theaetetus*, appearances were troublesome because of the epistemological claim underscoring its relevance; namely that *because* knowledge is derived from sense-perception, *whatever* is perceived for any individual, in fact, *is*—with that compromising addition, *at least for that individual*. And from there, the problem concerning whether any belief entertained in the mind of a percipient could really ever be of the object in question followed. By the end of the *Sophist* this difficulty can successfully be met with reference to the semantic theory of meaning in the same way that falsehood was accommodated. The consequence of this reply is that even, to take Cornford's example, 'when 'it appears to me' that a distant figure is a friend, that judgement may be true, and, if it is false, there is nothing wrong with the object: the falsity lies wholly in my *judgement*'.[23] The Stranger's interest in *appearances* must consequently be of a different kind. What is the philosophically pertinent problem which the Stranger feels persists with respect to *not-being*? The clue is to follow the Stranger's directives and pick up where the art of angling left off.

> The truth is my friend, that we are faced with an extremely difficult question. This *appearing* or *seeming* without really *being* and the saying of something which yet is not true—all these expressions have always been and *still* are deeply involved in perplexity. It is extremely hard, Theaetetus, to find correct terms in which one may say or think that falsehoods have a real existence, without being caught in contradiction by the mere utterance of such words (236e-237a3).

Coming full circle, when these remarks opening the debate on the problem of falsehood are matched with the respective remarks closing the same debate, it becomes evident that the Stranger is sweating over the actual status of 'that appearance of the man which seemed to be my friend, but who was not'. This presents a difficulty not immediately appreciable partly because the presumably analogous examples from the world are deceptively simple to solve. The painting of the *actual* man is not *the man*, *it is* an *image of the man*; in effect, it is a painting. This is a disappointing platitude; it is uninformative since nothing that we did not already know in calling this image a 'painting' has been disclosed. The issue draws from the same deceptiveness involving the metaphysical world in which sense-data or impressions lie. Empiricists often admit that because belief/knowledge is derived, either exclusively are ultimately, from sense-perception, and because the senses mediate to the mind sensations from experiencing the world, one is never immediately in touch with the experienced objects of the world, only with impressions of these. What is the metaphysical domain in which these impressions lie? Indeed, it may be that these are of or derived from *real* objects, but what does that make *impressions themselves*?[24] Real or unreal, yet existent? Of course, impressions are not nothing; but, in being something, they are not also *really real*. This topic is not exclusively a problem for catching the sophist, rather it will be a problem for any theory which fosters some notion about the *mind's eye* or the distinction between opinion and knowledge or true and false belief. The exact arguments presented need not be delivered here, it suffices to say that the Stranger does not provide an answer to this puzzle, and it need not trouble us any further in the specified objective of our inquiry.

Conclusion

The answer to the puzzle on falsehood is surprisingly obvious. People have been saying this for centuries (Aristotle *De Intepretatione*). It is obvious that sentences assert or make judgements and this is certainly different from naming. You would expect a word functioning as a name to indeed pick out some object for thought and for its name to in turn stand in for it when used in a sentence. But it was the semantic atomism stemming from Parmenides that suggested that all words function in this way. Consequently nothing would ever get asserted or no judgement made, since in effect what we would end up with is a string of words naming their objects, as in 'John tall'. The usage of the verb 'to be' is therefore not the culprit that Plato identifies. Surely a revised understanding would include an alternative usage of the verb, but this, as it has been argued, is not *how* the puzzle is solved. Once it is clear that language works in this way it seems a fairly easy process to figure out what statements do and how they become meaningful. Statements are meaningful not in virtue of the truth which they reflect about the world. In the *Theaetetus* there is a passage which significantly argues that *thinking/inquiring* and *stating/judging* are not the same because the second pair makes a claim to truth whereas the first, in being reflective alone, does not, though nonetheless meaningful. This, of course, does not mean that statements are *only* meaningful when they are true; rather, statements like thinking can be meaningful even when they fail to say what is true. Statements that are false would be meaningful in the same way that thoughts are meaningful which are not about the true; namely in virtue of what gets *said*.

Still the problem for Parmenides and Plato really began as an epistemological puzzle regarding the metaphysics of thought. When thoughts are entertained surely they must be of something. The alternative was no-thing which is a non-thought. This some-thing for thought created a series of difficulties. To think of some-thing it makes sense that what is thought is *that* thing and *nothing else whatsoever*. Complex objects and naming became a problem because it was not obvious how some-one-thing could be thought of with a sum of *distinguishable*, hence *nameable*, aggregate parts in this way. All words *name* as it were. Consequently, any thought which, in whatever form, involves *thinking what is-not* would be impossible since that would imply the thinking of some-thing which is not there to be named. Plato needed a philosophy to explain how words can be thought meaningfully without *naming*, therefore. This is what he provides us with. Once he says that we must embrace the assumptions which make the very activity we are engaging in possible, namely complex thought, he is able to stop the vicious circle which encourages scepticism (i.e. we need a starting point which can be taken as true since without this there is no point of fixity from which to erect any thoughtful discussion on any topic) and ask the right questions. Instead of asking what thoughts are of, he can now ask, what makes thoughts meaningful.

The solution is successful. Falsehood is possible because we have now dispensed with the required assumption that something must be thought *as* itself; and that all words name. The function of a word is going to be determined by how it contributes to the meaning of the sentence or by what is getting said. What the sentence is of will be expected to *name* and hence stand in for an object; and what gets said *about* it will be affirmed for it. The truth conditions are clear: an assertion is true when the thing named on the right hand side of the verb is a member of the things that the words on the left hand side of the verb—the predicate word—signify. It is meaningful when the speaker successfully communicates a thought. Truth and meaning have therefore been successfully divorced. That is, a statement is meaningful when the statement 'Theaetetus flies' successfully *relates* that the man Theaetetus belongs to the category of things that *fly*; so too for the statement 'Socrates is a sophist'. In effect, it could be argued that verbs acquire meaning in virtue of both the objects of which they are true and the objects of which they are not true. To think a false thought would be to think 'Socrates is really a woman' because the statement does not correspond to the facts; it is nonetheless meaningful because what it asserts or claims is clearly: Socrates refers to an object which is a member of things that the verb phrase 'really a woman' would be true of. We no longer have the problem of the so-called non-thought scenario because neither are statements as a whole expected to name their facts, nor are all words that make up a statement expected to always name the object(s) that they refer to. Thoughts relate or communicate thoughts. A truism, yes; enlightening nonetheless because it makes clear the obvious point that thoughts need *only* make an assertion in order to be meaningful. But that is just what we mean by 'thinking' , 'reflecting', 'contemplating' or indeed 'inquiring'.

Notes

[1] Though certainly the various usages of the verb 'to be' is not a negligible point, to suggest that Plato intended to solve the problem of falsehood, which was introduced as a special problem of *not-being*, by demonstrating a misconstrued application of this *verb* (identity as opposed to predicative) does not correspond to *how* the problem was developed. Hence, though by implication a different usage of the verb 'to be' must be in play for the solution, it does not also follow that this *is* the solution. In fact, construing and clarifying these different uses simply can not explain *predication*. That is, it can not explain how things can be understood to combine such that it corresponds to how things are in fact without that thing

ceasing to be *what it is*; nor still how things can be understood to combine such that it does NOT correspond to how things are without that thing ceasing to be *what it is*. Whether anyone wants to admit that Parmenides is centrally important to the dialogue is a matter of argument; but that this is the overall ambition of the dialogue is an undeniable fact.

[2] This is a rather popular point of view supported by Frede (though he argues that the *is of predication* distinguished from the *is of identity* is not the 'ordinary' copulative predicative *not-being*) in his *Pradication und Existenzaussage* (1967), Owen in his 'Plato on Not-Being', in Plato, I, ed. G. Vlastos (1972), as well as, Ackrill (1957) ' Plato and the Copula: *Sophist* 251-9', *JHS* 77.

[3] See R.W. Jordan (1984) 'Plato's Task in the *Sophist*' *Classical Quarterly 34*, pp. 113-129; esp. p. 122: 'Plato regards the accomplishment of his task as a refutation of Parmenides' criticisms of the route of enquiry embraced by the two-headed mortals. We must ask, I believe, just what point we would expect such a refutation to bring out. In fact, Parmenides' criticism of mortals does not lie at the core of his metaphysics. Parmenides in his poem raises difficulties both about the unintelligibility of "notbeing" (there is nothing to refer to) and also about the compresence of being with notbeing. But Parmenides' position rests on the first of these two claims, the one about the unintelligibility of "notbeing". Plato, like Parmenides, raises both difficulties. But Plato, unlike Parmenides, is primarily interested in the second of the two problems—that is, in the compresence of being with notbeing, and *not* in the unintelligibility of notbeing.'

[4] ibid. Jordan frames the problem solely in terms of the compresence of being and notbeing and consequently Plato's problem is understood solely in terms of combination which involves, as he says, showing why it is not that being (a cat) is not *opposed* [hence contradictory] to notbeing (an image, or an image of a cat), p. 124. This analysis plays on the distinctiveness between *opposition* and *negation* or *non-identity* and is therefore an argument which sees the resolution of the problem in terms of two senses of the prefixed word 'not'.

[5] This is neatly confirmed by the derogatory reference to the later learners who could not tolerate calling the same thing by different names precisely because *all naming expressions functioned in the same way*; transparently referential.

[6] This corresponds to the historical puzzle, as Frede calls it, which he takes to involve understanding a statement (*Tht* 202a6-8) or name (*Soph.* 251a5*ff*) as naming something only when it names the object of itself. Or in Frede's own words, 'each object should be addressed by its own name and not by a name of something else, so that we should not call, for example, an object "white", since "white" is the name of a colour and an object is not a colour'. Stough also acknowledges this as the problematic model of naming adopted by the late learners which holds that 'a Form cannot be called by the name of anything else other than itself'. See Frede 'The *Sophist* on False Statements' in R Kraut (ed.) (1992) *The*

Cambridge Companion to Plato, esp. p. 414; and C. Stough (1990) 'Two Kinds of Naming in the *Sophist*', *Canadian Journal of Philosophy*, Vol. 20, No.3, esp. 360.

[7] In Cornford's (1957) *Plato's Theory of Knowledge: The Theaetetus and the Sophist*. Cornford argues against the view—e.g. Taylor (*Plato* 1926)—which supports that this passage concerns *logic* since the science of dialectics which is being pursued is not interested in the formal symbolic patterns of reasoning (esp. p. 265), but rather with the rules for the correct procedure of Collection and Division with respect to Forms. Specifically, 'Dialectic is not Formal Logic, but the study of the structure of reality—in fact Ontology, for the Forms are the realities.' p. 266.

[8] Ibid, p. 277; Cornford agrees, adding that the analysis of the nature of being, sameness and difference reveals the senses of the words 'is' and 'is not'. Motion and Rest are employed as examples only because they are contraries, hence with the relation of incompatibility, and because (as the Stranger says) we have been discussing them, and for no ulterior reason. I am in complete agreement with Cornford on this matter.

[9] Ibid. Cornford, of course, sees the solution to the problem of *not-being*—as a case of thinking 'something different from the actual facts'—as involving the understanding that a statement requires the use of at least one Form which provides the meaning of the name(s) being employed in a given statement, see esp. pp. 299-301.

[10] In her article 'Two Kinds of naming in the *Sophist*', C Stough also argues that 'The nature of a Form explains its behaviour in relation to other Forms in the manner in which the meaning of a concept accounts for the way it functions in discourse', p. 356.

[11] op. cit., p. 280; Denyer, p. 129-130 where he argues that the perplexity of this passage can be attributed to Plato's ambition to explain two separate things at the same time. The first to explain negation by 'the other'; and the second, to clear up the ambiguity of identity and predication. Denyer argues that the latter is not explained by reference to two distinct usages of the verb 'to be', but rather by sentential analysis regarding the naming expressions before and after the 'is'. esp. pp. 134-137.

[12] Of course this was motivated by an interest to show how it is possible to objectively judge that something is the case without coming up against the relativism of application. That is, even for the more obviously relative concepts, like tallness, Plato wanted to show that in order for the name 'tallness' to be meaningfully operable in a sentence, in must have some logically prior meaning for thought.

[13] Examples of forms would render the same results. In the statement 'motion is circular' circular is not what it *means* to be motion, nor the converse; though, if it is true, we would expect all things that belong to the class of circularity, to also belong to the class of motion. Though, of course, all things in motion will not also

be in circular motion. Since these two expression or names do not mean the same thing according to (a) they will not also necessarily be co-referential. Only co-meaning names will also necessarily be co-referential.

[14] I find it irresistible not to quote the words found in *The History of Philosophy* regarding Frege, 'Clearly, if we are to respect the semantic unity of judgeable contents, the logically relevant contributions made by the different sorts of subsentential expressions out of which the sentences of our language are composed must be so characterised that it is clear from *their very nature* how they relate with each other in such a way as to issue in determinate truth conditions. The point here is, of course, that sentences are made up of various words that contribute differently to the meaning of the assertion, and that the value of any sentence (the true and the false) follows from the *nature* of subsentential expressions which determine the logical relatedness of each term.

[15] I am not presenting a philological analysis of the ancient Greek texts for the consideration of this very dense passage. I am relying on the generally accepted translation by Cornford, in *Plato: Collected Dialogues*, ed. E. Hamilton and H. Cairns.

[16] N. Denyer argues in his book (1991) *Language, Thought and Falsehood in Ancient Greek Philosophy* that the intended solution to the problem involves drawing a distinction between predication and identity by clearing up the ambiguity of the name 'the same'. That this is accomplished by tidying up the expressions that appear on either side of the 'is'. Specifically, that for Plato the difference between predication and identification is just a matter of the expression on the right side of the 'is'. Specifically, that the expression on the right of the 'is' for predication is a general term that applies indifferently to a class of things, whereas for identity the expression is a proper name, pp. 134-137.

[17] I take it that the argument raised against the sophist regarding his use of blatant contradiction and its stemming from 'a too recent contact with reality' to hinge upon the fact that the sophists are empiricists, and consequently they literally describe the array of things and the circumstances in which they are found as they appear at any particular time (so that at one time a man appears short [beside an elephant] and tall [beside a rat] by taking them out of context to say only that 'man is short and tall'.

[18] 'It is' translates *esti* which more accurately grasps the monistic picture which would easily suggest a purely indexical form of communication in the absence of discourse proper since in the Greek use of verbs the pronoun is admitted in its conjugation, and therefore there is no need to separate subject (it) from verb (is).

[19] Stough also argues in favour of two kinds of naming in the *Sophist* but she limits this claim to a purely referential interpretation. So that though the straight name-thing correspondence relation is suspended, no secondary function of a name is introduced. Namely, in both kinds of naming the function is purely referential. The

name₁ 'Motion', for instance, is the proper name for motion (stands in for the individual thing); but it is also the name₂ of any form that blends with motion. Hence in the second kind of naming, again individuals are picked out, but this time a class of individual forms defined by its members' combination with the form named₁. She adds 'Two terms may name the same thing without having the same meaning if one names it naturally [proper name] and another by participation.' Later in her analysis of the passage introducing an important syntactic distinction between *onomata* and *rhemata* again she argues that Plato's intention is only to show that a simple stringing together of various names can not by itself constitute a meaningful statement. That the point is only be make the purely syntactic point that for a complex linguistic statement to be successful in stating something must satisfy certain syntactic conditions, otherwise it is *just* a string of words with no larger function beyond that of naming it components. Surely, however not only does Plato introduce two distinct words—*onoma* and *rhema*—instead of saying one word, *esti*, can be used in each of the distinct ways [see Vlastos, 'The Unity of Virtues', reprinted in *Platonic Studies,* p. 238], but it would seem to ignore completely what this syntactic distinction involves. Namely, that a statement entails a naming of something so as to then go on and say something about it, and here the argument of syntax clearly points this out. Consequently, this lends itself to a two function interpretation of naming: the first a subject [phrase] which is the so-called object of thought, and the predicate or verb that says something about it without actually [as originally misconstrued] also standing in for some other objects or class of objects necessarily. See C. Stough (1990) 'Two Kinds of Naming in the *Sophist*', *Canadian Journal of Philosophy*, Vol. 20, No.3, p. 369.

[20] Cornford too adopts this line of argument in his (1957) *Plato's Theory of Knowledge: The Theaetetus and the Sophist*, p.311. He says, 'if we define true statement by the correspondence of its structure with the structure of an existing fact which it refers to, the Sophist will object that a false statement cannot be defined as corresponding to anything, because there are no non-existent facts for it to correspond with or refer to. A false statement, therefore, means nothing.' And he adds that, 'This involves a problem which modern logicians are still discussing. 'Charles I died on the scaffold' corresponds to the fact; 'Charles I dies in bed' and 'Charles I did not die on the scaffold' do not. If I judge or believe either of these statements, how can there be an 'objective falsehood' or 'negative fact' to provide an object for my belief?'

[21] The actual use of prepositions is not mentioned presumably because the problem with which Plato wanted to deal was the complexity of thought such that something gets said. In its most economic form, the Stranger reminds us, the subject-predicate form requires only some thing to which the assertion applies, and another name actually making a claim about it. Emphasis can successfully be given to the act of judgement, which is explicated immediately following, without involving the use

of prepositions.

[22] Clearly this flies in the face of any statement for which the subject name is non-existent, like in the Russell's' famous example, 'The Present King of France such and such', where there is no man who at the time of this assertion held the title and could be identified by the definite description 'The King of France' (there are, of course, proper names which are equally puzzling; e.g. Mickey Mouse).

[23] See F.M. Cornford (1957) *Plato's Theory of Knowledge: The Theaetetus and the Sophist of Plato* [my italics], p. 321.

[24] Recall *Theaetetus* 155a where Socrates asks Theaetetus to consider the *status of the appearances in us*. See Chapter Three—Knowledge as Perception in the *Theaetetus*, p. 25.

Conclusion

The *Meno, Theaetetus*, and the *Sophist* as well as the *Sophistic School* and *Parmenides* have been shown to be philosophically interwoven into a single puzzle on falsehood. The topic has been falsehood and each subsidiary puzzle, first on knowledge and then on language, had the same starting point, *what is not*. The topic of falsehood is genuinely important to Plato in order to resist the relativism of sophistic speech. Socrates had, of course, been tried, convicted and executed because he was unable to defend the *elenchus* from the grievances of those who had suffered the ill-effects of its exercise. The premise Socrates was unable to support was the constructivism of the elenctic objective since he was unable to say what knowledge is and how it might be attained once its need had become embarrassingly apparent to his interlocutors. Knowing not what knowledge is, the elenchus could do no more than show that what the interlocutor believed true is what another one of his beliefs would surely lead him to believe is false. Relativism seems the easy route out of despair. Were truth relative, the so-called contradictory beliefs need only be shown to belong to a different set of circumstances and time. Indeed, this may be the route transgressed by such men. Still that which remained philosophically significant was that Plato could meet the premise half way by demonstrating that false belief is possible, and thereby undermine the relativity of truth and show this route to be a flagrant escape. Given the possibility of falsehood the elenctic objective would have to be acknowledged; the interlocutor would be forced to surrender to contradiction and its implication, namely that he knows not what he believed he knew.

The possibility of falsehood would truly counter relativism; but the elenchus had an even deeper difficulty. Its conditions made it impossible for inquiry to proceed. In the *Meno* the *Meno Paradox* is developed as a problem for knowledge which is in turn picked up as a general problem for thought in the *Theaetetus* and *Sophist* afterwards. Knowledge can not be acquired via the elenchus because the availability constraint and doxastic constraint together placed knowledge outside of the interlocutors' reach. Still the paradox does not frustrate inquiry altogether as it is sometimes argued. Socrates trips up because in searching for the knowledge of x he makes it painfully clear that instances of x cannot legitimately produce knowledge since that would already beg the question since it would presume already that *xs* can be correctly identified. Were it the case that *x* was already known inquiry would be pointless; were it otherwise not known the elenchus could not produce knowledge. The paradox was threefold: (1) 'how, if you do not know what *x is*, will you look for it?, (2) what sort of thing among the things that you do not know will you set before yourself as the object of your search?, and (3) if you did chance upon it, how would you know that it was the thing that you did not know to begin with?' (*Meno* 80c). In turn Socrates argued that the paradox will be damaging only if inquiry is shown to be (4) incompatible with knowing *x* or (5) incompatible with not knowing *x*.

Belief either was arbitrary and therefore of no help to acquire knowledge, or else it presupposed knowledge in which case inquiry would be pointless. The attempts to respond to the puzzle set up by Meno introduced a serious misunderstanding regarding *thought itself* which was to takeover the debate and which would in turn introduce *'what is not'* in an incredibly puzzling manner. Thought must be full; it must be of some-thing; that thing in turn must be identifi*able*; hence, it must also be known. Falsehood is therefore impossible because to think of some-thing requires knowing it; hence there is no way to entertain a belief of the form *'x* is F' where F *belongs* to *y* instead, as a result of thinking *y* when mis-takingly you got hold of *x*. The knowledge of *x* would counter the possibility of ever getting the wrong thing in mind and attribute things that don't belong to it; and it would be impossible to get hold of the right object and then go on and think about it in terms of what does not belong to *it*. Knowledge is a hit or miss affair; either something is in mind and it is known completely or not all. Ignorance is here comparable to oblivion; or thinking *what is not*. All names, it follows, must represent *things* for thought to grab hold of and this implies a purely referential capacity for all naming expressions. *What is not* is no exception; to think *what is not* is impossible precisely because it does not *name* anything. In effect, it is a non-thought.

Parmenides sets the puzzle up in the appropriately perplexing way. Thought involves the assumption of semantic atomism. All *words* name objects in the world; and *names* can either name the things that they are of or else they are only a name of a name which is, in effect, no-thing. On the condition that thought must be full, an empty name would be meaningless. As a result language was rendered impotent to convey *thought* and the only thing that could be *uttered* without contradiction was *esti*. Thinking, of course, is necessarily complex—i.e. in its more economical form it requires attributing a property to an object—, like '*x* is *F*', but this involves thinking of first the object-*x* and then the object-*F* and claiming therefore that the one *is* the other. This would be a straight contradiction since it involves thinking of *x* in terms of *what it is not as itself*. The radical monism of Parmenides is intended as a challenge since it demonstrates *through* language that language is impossible because nothing can properly *get said*, if thought means to identify.

Thought does not *name* but it communicates reflections—either silently to oneself or to others aloud; and at once it is obvious that falsehood is possible because '*what is not*' does not mean to think of something that does not exist. Instead, *both what is and 'what is not'* acquire meaning in the same way. Words do not all function in the same way for thought; and their function always depends upon their use in a statement. Truth and meaning are distinguished. A statement can be true or false; but it is always meaningful irrespective so long as something gets asserted. Thoughts and inquiry are reflections which unlike statements and judgements do not intend to say the true; and these are meaningful because they convey ideas so to speak. Statements are true when the facts asserted correspond to what actually is the case for the world; however, a thought or statement is successfully meaningful when the relation of the words in the sentence is clear.

So what was all the fuss about? And how does this affect the *Meno Paradox*? Plato had a hard time with the puzzles on '*what is not*' because for him it was clear that having a thought of something required having an *object* as such in mind and hence the analogy of thought to reflections in water; this tacitly says that anything that is thought with its regard must also *belong* to it; i.e. the proprietary assumption. Knowledge defined as true belief plus an account was not a bad definition as such; but Plato could not really explain what an account could add to truth unless somehow the ulterior things asserted of it somehow involved what the thing in question *is itself*. In terms of language the only words that could legitimately be used to talk about some-thing would be the names of the bits of things which make it up; but a list of aggregate parts adds nothing to true belief. These bits tacitly condoned the semantic atomism troubling us since Parmenides, though the counter-argument used to refute it hinged on the parts comprising something not being sufficient to distinguish the knowledge of two distinct things made up of the same bits. Though semantics was not yet at issue, curiously an example from the alphabet was employed to illustrate the point; the same letters (bits) may make up the spelling of the words 'god' and 'dog' but the arrangement is different. In this way, like in the *Allodoxia Model*, some-one-thing may have alternative names and because this would be suggestive of a non-referential capacity for a naming expression which would be rendered impossible on Parmenidean grounds–i.e. naming pluralises–there must have already been a tacit rejection of semantic atomism.

With the new appreciation of language Plato is able to explain a lot more than just the problem of falsehood. First, it becomes obvious that thinking falsely does not require the presupposition of knowledge for an identifi*able* object. Again thinking is complex and never just consists of naming. Never does having a thought as a whole come to make sense in terms of getting some kind of corresponding visual image of the actual thing thought reflects.[1] Thought is *meaningful* in virtue of getting something said. What needs to happen for something to acquire meaning is for the words employed to be related somehow such that something gets asserted. It does not really matter whether what is actually said is fictitious or not. It would make just as much sense to say that 'Superman is stronger than Popeye' as it would to say 'My husband is stronger than my father'. The meaning of these two statements is derived from what gets related: in both cases a predicate phrase is said to be true of a subject phrase, so that what is being conveyed, what gets said, is that the latter must be a member of the former. The *Meno Paradox* was incited as a result of Socrates' insistence that instances of what can be *named* by the inquiring topic, e.g. virtue, can not produce knowledge. That is, were Meno to say that virtue is when 'women keep good house', etc. and that he believes this exhibits knowledge of what virtue is, Socrates would respond that he has only provided a list of virt*uous* acts or acts that can be *called* by the name 'virtue'. Flabbergasted Meno set-up the Meno paradox, which Socrates in turn reformulated as the impasse to inquiry altogether. To be able to legitimately call the list of beliefs regarding virtuous acts knowledge—in order to legitimately call these acts *virtuous*—first one would have to be sure that he knew what virtue is. A reasonable claim. After all if together with your 3 year-old daughter you set out to find examples of fuchsia on your walk in the forest, and she proclaimed, 'here mummy, I found some!' you would probably have a good chuckle since your daughter could not possibly *know* what fuchsia *is* (by the way it is a onagraceous shrub which has showy drooping purple, red or white flowers; also known as the California fuchsia). Surprisingly, she *accidentally* did *find* a fuchsia plant!

From there Meno concluded that inquiry must be an altogether pointless effort; either because some of your beliefs may be true others false, which the elenctic aporetic end would imply, and therefore the acquisition of knowledge becomes impossible; or else, the ability to cite examples to illustrate your knowledge, means that you must already know *what virtue is*, and consequently you need not search for it. Strictly speaking this is a *re*formulation of the puzzle previously developed by Meno. Meno's claim suggests middle ground which Socrates does not explore as he is already working on the 'all or nothing' premise regarding knowledge. Meno's precursory enunciation of (3) stages in the puzzle sets us up for Socrates' exhaustive logical alternatives: either inquiry is compatible with (i) knowing x or (ii) not knowing x. There is a problem regarding the interpretation of this proposal: in terms of the Socratic *re*formulation of the dilemma we might just argue that at each stage the same problem is raised regarding the ability to identify some-thing and name it for thought to think of. This is easily dismissed by appealing to the meaningfulness of *thinking* in terms of contemplation; i.e. getting something asserted. This is not the view that is being endorsed here since it has been argued that stages (1)-(3) may indeed be taken this way when the hit-or-miss assumption is exposed, but that we must be able to show why stages (1) and (2) suggest something different from the problem regarding knowledge at stage (3). Moreover, the 'all or nothing' premise could commit us to the conclusion that *belief presupposes knowledge* which would counter the possibility of having beliefs short of knowledge which would in turn negate the very *conditions* which set up the paradox—i.e. Meno's beliefs when employed by the elenchus could not produce knowledge. Stage (1) regards the actual conditions of the method; namely are we entitled to the doxastic constraint, namely to the pre-existing beliefs of interlocutors; stage (2) asks which of all the *things* you do not know will be *named* as the object of the pursuit; and finally stage (3) questions the ability to recognise the knowledge of what x is as a result of such an inquiry (the doxastic and availability constraint would, of course, apply). Since the puzzle is initiated as a response to the use of instances in the inquiry for knowledge, and stage (1) asks *how* inquiry would proceed, it must be concerned with the legitimacy of employing the existing beliefs of the interlocutor. Of course, based on Socrates' ultimatum, you either know or do not know at all, such beliefs would already presuppose knowledge. He offers no middle ground; thought is otherwise impossible. Yet, it seems to follow straightforwardly from Socrates' reproach just before Meno's utter frustration with the and pronounced the paradox, that to be entitled to employ such beliefs, these *beliefs fall short of knowledge*. Indeed Socrates himself actually draws from examples to illustrate points; for instance, the *Jury Example* in the *Theaetetus* is used to swiftly dispose of the opinion that true belief is knowledge. The incongruity between Meno's presentation of the paradox and Socrates' basic evaluation of its implications, would suggest that Plato does not really endorse the 'all or nothing' premise regarding knowledge, but at the time he was not yet sure of how to solve it. All beliefs which figure in the elenctic search—doxastic constraint—must be meaningful; and yet these necessarily comprise *both* true and false beliefs—the contradictory end of the elenchus confirms that—in which case the puzzle about falsehood should be expected to directly overturn this difficulty. That is, because both true and false beliefs are equally meaningful—corresponding to stages (1) and (2)— and the 'all or nothing' premise could not license this when fully worked out, Meno's view tacitly confirms that truth and meaning are distinct. However, because stage (3) is a historically and epistemologically confirmed paradox there must be something left over after resolving this distinction which leaves its resolution uncomfortably unexplained.

For the *Meno Paradox* the difficulty proposed can only be dismissed if we seek refuge in the semantic solution for falsehood which would support that beliefs are meaningful in virtue of getting something asserted. So the problem regarding the rightful *use* of beliefs whose truth-value is, in effect, dependent upon the criteria set by the terms being used can be bypassed altogether. We are entitled to these, not on epistemological grounds, but on semantic grounds. Beliefs are meaningful even when they fall short of truth; however, whether we are epistemologically entitled to these is a question for another day. Stage (2) presupposes the possibility of (1). Once it is shown that we are entitled to *have* beliefs as such, we need to show why it is meaningful to *name* some-thing as the subject of inquiry when that thing is not yet known. Again, in order to move on to stage (2) stage (1) must have already been successfully overturned, so we must now be working on the assumption that beliefs are meaningful even when these are short of truth. Hence, that which in turn might stump inquiry is the possibility to attend upon something as the subject of what is as of yet unknown. We have already said that beliefs are meaningful because of what gets asserted by them, rather than what they are about. The problem which remains would therefore seem to be how it becomes meaningful to *name* something as the object of your search without that already presupposing knowledge of that thing. Meno asks specifically 'what of all things that you *do not know* will you *name* as the *object* of your search?' Stage (1) would have been impossible on Parmenidean grounds since all words would be expected to name. However, even the response proposed to resolve the enigma of falsehood would say that *names name*; the sentential subject—names vs. verbs—is meaningful in virtue of *what it names or in virtue of referring*. In this case would it not indeed presuppose that the thing named as the object of the search can be *identified* by the person inciting the search? The solution proposed is flexible enough to accommodate even this somewhat disturbing problem. Once again it need not be the case that the subject term *actually* names anything. It makes sense to say 'Superman is strong' because eventhough the *name* Superman does not *actually name* anything (Superman is a fictitious character) it does successfully stand in for something for the predicate phrase 'is strong' to be true of. Once again, it will be unnecessary to be able to identify the object of inquiry as such in order to name it as the subject of the search in a meaningful way.

The final stage (3) truly presents a problem which I will argue Plato is unable to defend since it would require a previous account of *how* words come to have meaning at all. Once entitled to express beliefs and propound knowledge, what remains is to show whether Socrates can be defended against charges of deceitful trickery in argument. Even if it is to be argued that words acquire meaning for statements regarding their particular contribution to what is getting asserted, and that statements are then judged to be true when the object named by the subject term is a member of the things that the predicate term is true of, still there is the question of *how* the predicates come to have the meaning and therefore be true of whatever objects they are of and false of those that they are not of. Left with the epistemological puzzle regarding the possibility of detecting which of all supplanted beliefs are true and which false, we are once again faced with the difficulty of explaining our knowledge of what can be taken to be true or false of some term. The discussion of *logos* in Part III of the *Theaetetus* did suggest that thinking of knowledge in terms of the proprietary assumption was the result of the misplaced assumption regarding thought and what makes a statement true. By the end of the dialogue a shift in emphasis had placed the semantics responsible for the mishap on thought at the centre. *Logos* was the focus of the debate: we are trying to figure out what *logos* could add to true belief that would produce knowledge, and how this obtains. The proprietary assumption already mentioned of course introduced the problem of foundationalism in terms of facts. That is, *logos* is compared to a catalogue of parts/elements of the complex thing in question, so that if you can acquire [knowledge of?] the list you would have knowledge. However, were that the case something, namely partless things, would remain unknown, and this would in turn undermine the knowledge of complex things. This version of *logos* was rejected, and replaced with the view that *logos* should be expected to provide criteria that distinguish the thing in question from all other things. This in turn also failed because again it presupposed knowledge. Clearly, however this is leading towards the notion of *difference* presented in the *Sophist* and it might be offered that the solution to the problem of knowledge acquisition could be solved by indeed working out the truth conditions for any statement. Specifically by determining what objects a predicate phrase is true of and what things it is false of. Unfortunately, Plato does not present a theory that explains how the truth value of any statement is actually determined, nor is it clear how truth, once determined, would lead to knowledge.

It can now be concluded that the solution to the problem of false belief was flexible enough to also explain to Meno how it is possible to entertain beliefs more generally and how it is also possible to search for something and name that thing without knowing it. That which is left unexplained is how knowledge in is thereby acquired. The sophists no longer can hide in their niche of relativism and must now either give up the eristic method of reasoning or else show that despite the reinstatement of falsehood, in the absence of knowledge there would be no way to distinguish true from false beliefs and for this reason they need not alter their ways. The elenctic method is, therefore, still in trouble because the ability to acquire knowledge is not spelled out.

Note

[1] This view is reminiscent of the Idea Theory of Meaning of empiricists like Locke, Berkeley and Hume. See R.M. Martin (1989) *The Meaning of Language*, ch. 2.

Bibliography

Ackrill, J. (1966) 'Plato on False Belief: *Theaetetus* 187-200', *Monist*, pp. 383-402.

Allen, R. E. (ed.) (1965) *Studies in Plato's Metaphysics*, London.

Angene, L.E. (1978) 'False Judgement in the *Theaetetus*', *Philosophical Studies* 33, pp. 351-365.

Annas, J. (1990) *Oxford Studies in Ancient Philosophy*, Supplementary Vol., Oxford: Clarendon Press.

Aristotle (1955) *On Sophistical Refutations*, in Loeb Classic Series, US: Harvard University Press.

Armstrong, D.M. (1969-70) 'Does Knowledge Entail Belief?', *ASP*, pp. 21-36.

Austin, J.L. (1962) *Sense and Sensibilia*, London: OUP.

Austin, J.L. (1970) *Philosophical Papers*, London: OUP.

Barnes, B. (1982) *The PreSocratic Philosophers*, London: Routledge & Kegan Paul Publishers.

Barnes, J. (1979) 'Parmenides and the Eleatic One', *AGP*.

Bedu-Addo, J.T. (1983) 'Sense-Experience and Recollection in Plato's *Meno*', *American Journal of Philology*, pp. 229-248.

Bedu-Addo, J.T. (1984) 'Recollection and the Argument 'From Hypothesis' in Plato's *Meno*', *Journal of Hellenic Studies*, pp. 1-14.

Benardete, S. (1986) *Plato's Sophist: Part II of The Being of the Beautiful*, Chicago: University Press.

Benson, H.H. (1987) 'The Problem of the Elenchus Reconsidered', *Ancient Philosophy* 7, pp. 67-85.

Benson, H.H. (1990) 'Meno, the Slave Boy and the *Elenchus*', *Phronesis*, pp. 128-158.

Benson, H.H. (1990) 'The Priority of Definition and the Socratic Elenchus', *OSAP*, Vol. VIII, pp. 19-65.

Benson, H.H. (1992) 'Why is There a Discussion of False Belief in the *Theaetetus*?', *Journal of the History of Philosophy*, 30:2, April.

Beversluis, J. (1987) 'Does Socrates Commit the Socratic Fallacy?' *American Philosophical Quarterly*, July, pp. 211-223.

Bluck, R.S. (1957) 'False Statement in Plato's *Sophist*', *Journal of Hellenic*

Studies 77, pp. 181-6.

Bluck, R.S. (1961) *The Meno*, Cambridge: University Press.

Bluck, R.S. (1975) *Plato's Sophist*, Manchester: The Humanities Press.

Bosley, R. (1976) 'Monistic Argumentation', *Canadian Journal of Philosophy, Supplementary Volume II*, pp. 23-44.

Bostock D. (1994) 'Plato On Understan-ding Language' in S. Everson (ed.) *Language: Companions to Ancient Thought 3*, Cambridge: CUP.

Bostock, D. (1984) 'Plato On 'Is Not' (*Sophist* 254-9)' in *OSAP 2*, pp. 89-119.

Bostock, J. (1988) *Plato's Theaetetus*, Oxford: Clarendon Press.

Brickhouse T.C., Smith, D. S. (1984) 'Socrates' Elenctic Mission' *Phronesis*, pp. 132-160.

Brickhouse, T.C., Smith, D.S (1984) 'Vlastos on the Elenchus', *OSAP*, pp. 185-195.

Brickhouse, T.C., Smith, D.S. (1991) *Socrates On Trial*, Oxford: OUP.

Brickhouse, T.C., Smith, D.S. (1994) *Plato's Socrates*, Oxford: OUP.

Brown, L. (1986) 'Being in the *Sophist*: A Syntactic Enquiry', *Phronesis*.

Brown, L. (1991) '*Being in the* Sophist', *OSAP*, Oxford: OUP.

Brown, L. (1994) 'The Verb 'to be' in Greek Philosophy: Some Remarks' in Everson (ed.) *Language: Companions to Ancient Thought 3*, Cambridge: CUP.

Burnet, J (1962) *Greek Philosophy: From Thales to Plato*, UK: St. Martin's Press.

Burnyeat, M. (1990) 'Protagoras and Self-Refutation in Plato's *Theaetetus*' in S. Everson (ed.) *Epistemology: Companions to Ancient Thought 1*, Cambridge: CUP.

Burnyeat, M.F. (1976) 'Protagoras and Self-refutation in Plato's *Theaetetus*', *The Philosophical Review 85*.

Burnyeat, M.F. (1990) *The Theaetetus of Plato*, with trans. and intro. by M.L. Levitt, Indianapolis: Hackett.

Charles, D. (1994) 'Aristotle on Names and Their Significance' in S. Everson (ed.) *Language: Companions to Ancient Thought 3*, Cambridge: CUP.

Crombie, I.M. (1971) *An Examination of Plato's Doctrine's*, Routledge & Kegan Paul, NY: The Humanities Press.

Curd, P.K. (1991) 'Parmenidean Monism', *Phronesis*, pp. 241-264.

Denyer, N. (1991) *Language, Thought and Falsehood In Ancient Greek*

Philosophy, Cambridge: CUP.

Descartes, R. (1986) 'Meditations on First Philosophy' trans. by J. Cottingham, Cambridge: CUP.

Everson, S. (1994) *Language: Companions to Ancient Thought 3*, Cambridge: CUP.

Everson, S. (ed.) (1990) *Epistemology: Companions to Ancient Thought 1*, CUP.

Fine, G. (1979) 'False Belief in the *Theaetetus*', *Phronesis*, pp. 70-80.

Fine, G. (1979) 'Knowledge and *Logos* in the *Theaetetus*', *Philosophical Review 88*, pp. 366-397.

Fine, G. (1990) 'Knowledge and Belief in *Republic* V-VII' in S. Everson (ed.) *Epistemology: Companions to Ancient Thought 1*, Cambridge: CUP.

Fine, G. (1992) 'Inquiry in the *Meno*' in R. Kraut (ed.) *The Cambridge Companion to Plato*, Cambridge: CUP.

Fitch, G. W. (1990) 'Thinking of Something', *Nous,* 24, pp. 675-696.

Frankel, H. (1975) 'Studies in Parmenides', from R.E. Allen & D.J. Furley (eds), *Studies in PreSocratic Philosophy*, Vol. II.

Frede, D. (1986) 'The Impossibility of Perfection: Socrates' Criticism of Simonides' Poem in the *Protagoras*', *Review of Metaphysics* 39, pp. 729-753.

Frede, M. (1992) 'Plato's *Sophist* on False Statements' in R. Kraut (ed.) *The Cambridge Companion to Plato*, Cambridge: CUP.

Frede, M. (ed.) (1991) *Plato's Protagoras*, Indianapolis : Hackett Publishing Company.

Frege G. (1952) 'On Sense and Reference' in his *Philosophical Writings*, (eds) P.T. Geach and M. Black, Oxford, OUP.

Furley, D (1973) 'Notes on Parmenides' *Exegesis and Argument*, ed. E.N. Lee, A.P.D. Mourelatos, and R. Rorty, Assen.

Furley, D. (1988) 'Truth as What Survives the *Elenchus*' in his *Cosmic Problems: Essays on Greek and Roman Philosophy of Nature*, NY: CUP.

Furth, M. (1968) 'Elements of Eleatic Ontology', *History of Philosophy 6*, pp. 111-132.

Geach, (1966) 'Plato's *Euthyphro*: An Analysis and Commentary', *Monist*, pp. 369-402.

Gomperz, T. (1964) *Greek Thinkers: A History of Ancient Philosophy*, Vol.

I, Humanities Press.

Grant, C.K. (1972-3) 'On a Definition of Knowledge', *ASP*, pp. 157-166.

Griswold, C.L. (1988) 'Plato's Metaphilosophy: Why Plato Wrote Dialogues' in C.L. Griswold (ed.) *Platonic Writings: Platonic Readings*, New York: Routledge.

Griswold, C.L. (1988) *Platonic Writings: Platonic Readings*, New York: Routledge.

Groarke, L. (1990) *Greek Scepticism: Anti-Realist trends in Ancient Thought*, Montreal: McGill-Queen's UP.

Gulley, N. (1968) *The Philosophy of Socrates*, London: Macmillan.

Guthrie, W.K.C. (1969) *History of Greek Philosophy II*, Cambridge: CUP.

Guthrie, W.K.C. (1992) *Socrates*, Cambridge: CUP.

Guthrie, W.K.C. (1993) *The Sophists*, Cambridge: CUP.

Guttenplan, S. (1989) *The Language of Logic*, London: Blackwell.

Hale, B. (1972) 'Frege' Platonism' *The Philosophical Quarterly* Vol. 34 no. 136, pp. 225-241.

Hamilton, J. (1991) *A History of Philosophy*, New York: The Humanities Press.

Harrison, E.L. (1964) 'Was Gorgias a Sophist?', *Phoenix*, pp. 183-192.

Harrison, J. (1978-79) 'If I Know, I Cannot Be Wrong', *ASP*, pp. 137-150.

Irwin, T. (1974) *Plato's Moral Philosophy*, Oxford: Oxford University Press.

Irwin, T.H. (1992) 'Plato: The Intellectual Background' in R. Kraut (ed.) *The Cambridge Companion to Plato*, Cambridge: CUP.

Jordan, R.W. (1984) 'Plato's Task in the *Sophist*', *Classical Quarterly* 34, pp. 113-129.

Jordan, W. (1990) *Ancient Concepts of Philosophy*, London: Routledge.

Kahn, C. (1969) 'The Thesis of Parmenides' *The Review of Metaphysics* 22, pp. 704-6.

Kant, I. (1985) *Prolegomena to Any Future Metaphysics That Will be Able to Come Forward as a Science*, US: Open Court Publishers.

Kerferd, G.B. (1981) *The Sophistic Movement*, Cambridge: CUP.

Ketchum, R.J. (1990) 'Parmenides On What There Is', *Canadian Journal of Philosophy*, Vol. 20, pp. 167-190.

Keyt, D. (1973) 'Plato on Falsity: *Sophist* 263B', in *Exegesis and Argument,* (eds) E.N. Lee, A.P.D. Mourelatos and R. Rorty, Assen, pp. 285-305.

Klein, J. (1989) *Commentary on Plato's* Meno, Chicago: University of Chicago Press.

Kostman, J. (1989) 'The Ambiguity of 'Partaking' in Plato's *Sophist'*, *Journal of the History of Philosophy* 27:3, July, pp. 343-363.

Kraut, R.. (1992) *The Cambridge Companion to Plato*, Cambridge: CUP.

Lacey, A.R. (1980) 'Our Knowledge of Socrates' in G. Vlastos (ed.) *The Philosophy of Socrates: A Collection of Critical Essays*, UK: University of Notre Dame Press.

Lewis, F.A. (1973) 'Two Paradoxes in the *Theaetetus*' in *Patterns in Plato's Thought*, (ed.) J.M.E. Moravesik, Dordrecht, pp. 123-49.

Lewis, F.A. (1979) 'Knowledge and the Eyewitness: Plato *Theaetetus* 201a-c', in *Philosophical Review*, pp. 185-197.

Long, A.A. (1963) 'The Principles of Parmenides' Cosmology', *Phronesis* 8, pp. 90-107.

Luntley, M. (1962) 'The Sense of a Name', *The Philosophical Quarterly* Vol. 34 No. 136, pp. 265-282.

Macintosh, J.J. (1979-80) 'Knowing and Believing', *Aristotelean Society Proceedings*, pp. 169-185.

Mackenzie, M.M. (1982) 'Parmenides' Dilemma', *Phronesis*, pp. 1-12.

Mackenzie, M.M. (1988) 'Socratic Ignorance', *Classical Quarterly* 38, pp. 331-350.

Martin R.M. (1989) *The Meaning of Language*, Cambridge, Massachusetts: The MIT Press.

McDowell, J. (1973) *Theaetetus*, Oxford: OUP.

McDowell, J. (1977) 'On the Sense and Reference of a Proper Name', *Mind*, pp. 159-185.

McKirahan, R.D. (1994) *Philosophy Before Socrates*, Indianapolis: Hackett Publishing Company Inc.

Miller, L.W. (1962) 'Knowledge, False Belief, and Dialectic in Plato', *Tulane Studies*, pp. 125-151.

Moline, J. (1988) 'Recollection, Dialectic, and Ontology: Kenneth M. Sayre on the Solution to a Platonic Riddle' in C.L. Griswold (ed.) *Platonic Writings: Platonic Readings*, New York: Routledge.

Morgan, M.L., (1989) 'How Does Plato Solve the Paradox of Inquiry in the Meno?', in J.P. Anton & A. Preus (eds) *Essays in Ancient Philosophy III*, Albany: State of NY Press.

Mourelatos, A.P.D. (1976) 'Determinacy and Indeterminacy, Being and

Non-Being in the Fragments of Parmenides', *Canadian Journal of Philosophy, Supplementary Volume II*, pp. 45-60.

Nakhnikian, G. (1980) 'Elenctic Definition' in G. Vlastos (ed.) *The Philosophy of Socrates: A Collection of Critical Essays*, UK: University of Notre Dame Press.

Nehemas, A. (1985) 'O Sokratis Peri tis Proteraiotitas tou Orismou', *I Elliniki Filosophiki Etairia*, Athens, pp. 116-123.

Nehemas, A.(1985) 'Meno's Paradox and Socrates as a Teacher', *OSAP*, Vol. III, pp. 1-30.

Owen, G.E.L. (1960) 'Eleatic Questions', *CQ NS 10,* pp. 84-102.

Owen, G.E.L. (1972) 'Plato On Not-being', *Modern Studies in* Philosophy*: Plato I*, New York: Anchor Books.

Penner, T. (1992) 'Socrates and the Early Dialogues' in R. Kraut (ed.) *The Cambridge Companion to Plato*, Cambridge: CUP.

Popper, K.R. (1992) 'How the Moon Might Throw Some of Her Light Upon the Two Ways of Parmenides', *Classical Quarterly 42*, pp. 12-19.

Quine, W.V.O. (1961) 'Reference and Modality' in Quine W.V.O. *Logical Point of View*, NY: Harper and Row Publishers.

Quine, W.V.O. (1991) 'Quantifiers and Propositional Attitudes' in Quine W.V.O. *Ways of Paradox*, NY: Random House Publishers.

Ray, C.A. (1984) *For Images: An Interpretation of Plato's* Sophist, University Press of America.

Reinhardt, K. (1974) 'The Relation Between the Two Parts of Parmenides' Poem', from A.P.D. Mourelatos (ed.) *The PreSocratics: A Collection of Critical Essays*, New York: Anchor Press.

Robinson, R. (1950) 'Forms and Error in Plato's *Theaetetus*', *Philosophical Review*, pp. 3-30.

Robinson, R. (1980) 'Elenchus' in G. Vlastos (ed.) *The Philosophy of Socrates: A Collection of Critical Essays*, UK: University of Notre Dame Press.

Robinson, R. (1980) 'Elenchus: Direct and Indirect' in G. Vlastos (ed.) *The Philosophy of Socrates: A Collection of Critical Essays*, UK: University of Notre Dame Press.

Robinson, R. (1980) 'Socratic Definition' in G. Vlastos (ed.) *The Philosophy of Socrates: A Collection of Critical Essays*, UK: University of Notre Dame Press.

Rosen, S. (1983) *Plato's* Sophist*: The Drama of the Original and Image*,

New Haven: Yale UP.

Rudebusch, G. (1985) 'Plato on Sense and Reference', *Mind*.

Russell, B. (1872) 'Knowledge by Acquaintance and Knowledge by Description', in *Logic and Mysticism*, London: G. Allen & Unwin.

Ryle (1990) *Collected Papers*, US: Thoemmes Antiquarian Books, Vol. 1 & 2.

Ryle, G. (1949) *The Concept of Mind*, New York: Barnes & Noble.

Ryle, G. (1990) 'Logical Atomism in Plato's *Theaetetus*', *Phronesis 35*, pp. 21-46.

Ryle, G., (1966) *Plato's Progress*, Cambridge: CUP.

Sayre, K. (1969) *Plato's Analytic Method*, Chicago: University of Chicago Press.

Sayre, K. M. (1988) 'Reply to Jon Moline' in C.L. Griswold (ed.) *Platonic Writings: Platonic Readings*, New York: Routledge.

Schmit, F.F. (1992) *Knowledge and Belief*, London: Routledge.

Scott, D. (1987) 'Platonic Anamnesis Revisited', *Classical Quarterly*, 37, pp. 347-366.

Searle, J.R. (1958) 'Proper Names', *Mind*, pp. 166-173.

Sharples, R.W. (1985) *Meno*, US: Aris & Phillips.

Sidgwich, H. (1872) 'The Sophists', *The Journal of Philosophy*, pp. 288-307.

Stough, C. (1990) 'Two Kinds of Naming in the *Sophist*', *Canadian Journal of Philosophy*,. pp. 355-382.

Strawson, P.F. (1950) 'On Referring', *Mind*, pp. 320-344.

Striker, G. (1990) 'The Problem of Criterion' in S. Everson (ed.) *Epistemology: Companions to Ancient Thought 1*, Cambridge: CUP.

Taylor, W. (1976) Plato's Protagoras, Oxford: OUP.

Thomas, J.E. (1980) *Musings on the* Meno, US: Nijhoff Publishers.

Trevaskis, J.R. (1965-6) 'The *Megista Geni* and the Vowel Analogy of Plato; *Sophist* 253', *Phronesis*, Vol. 10-11.

Turnball, R.G. (1965) '*Episteme* and *Doxa*: Some Reflections on Eleatic and Heraklitean Themes in Plato', in J.P. Anton & A. Preus (eds) *Essays in Ancient Greek Philosophy*, Vol. Two.

Vendler Z. (1973) 'Platonic Theory of Thinking' read to a Rice University Colloquium in the fall of 1973.

Vendler Z. (1974) 'Reference in Thought' read to a Rice University Colloquium in the fall of 1974.

Vlastos, G. (1946) 'Parmenides' Theory of Knowledge', *Transactions of the American Philological Association*, 77, (ed.), J. Heller, University of Minesota, pp. 66-77.

Vlastos, G. (1973) 'An Ambiguity in the *Sophist*' reprinted in G. Vlastos *Platonic Studies*, NY: Princeton University Press.

Vlastos, G. (1980) 'Introduction: The Paradox of Socrates' in G. Vlastos (ed.) *The Philosophy of Socrates: A Collection of Critical Essays*, UK: University of Notre Dame Press.

Vlastos, G. (1985) 'Socrates' Disavowal of Knowledge', *The Philosophical Quarterly*, pp. 1-31.

Vlastos, G. (1988) 'Elenchus and Mathematics', *American Journal of Philology*, pp. 362-394.

Vlastos, G. (1990) 'Is the 'Socratic Fallacy' Socratic?', *Ancient Philosophy* 10(1), pp. 1-14.

Vlastos, G. (1992) *Socrates: Ironist and Moral Philosopher*, Cambridge: CUP.

Vlastos, G. (ed.) (1980) *The Philosophy of Socrates: A Collection of Critical Essays,* UK: University of Notre Dame Press.

White, N. (1976) *Plato On Knowledge and Reality*, Indianapolis: Hackett Publishing Company.

White, N.P. (1992) 'Plato's Metaphysical Epistemology' in R. Kraut (ed.) *The Cambridge Companion to Plato*, Cambridge: CUP.

Wiggins, D. (1971) 'Sentence Meaning, Negation and Plato's Problem of Non-Being', in Vlastos (ed.) *Plato I*, Garden City, pp. 268-303.

William's, C.J.F. (1972) 'Referential Opacity and False Belief in the *Theaetetus*', *Philosophical Quarterly*, pp. 289-302.

Williams, B. (1994) '*Cratylus*' Theory of Names and its Refutation' in S. Everson (ed.) *Language: Companions to Ancient Thought 3*, Cambridge: CUP.

Williams, C.J.F. (1972) 'Referential Opacity and False Belief in the *Theaetetus*', *Philosophical Quarterly*, 22(89), pp. 289-302.

Woodruff, P. (1990) 'Plato's Early Theory of Knowledge' in S. Everson (ed.) *Epistemology: Companions to Ancient Thought 1*, Cambridge: CUP.

Xenakis, J. (1958-60) 'Plato's *Sophist*: A Defense of Negative Expressions and a Doctrine of Sense and of Truth', *Phronesis*, V(3,4,5) pp. 29-43.

Zemach, E.M. (1986) 'From Meaning to Sense and Reference', *Philosophical Papers*, XV (1), pp. 23-39.